AMERICAN
PERSPECTIVES

READINGS ON CONTEMPORARY U.S. CULTURE

SUSAN EARLE-CARLIN
COLLEEN HILDEBRAND

**University of California,
Irvine**

Longman

American Perspectives: Readings on Contemporary U.S. Culture

Pearson Education, 10 Bank Street, White Plains, NY 10606

Editorial director: Allen Ascher
Executive editor: Louisa Hellegers
Development editor: Carolyn Viola-John
Director of design and production: Rhea Banker
Associate director of electronic production: Aliza Greenblatt
Production manager: Alana Zdinak
Managing editor: Linda Moser
Production editor: Martin Yu
Electronic production editor: Rachel Baumann
Associate technical production manager: Steven Greydanus
Senior manufacturing manager: Patrice Fraccio
Manufacturing supervisor: Edith Pullman
Photo research: Matthew McConnochie
Cover design: Lissi Sigillo
Cover credits: Baseball © Duomo Photography Incorporated; Statue
    of Liberty © McDaniel Wolf/PhotoDisc; Capitol Hill © The Stock
    Connection; Girl rollerblading © Renee Lynn/Photo Researchers,
    Inc.; Street musician © D. Falconer/PhotoDisc, Inc.
Text design: Lissi Sigillo
Text credits: see page xii
Photo credits: see page xiii

Library of Congress Cataloging-in-Publication Data

American perspectives: readings on contemporary U.S. culture / Susan
    Earle-Carlin, Colleen Hildebrand.
        p.   cm.
    Includes bibliographical references.
    ISBN 0-201-52075-3
    1. English language Textbooks for foreign speakers.   2. United
States—Civilization—20th century Problems, exercises, etc.
    3. Readers—United States.   I. Earle-Carlin, Susan.
    II. Hildebrand, Colleen.
    PE1128.A4774   1999   99-31284
    428.6'4—dc21   CIP

6 7 8 9 10-CRW-05

CONTENTS

Chapter 10: Pursuing Happiness   **236**

READINGS

PREFACE

What makes *American Perspectives: Readings on Contemporary U.S. Culture* different from other cultural readers? *American Perspectives* concentrates on examining the present-day American psyche. Balancing the light and the more serious sides of American culture, it provides students with authentic readings and short, thought-provoking quotations on American life, values, and beliefs. The wide variety of reading and writing activities engages students, reinforces their comprehension, and helps them apply what they have learned. Written for high-intermediate and low-advanced students, this text invites them to explore attitudes and stereotypes of the United States and its people.

The authentic materials in *American Perspectives* come from current newspapers, magazines, books, journals, and websites. Instead of a watered-down, one-sided view of American society, the materials have been chosen to stimulate lively discussions about issues, people, and events, as well as comparisons to other cultures. As a reading/writing textbook, *American Perspectives* prepares students for the transition to academic discourse by developing a wide range of useful skills for comprehending and interacting with the text. Each of the activities provides opportunities for students to work individually, as well as in pairs or small groups.

THEMATIC UNITS

The themes in *American Perspectives* were developed to reflect the American character, from the way Americans work to the way they play. In his brochure for visitors to the United States, *The Values Americans Live By,* L. Robert Kohls, former executive director of the Washington International Center, lists thirteen values : personal control over the environment; change; time and its control; equality/egalitarianism; individualism and privacy; self-help concept; competition and free enterprise; future orientation; action/work orientation; informality; directness, openness, and honesty; practicality and efficiency; and materialism/acquisitiveness. The readings try to reflect as many of these values as possible, and the quotations and facts in the margins highlight these descriptions of the American character. For example, the article "Fresh Start" shows how both the belief in change and the self-help concept inspire adults to return to school to improve their lives. The heroes in "Heroes We Have Known and Loved" show American individualism, and the reading on Jackie Robinson describes a hero's struggle for equality. While Americans are often criticized for the disintegration of family values, "What Is a Family?" explains the new open attitude toward this changing institution. These readings give insight into the American psyche from many different points of view, and the reader is encouraged to add his or her own.

CHAPTER DESIGN

Each chapter in *American Perspectives* is theme-based and provides activities in reading, writing, vocabulary development, and speaking. The format of the tasks is varied so that students and teachers are not bored with predictable exercises. Many skills are introduced and also reviewed and reinforced in later chapters.

Previewing the Chapter

A picture, a thought-provoking quotation, and a short introductory text orient readers to the theme of each chapter. In the **Focusing In** section, students are invited to activate their knowledge and examine their preconceptions by discussing the picture and sharing their answers on short preview quizzes.

Readings

Background information on the topic and the author introduces each of the three readings in a chapter. Preview and prediction questions help the readers focus in on the content.

Understanding the Reading

The comprehension activities following each reading focus on different reading skills, including finding facts and details, identifying topics and main ideas, making judgments and inferences, paraphrasing, distinguishing fact from fiction, and summarizing. Students are also encouraged to try different reading strategies such as predicting, skimming, scanning, annotating the text, charting information, and outlining.

Using the Vocabulary

In the readings, difficult words are glossed at the bottom of the page so students do not become frustrated with the vocabulary demands of authentic material. Students then reexamine this vocabulary through activities that include vocabulary in context exercises, synonym and antonym distinctions, dictionary usage, word classifications, word games, word-form analysis, and analogies. Every reading also has a vocabulary cloze activity that is designed to review and reinforce word knowledge.

Thinking Together

Collaborative tasks encourage students to apply the information from the reading in a different way by going beyond the text and examining the issues raised in American society and in other cultures.

Writing about It

These creative prompts can be used to test the students' comprehension of the reading. They can function as in-class short writes or as homework assignments.

Reacting to the Reading

Thought-provoking questions allow students to voice their opinions on a specific aspect of the beliefs or values underlying the reading. Teachers can assign these as short in-class writings, tests, group discussions, or class debates.

In addition, each chapter contains a collaborative task that focuses on interpreting graphic material such as maps, charts, or graphs; a timed reading activity, **Keeping Track of Your Reading Rate**, helps students try out techniques for more efficient reading while keeping track of their speed.

Making Connections

Each chapter ends with activities that help students pull together the ideas that have been presented.

- **Responding to the Reading** This section provides additional opportunities for students to present written or oral responses to the topics and to examine the ideas in relation to their own experiences and cultures.
- **Editing Your Work** These exercises remind students to edit their work for a particular grammar trouble spot that might be elicited through the writing activities in the chapter. The paragraphs to be edited were all written by students in response to the assignments in *American Perspectives*.
- **Writing an Essay** Essay topics may be assigned by teachers in more writing-intensive courses. The topics vary in rhetorical demands; each chapter includes at least one topic for research.
- **Finding More Information** Students who wish to investigate the themes in more depth can refer to these lists of related books, magazines, movies, and websites.

TO THE STUDENT

We hope you enjoy using *American Perspectives: Readings on Contemporary U.S. Culture*. In order to become more familiar with this book, work with a partner to preview the text and answer these questions.

1. How many chapters does this text have?

2. Which chapter concentrates on American music?

3. How is new vocabulary defined in each reading?

4. How many photographs are there in each chapter?

5. What map is included after the reading "Return to Ellis Island Evokes Memories and Pride" in Chapter One?

6. Where can you find the publication information on the articles included in the text?

7. Which reading comes directly from a website? What is the address?

8. What is the address of one website that provides additional information on American health?

9. What appendices are included in the back of the book?

10. What are some of the suggestions that the authors provide for reading more efficiently and writing more effectively?

ACKNOWLEDGMENTS

We would first like to thank our students at the University of California, Irvine who inspired us to compile a book of readings on American culture and who contributed their own writing to the development of exercises. Over the years, they have piloted material in the text and offered helpful comments and insightful suggestions for improvement. We appreciate the assistance of Theresa Jones and Susannah Abbey in the preparation of our manuscript. The constructive criticism of our colleagues, Robin Scarcella and Joyce Cain, was also invaluable in helping to shape and refine our work.

Without the strong support of the editorial staff at Pearson Education, this book would never have been published. We thank Louisa Hellegers, executive editor, for her steadfast belief in our project and her enthusiasm throughout its development. We are especially grateful for the dedication of our editing team at Pearson Education: Carolyn Viola-John, development editor; Martin Yu, production editor; Alice Vigliani, copy editor; and Matt McConnochie, editorial assistant and photo researcher. Their advice and expertise are evident in the high quality of this book.

We would also like to thank the many writers who contributed their work to our text. Their varied perspectives helped us paint a broad picture of American culture.

Finally, we want to thank our children, Matt and Todd Carlin and Calisa and Kaela Hildebrand, for their never-ending patience, and our husbands, Chris Carlin and Garrett Hildebrand, whose encouragement, support, and computer expertise kept us up and running. We dedicate this book to them.

CREDITS

Text Credits

Page 4, by Chuck Sambar, from http://www.sambarpress.com. Reprinted by permission of Chuck Sambar. **Page 10,** by Lewis Sawaquat, from *Newsweek,* September 5, 1983. Reprinted by permission of Lewis Sawaquat. **Page 16,** by Marcus Bleecker, from *The New York Times Magazine,* October 15, 1995. Copyright © 1995 by the New York Times Co. Reprinted by permission. **Page 21,** by Meghan Sweeney, from the *New University,* November 7, 1994. Reprinted by permission of *New University Newspaper.* **Page 28,** by Bernard Gavzer, from *Parade,* November 22, 1992. Copyright © 1992. Reprinted with permission from *Parade.* **Page 36,** by Elizabeth Mehren, from the *Los Angeles Times,* August 20, 1995. Copyright © 1995. Los Angeles Times Syndicate. Reprinted with permission. **Page 41,** by Marcia Schnedler, from *The Salt Lake Tribune,* March 10, 1996. Taken from a MARCIA SCHNEDLER column by MARCIA SCHNEDLER. Copyright © UNIVERSAL PRESS SYNDICATE. Reprinted with permission. All rights reserved. **Page 45,** by Kaitlyn Kerry, from http://rainbowkids.com, May/June 1996. Courtesy of Martha Osborne and rainbowkids.com. **Page 52,** by Mike Tharp, from *U.S. News and World Report,* July 15, 1996. Copyright © 1996. *U.S. News and World Report.* **Page 58,** by Jeff Lenburg, from *Baseball's All-Star Game: A Game by Game Guide.* Copyright © 1986 by Jeff Lenburg. Reprinted by permission of the author. **Page 65,** reprinted by permission of the Boston Athletic Association. **Page 71,** from http://www.specialolympics.org. Courtesy of Special Olympics International. **Page 78,** by Horace Miner, from *AMERICAN ANTHROPOLOGIST,* 58:3, June 1956. Reproduced by permission of the American Anthropological Association. Not for further reproduction. **Page 86,** by Doris Williams, from *The Salt Lake Tribune,* September 20, 1994. Reprinted by permission of *The Salt Lake Tribune.* **Page 93,** from http://shapeup.org/dated. Reprinted with permission of the Shape Up America! Organization. **Page 99,** by Dennis Fiely, from the *Columbus Dispatch,* February 21, 1997. Reprinted by permission of *Columbus Dispatch.* **Page 106,** by Mercedes Hardey. Reprinted by permission of Mercedes Hardey, Executive Director of Cultural Horizons, Inc. **Page 115,** by Dan McGraw. *U.S. News and World Report,* April 14, 1997. Copyright © 1997. *U.S. News and World Report.* **Page 122,** by Alan Bunce, from *The Christian Science Monitor,* February 16, 1989. Copyright © 1989. The Christian Science Publishing Society. All rights reserved. Reprinted with permission. **Page 128,** from http://kennedy-center.org/honors/years/jacdam.html. Reprinted with permission from the John F. Kennedy Center for the Performing Arts.

Page 136, by John F. Dickerson, from *TIME* Magazine, Cyberspace, Spring 1995. Copyright © 1995. TIME INC. Reprinted by permission. **Page 141,** by Randy Hecht, from http://www.mixnmatch.com, August 6, 1997. Copyright © 1997. Mix 'n Match. Courtesy of Match.Com™. **Page 149,** by Peter Theroux, from *Avenues,* January/February 1997. Copyright © by Peter Theroux. **Page 155,** by Robert Waldron, from *OPRAH!* by Robert Waldron. Copyright © 1987 by Robert Waldron. Reprinted by permission of St. Martin's Press, Incorporated. **Page 162,** from http://www.redcross.org. Courtesy of the American Red Cross. All rights reserved in all countries. **Page 169,** by Avonie Brown, from http://www.afroam.org/history. Reprinted by permission of the Baltimore Afro-American Newspapers. **Page 176,** by Robert McG. Thomas Jr., from *The New York Times,* May 16, 1993. Copyright © 1993 by The New York Times Co. Reprinted by permission. **Page 181,** by Susan Ware. Abridged from "Amelia Earhart" in *THE READER'S COMPANION TO AMERICAN HISTORY,* edited by Eric Foner and John A. Garraty. Copyright © 1991 by Houghton Mifflin Company. Reprinted by permission of Houghton Mifflin Company. All rights reserved. **Page 189,** by Secretary Richard W. Riley, from the U.S. Department of Education, the National Library of Education. **Page 195,** by Peggy Goetz, from *Irvine World News,* June 5, 1997. **Page 200,** by Dennis Hevesi, from *Education Life,* a supplement to *The New York Times,* August 5, 1990. Copyright © 1990 by The New York Times Co. Reprinted by permission. **Page 208,** Copyright © 1997. American Federation of Teachers. Reprinted from the April 1997 issue of *AFT On Campus.* Used by permission. **Page 214,** by Martha Groves, from the *Los Angeles Times,* February 26, 1996. Copyright © 1996. Los Angeles Times Syndicate. Reprinted with permission. **Page 220,** by Jan Norman, from the *Orange County Register,* August 29, 1992. Copyright © 1992. Reprinted with permission of the Orange County Register. **Page 225,** by the California Curriculum Project, Hispanic Biographies. Reprinted with permission of the Cesar E. Chavez Foundation. **Page 231,** by Jennifer Kossak, from *Home Business News,* Spring 1996, published by American Home Business Association, Salt Lake City, Utah. **Page 238,** by Leslie Dreyfous, from *The Salt Lake Tribune,* September 13, 1992. Reprinted by permission of Associated Press. **Page 245,** by Shari Caudron, from *Industry Week,* September 2, 1996. Copyright © 1996. Penton Publishing Inc. **Page 252,** by Margaret Dwiggins, from *The Courier,* March 12, 1996. Reprinted by permission of *The Courier.* **Page 256,** by David Barton, from *The Sacramento Bee,* August 6, 1997. Copyright © 1997. *The Sacramento Bee.*

Photo Credits

Page 2, The Granger Collection. **Page 6**, courtesy of Chuck Sambar. **Page 11**, courtesy of Terry Young, *New University News*. **Page 17**, Marc Riboud/Magnum Photos. **Page 26**, Tony Freeman/PhotoEdit. **Page 28**, Robert Brenner/PhotoEdit. **Page 36**, Keith Brofsky/ PhotoDisc. **Page 41**, courtesy of Dr. W. D. Harmon. **Page 50**, courtesy of Sports on Wheels and Colours by Permobil. **Page 54**, courtesy of Merry McConnochie. **Page 59**, Duomo Photography Incorporated. **Page 67**, courtesy of Victah Siler/Photo Run and the Boston Athletic Association. **Page 76**, David Young-Wolff/PhotoEdit. **Page 80**, courtesy of Tracy Rousselot. **Page 87**, Charles Gupton/The Stock Market. **Page 95**, Donna Day/Tony Stone Images. **Page 104**, J-F Néron. **Page 108**, photo by Flo Hendry. Courtesy of Mercedes Hardey, Executive Director of Cultural Horizons, Inc. **Page 116**, John Chaisson/Liason. **Page 123**, Allan Tannenbaum/Sygma. **Page 134**, Alan L. Detrick/Photo Researchers. **Page 137**, courtesy of William Ryan and Springbrook Elementary School. **Page 143**, Doug Menuez/PhotoDisc. **Page 151**, photo by Jeffrey Weiss from *Avenues*. Jeffrey Weiss Photography. **Page 160**, Library of Congress. **Page 163**, courtesy of the American Red Cross. All rights reserved in all countries. **Page 171**, AP/Wide World Photos. **Page 177**, Chris Falkenstein/PhotoDisc. **Page 186**, Anne Vega/Merril Education. **Page 190**, Beryl Goldberg. **Page 196**, photo by Michael M. Schwartz. Courtesy of *Irvine World News*. **Page 201**, Kevin Horan/Tony Stone Images. **Page 212**, John Feingersh/The Stock Market. **Page 215**, John Feingersh/The Stock Market. **Page 221**, photo by Ignacio Nanetti. Courtesy of the *Orange County Register*. **Page 227**, AP/Wide World Photos. **Page 236**, Michelle Bridwell/PhotoEdit. **Page 239**, courtesy of Mickey Ryan. **Page 246**, photo by Steve Craig. **Page 253**, courtesy of Habitat for Humanity, Orange County.

CHAPTER 1

Going Back to Our Roots

> Give me your tired, your poor, your huddled masses yearning to breathe free, the wretched refuse of your teaming shore. I lift my lamp beside the golden door.
>
> Emma Lazarus (1849–1887), American poet and essayist

By the early nineteenth century, four primary groups made up the American people—Native Americans, descendents of the original colonists who were primarily from England, Africans (as forced immigrant slaves), and European immigrants. With the arrival of Christopher Columbus in 1492, the New World was opened to settlers from Europe. Many were refugees fleeing religious or political persecution, while others came searching for personal gain. The thirteen colonies which first formed the United States were along the eastern coast. The development of the southern states and their reliance on agriculture caused southern landowners to search for cheap labor through the slave trade in Africa.

In the early 1800s, the country was expanding westward. Many newcomers arrived as indentured servants who were required to work for free to pay for their passage to America. While some pioneers prospered, other ethnic groups suffered as a result of the country's rapid development. As they moved westward, new settlers pushed the Native American population off their land and eventually onto reservations. The nation's rapid expansion brought Chinese laborers to the West Coast to work on the railroads. In spite of the contributions of different groups to the growth of America, there were times in the nation's history when quotas were established in an attempt to stem the tide of immigration.

Since the early 1800s, the United States has been a land of immigrants who have come in search of the "American Dream"—a better life for themselves and their children. Some, such as Chuck Sambar, author of "Return to Ellis Island Evokes Memories and Pride," have come seeking a fresh start. In recent years, diverse groups of Americans have developed a sense of pride in their cultural heritage. This can be seen in the readings "For My Indian Daughter" by Lewis Sawaquat and "My Father's Black Pride" by Marcus Bleecker and in ethnic celebrations such as the one described in "Reflecting on UCI's Diversity: Rainbow Festival Offers Color, Culture, Cuisine."

What does it mean to be or become an American? Discuss this question in small groups. Then talk about the picture on page 2 and answer the question: *As this family gazes across New York Harbor, what does the statue in the distance symbolize to them?*

Can You Pass This "Citizenship" Test?

Work with a partner to decide which of these statements about the United States are true *(T)* or false *(F)*.

_____ 1. All American immigrants must become citizens.

_____ 2. Many immigrants had their names shortened or changed at Ellis Island.

_____ 3. An Englishman discovered America.

_____ 4. Early immigrants believed the streets of America were paved with gold.

_____ 5. All immigrants to the United States are welcomed.

_____ 6. Only U.S. citizens can vote.

_____ 7. The Statue of Liberty was a gift from France to the United States.

_____ 8. Most immigrants to the United States today come from Europe.

_____ 9. The second most common language spoken in the United States is Chinese.

_____10. Many U.S. states, streets, and cities have Native American and Spanish names.

Test Your Word Power

Take this vocabulary quiz. Match the words with their definitions. Then compare your answers with a partner so you will be better prepared to understand the readings.

_____ 1. immigrant (n)

_____ 2. descendant (n)

_____ 3. ancestor (n)

_____ 4. heritage (n)

_____ 5. ethnic (adj)

_____ 6. racism (n)

_____ 7. diversity (n)

_____ 8. immigration quota (np)

_____ 9. genealogy (n)

_____10. refugee (n)

a. person who moves to another country to live

b. person leaving a country due to bad conditions, such as war

c. beliefs, traditions, history passed from one generation to the next

d. related to characteristics of race, origin, culture

e. names and history of a family

f. limit on number of immigrants

g. someone born into a certain family line

h. variety

i. prejudice against people based on color

j. person from whom one is descended

> In the 1990s, more than 40 percent, or over 100 million, of all living Americans could trace their roots to an ancestor who came through Ellis Island.
>
> U.S. Census Bureau

■ In his introduction to this essay, California columnist and educator Chuck Sambar writes, "I was among those who came aboard a ship loaded with people escaping the devastation of war and fleeing hardships such as poverty, religious persecution, and political unrest."

■ Do you know where Ellis Island is and how many immigrants passed through this inspection point when entering the United States by boat? Why would someone like Sambar want to return there? Read his essay to find out.

Return to Ellis Island Evokes Memories and Pride

CHUCK SAMBAR

1   Forty-four years ago, I stood and gazed with absolute awe and wonder at the Statue of Liberty as the Italian ship, the S.S. *Queen Frederica*, sailed into New York Harbor with a load of more than 1,200 immigrants. I was barely in my teens and among those who entered this great land of ours through Ellis Island.

2   Recently, I went back after all these years to view and remember my early days, when, as a little boy, I was *smuggled*[1] out of Lebanon to sail to America in search of life, liberty, and the pursuit of education and happiness. Thank God, I found them all. My return to New York was a trip I have dreamed about for years. I am an educator and businessman, and I have traveled all over the world, so what's so special about a trip to New York? Well, it was 10 years ago when my sons honored me by making a donation in my name to help in the *restoration*[2] of Ellis Island.

3   Little did I know when I came to my new country that Ellis Island was, and still is, the symbol of America's immigrant heritage. Ellis Island was the gateway to the largest tide of incoming humanity in our nation's history. And I was among those fortunate enough to have passed through its gate into my new country.

4   For six decades, from 1892 to 1954, Ellis Island was the entry point to some 12 million people, 40 percent of our nation's population at the time.

5   I was among those who came aboard a ship loaded with people escaping the *devastation*[3] of war and fleeing hardships such as poverty, religious *persecution*,[4] and political unrest. All of us came to America in search of free-

---

[1] *smuggle* (v) to bring things into another country illegally
[2] *restoration* (n) act of making something look new
[3] *devastation* (n) total destruction
[4] *persecution* (n) act of treating someone cruelly or unfairly because of one's beliefs

dom and opportunity. All of us passed through the gates and the great hall of entry at Ellis Island. I remember it well.

6   My wife, my son Al, his wife Phyllis, and my 20-month-old grandson Nathan joined me for the return journey. It was an anxious and tense day for me as we approached by train first, then subway, then boarded the ferry to Ellis Island. As we approached the island, I tried to remember every little detail of my first entry. I found myself talking to myself out loud.

7   I remembered large numbers of people lined up in many rows waiting to be interviewed and processed. I could hear loud voices, many foreign languages, people who communicated with gestures of hope, anger, and anticipation. I remembered masses of *huddled*[5] women and children with bundles of clothing, trunks, suitcases, some with little other than the clothes they were wearing.

8   More than 5,000 people a day were processed through Ellis Island. Many waited for hours to be questioned, processed, given papers, and allowed to enter our new country. Unfortunately, some were excluded and returned home on the same ship that brought them. It was very emotional.

9   Here I am with my grandson, tracing the steps I took years ago, remembering my early days, how I was lost, *disoriented*,[6] uninformed, and barely able to speak English or communicate with anyone. Here I am again in the massive processing hall of Ellis Island, overwhelmed visually and emotionally by the displays in the museum. Galleries filled with artifacts, historic photos, posters, ethnic music, and two theaters featuring *Island of Hope and Island of Tears*, an award-winning film documenting the Ellis Island experience. It has not changed at all.

10   Thousands of people from all over the world are there now with us today, talking in various languages, reading, viewing, and some crying. It is an *overwhelming*[7] and touching recollection. Inside the main hall where the museum's Baggage Room is located, there is an *innovative*,[8] *interactive*[9] computer registry that contains every name inscribed on the American Immigrant Wall of Honor.

11   We huddled around the computer and did a name search for Chakib Sambar. Sure enough, there is my name, country of origin, and date of entry. With feelings of joy and pride, I read where my own sons had honored me nearly 10 years ago by making a donation to the Ellis Island restoration effort.

---

[5] *huddled* (adj) pressed closely together
[6] *disoriented* (adj) confused
[7] *overwhelming* (adj) beyond one's ability to control; upsetting
[8] *innovative* (adj) creative and new
[9] *interactive* (adj) involving communication and activity between machine and user

In 1900, 85 percent of U.S. immigrants came from Europe. In 1990, more than two-thirds came from Asia and Latin America.

Doug Brugge, health scientist for *Public Eye*

The U.S. received about 60 percent of the world's immigrants from 1820 to 1930.

New Columbia Encyclopedia

12   It was my children's Christmas gift to me that year, 1986. Without a doubt, it stands as the most meaningful and sensitive gift I have ever and will ever receive. Through their donation, my name is inscribed on the American Immigrant Wall of Honor, along with such distinguished Americans as Col. John Washington, great-grandfather of George Washington, and the great-grandparents of Sen. Bob Dole, Barbra Streisand, Boris Karloff, Marlene Dietrich, and President John F. Kennedy. Virtually every nationality is represented on the wall, and the famous take their place among the hundreds of thousands of unsung individuals who are heroes to their descendants and children.

Author Chuck Sambar points to his name on the American Immigrant Wall of Honor.

13   I am a grateful and proud immigrant. More importantly, my children know how proud I am to be an American immigrant. Their gift honoring me does in fact honor my new country and keeps the memory and history of Ellis Island alive.

14   America may not be the most perfect country on Earth, but without a doubt, it is the best country on Earth. And I feel good now knowing that my children and grandson know the reality of my immigrant status and my belief that we must never take our country for granted.

15   We have been to Ellis Island.

Understanding the Reading: Recalling Facts and Details

See how many of these facts you now know about Ellis Island and Chuck Sambar's visits there. First try to write short answers to the questions without looking back at the reading. Then check your answers by **scanning***, or looking for key words and dates, to find specific information in the article.*

1. Sambar wrote this article in 1996. In what year did he arrive in the United States?
2. What country was Sambar originally from?
3. What famous symbol stands in New York Harbor near Ellis Island?
4. About how many people passed through Ellis Island between 1892 and 1954?
5. About how many immigrants were processed through Ellis Island each day?
6. Were all immigrants admitted?
7. What means of transportation does a person take to get to Ellis Island?
8. What special gift did Sambar's children give him in 1986?
9. Whose names are on the American Immigrant Wall of Honor?
10. What is the title of the movie about Ellis Island?

> According to the United Nations, the United States admits about 75,000 refugees each year, about 60 percent of the total number of resettled refugees.

Using the Vocabulary: Descriptive Adjectives

Since "Return to Ellis Island" is a personal narrative, Sambar uses many adjectives to describe his emotions at various points. Match the adjectives with the situation, person, or thing being described. The numbered adjectives on the left are listed as they appear in the text so that you can check your answers.

_____ 1. fortunate

_____ 2. overwhelmed visually and emotionally

_____ 3. anxious and tense

_____ 4. lost, disoriented, uninformed

_____ 5. innovative, interactive

_____ 6. meaningful and sensitive

_____ 7. grateful and proud

a. the day Sambar and his family traveled to visit Ellis Island in 1996

b. all the immigrants who passed through the gate of Ellis Island

c. the young Sambar arriving in New York

d. the family gift of a contribution and inscription on the wall

e. Sambar's description of himself as an American immigrant today

f. Sambar's reaction to the displays in the Ellis Island museum

g. the computer registry containing inscriptions

Reading Maps

The New York City subway system is one of the most extensive in the world. A tourist can get anywhere in the city by train. However, there are twenty-four subway lines and getting around the city is not always easy. Study the map with a partner and then answer these questions.

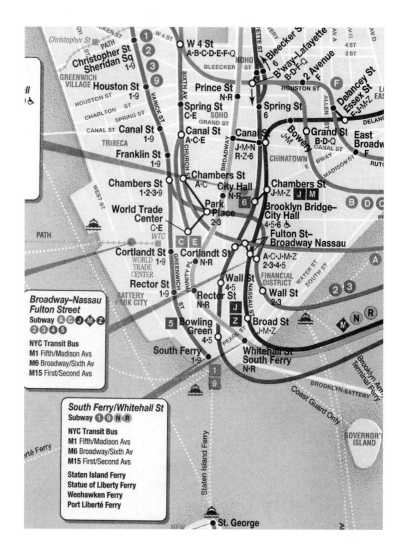

1. From West Fourth Street, which two of the seven trains will take you to the World Trade Center?

2. What is the stop on the Number 1 and 9 trains for the Statue of Liberty and the Staten Island Ferry?

3. What bridge is closest to City Hall?

4. Which train lines stop at the Wall Street stations in the financial district?

5. Which stop on the J-M-N lines is closest to Chinatown?

Thinking Together

Work in small groups to write the names of these ethnic groups in the regions on the map where they settled. What factors do you think influenced their decisions to settle there?

Swedes and Norwegians (Minnesota, Wisconsin)

Germans (Missouri)

Chinese (Northern California)

Japanese (Hawaii)

Italians (New York)

Indochinese (Southern California)

Portuguese (Connecticut, Massachusetts)

Irish (Massachusetts)

Mexicans (Texas, Arizona)

Cubans (Florida)

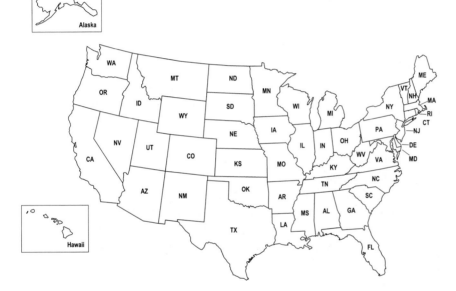

Writing about It

*Write one to two paragraphs on one of the following topics. Try to use some of the vocabulary from this reading and from **Focusing In**.*

1. Describe some of the hardships Sambar had to face as a young immigrant.

2. Summarize the importance of Ellis Island and the Statue of Liberty as symbols of American immigration.

3. Write a short report for a New York City newspaper of a day in the early 1900s when immigrants were arriving at Ellis Island.

Reacting to the Reading

Do you think it is important to preserve national monuments to a country's heritage, such as Ellis Island and the Statue of Liberty?

■ In this article, Lewis P. Sawaquat, a Native American, writes a memoir for his daughter about the prejudice he has encountered and the pride he has found in his heritage. As you read, you will discover what Sawaquat realizes about human nature.

■ What do you know about the history of Native Americans in the United States? What advice do you think Sawaquat will give to his child?

For My Indian Daughter

Lewis P. Sawaquat

from *Newsweek*

1　My little girl is singing herself to sleep upstairs, her voice mingling with the sounds of the birds outside in the old maple trees. She is two and I am nearly 50, and I am very taken with her. She came along late in my life, unexpected and unbidden, a startling gift.

2　Today at the beach my chubby-legged, brown-skinned daughter ran laughing into the water as fast as she could. My wife and I laughed watching her, until we heard behind us a low *guttural*[1] curse and then an unpleasant voice raised in an imitation war whoop.

3　I turned to see a fat man in a bathing suit, white and soft as a *grub*,[2] as he covered his mouth and prepared to make the Indian war cry again. He was middle-aged, younger than I, and had three little children lined up next to him, grinning foolishly. My wife suggested we leave the beach, and I agreed.

4　I knew the man was not unusual in his feelings against Indians. His beach behavior might have been socially unacceptable to more civilized whites, but his basic view of Indians is expressed daily in our small town, frequently on the editorial pages of the county newspaper, as white people speak out against Indian fishing rights and land rights, saying in essence, "Those Indians are taking our fish, our land." It doesn't matter to them that we were here first, that the U.S. Supreme Court has ruled in our favor. It matters to them that we have something they want, and they hate us for it. *Backlash*[3] is the common explanation of the attacks on Indians, the bumper stickers that say, "Spear an Indian, Save a Fish," but I know better. The hatred of Indians goes back to the beginning when white people came to this country. For me it goes back to my childhood in Harbor Springs, Michigan.

Theft

5　Harbor Springs is now a summer resort for the very *affluent*,[4] but a hundred years ago it was the Indian village of my Ottawa ancestors. My grandmother, Anna Showanessy, and other Indians like her, had their land there taken by treaty, by *fraud*,[5] by violence,

---

[1] ***guttural*** (adj) making a sound from the throat
[2] ***grub*** (n) insect larva that looks like a small worm
[3] ***backlash*** (n) strong reaction against a particular event, decision, or social development
[4] ***affluent*** (adj) wealthy, prosperous
[5] ***fraud*** (n) deceit with the purpose of gaining someone's property or money

by theft. They remembered how whites had burned down the village at Burt Lake in 1900 and pushed the Indians out. These were the stories in my family.

6 When I was a boy my mother told me to walk down the alleys in Harbor Springs and not to wear my orange football sweater out of the house. This way I would not stand out, not be noticed, and not be a target.

7 I wore my orange sweater anyway and deliberately avoided the alleys. I was the biggest person I knew and wasn't really afraid. But I met my *comeuppance*[6] when I enlisted in the U.S. Army. One night, all the men in my barracks gathered together and, gang-fashion, pulled me into the shower and scrubbed me down with rough brushes used for floors, saying, "We won't have any dirty Indians in our *outfit*."[7] It is a point of irony that I was cleaner than any of them. Later in Korea I learned how to kill, how to *bully*,[8] how to hate Koreans. I came out of the war tougher than ever and, strangely, white.

8 I went to college, got married, lived in La Porte, Indiana, worked as a *surveyor*[9] and raised three boys. I headed Boy Scout groups, never thinking it odd when the Scouts did imitation Indian dances, imitation Indian *lore*.[10] One day when I was 35 or thereabouts I heard about an Indian *powwow*.[11] My father used to attend them and so with great curiosity and a strange joy at discovering a part of my heritage, I decided the thing to do to get ready for this big event was to have my friend make

A young dancer performs at the Annual Pan-Indian Pow Wow at the University of California, Irvine.

me a *spear*[12] in his *forge*.[13] The steel was fine and blue and *iridescent*.[14] The feathers on the shaft were bright and proud.

9 In a dusty state fairground in southern Indiana, I found white people dressed as Indians. I learned they were "hobbyists," that is, it was their hobby and leisure pastime to *masquerade*[15] as Indians on weekends. I felt ridiculous with my spear, and I left.

---

[6] *comeuppance* (n) well-deserved punishment

[7] *outfit* (n) group of people working together, such as in the military

[8] *bully* (v) to force others to do things by using fear or strength

[9] *surveyor* (n) person who measures and records details of land

[10] *lore* (n) knowledge and traditions passed down by word of mouth

[11] *powwow* (n) Native American dance ceremony and/or meeting to discuss problems

[12] *spear* (n) long, thin pole with a sharp point, used in hunting, warfare, and rituals

[13] *forge* (n) machine or apparatus used for melting and shaping metals

[14] *iridescent* (adj) showing colors of the rainbow, usually shiny

[15] *masquerade* (v) to pretend to be someone else

10   It was years before I could tell anyone of the embarrassment of this weekend and see any humor in it. But in a way it was that weekend in all its silliness, that was my awakening. I realized I didn't know who I was. I didn't have an Indian name. I didn't speak the Indian language. I didn't know the Indian customs. Dimly I remembered the Ottawa word for dog, but it was a baby word, *kahgee*, not the full word, *muhkahgee*, which I was later to learn. Even more hazily I remembered a naming ceremony (my own). I remembered legs dancing around me, dust. Where had that been? Who had I been? "Suwaukquat," my mother told me when I asked, "where the tree begins to grow."

11   That was 1968, and I was not the only Indian in the country who was feeling the need to remember who he or she was. There were others. They had powwows, real ones, and eventually I found them. Together we researched our past, a search that for me *culminated*[16] in the Longest Walk, a march on Washington in 1978. Maybe because I now know what it means to be Indian, it surprises me that others don't. Of course there aren't very many of us left. The chances of an average person knowing an average Indian in an average lifetime are pretty slim.

Circle

12   Still, I was amused one day when my small, four-year-old neighbor looked at me as I was hoeing in my garden and said, "You aren't a real Indian, are you?" Scotty is little, talkative, likable. Finally I said, "I'm a real Indian." He looked at me for a moment and then said, *squinting*[17] into the sun, "Then where's your horse and feathers?" The child was simply a smaller, whiter version of my own ignorant self years before. We'd both seen too much TV, that's all. He was not to be blamed. And so, in a way, the *moronic*[18] man on the beach today is blameless. We come full circle to realize other people are like ourselves, as *discomfiting*[19] as that may be sometimes.

13   As I sit in my old chair on my porch, in a light that is fading so the leaves are hardly distinguishable against the sky, I can picture my girl asleep upstairs. I would like to prepare her for what's to come, take her each step of the way saying, there's a place to avoid, here's what I know about this, but much of what's before her she must go through alone. She must pass through pain and joy and solitude and community to discover her own inner self that is unlike any other and come through that passage to the place where she sees all people are one, and in so seeing may live her life in a brighter future.

---

[16] *culminate* (v) to result in
[17] *squint* (v) to look with partly opened eyes
[18] *moronic* (adj) stupid, foolish
[19] *discomfiting* (adj) distressing, upsetting

Understanding the Reading: Recalling Facts and Details

Readers may recall some facts and details after a first reading of a text, but answering specific questions usually requires rereading some sections. Read the beginning of each sentence and circle the letter for the phrase that best completes it. If you are not sure of your choice, cross out any answer you are sure is wrong before you look back at the text. Then check your answers with a partner.

1. Lewis Sawaquat and his family probably leave the beach because
   a. they are tired of fishing.
   b. they are bothered by the prejudice of the white man and his children.
   c. they are worried about being late.

2. Sawaquat feels that white people's basic views about Indians are that Indians
   a. eat fish more often than white people do.
   b. are taking something that doesn't belong to them.
   c. are too noisy.

3. The author wants to go to his first powwow because he is
   a. curious about understanding a part of his heritage.
   b. trying to earn approval from his people.
   c. interested in buying a new spear.

4. When Sawaquat was a boy, he didn't walk in alleys because he
   a. wasn't wearing an orange football sweater.
   b. knew he might be attacked in them.
   c. wasn't afraid of the people he would meet in the street.

5. The hobbyists that the author meets spend their leisure time
   a. dressing and acting like Indians.
   b. hunting buffalo.
   c. traveling in military outfits.

6. The author says that the chances of meeting a real Indian today are
   a. very likely.
   b. slim.
   c. impossible.

If you pen an Indian up on a small spot of earth, and compel him to stay there, he will not be contented, nor will he grow and prosper.

Chief Joseph (1840–1904), Nez Percé leader

7. Sawaquat writes that he and the little boy are similar because

   a. they like to masquerade as Indians.

   b. they both ride a horse and wear feathers.

   c. they are both ignorant.

8. At the end of the story, the author realizes that

   a. people are discomfiting.

   b. people are very similar.

   c. people are very different.

Using the Vocabulary: Synonyms

A. *Each of the following sentences from the reading has a new vocabulary word followed by two words or phrases. One is a* **synonym** *or a word close in meaning to the new word. Read the whole sentence carefully to help you remember the meaning of the first word. Then cross out the word that does* <u>not</u> *have the same meaning. Check your answers by looking at the definitions in the footnotes.*

1. Harbor Springs is now a summer resort for the very *affluent* (rich/needy), but a hundred years ago it was the Indian village of my Ottawa ancestors.

2. Together we researched our past, a search that for me *culminated* (began/ended) in the Longest Walk, a march on Washington in 1978.

3. "We won't have any dirty Indians in our *outfit* (fitting room/military company)."

4. Later in Korea I learned how to kill, how to *bully* (overpower by force/heat water), how to hate Koreans.

5. One day when I was 35 or thereabouts I heard about an Indian *powwow* (meeting/reservation).

6. The steel was fine and blue and *iridescent* (pasty white/shining).

7. . . . it was their hobby and leisure pastime to *masquerade* (wear costumes and masks/have parties in the streets) as Indians on weekends.

8. He looked at me for a moment and then said, *squinting* (making high-pitched sounds/peering out of half-closed eyes) into the sun, "Then where's your horse and feathers?"

9. And so, in a way, the *moronic* (talkative/foolish) man on the beach today is blameless.

10. We come full circle to realize other people are like ourselves, as *discomfiting* (upsetting/unnatural) as that may be sometimes.

B. *Complete the sentences with the appropriate words from this list.*

affluent	discomfited	moronic
culminated	iridescent	powwows

Many Americans today are (1)_____ by the past treatment of
Native Americans. The Indians were often attacked by pioneers and troops moving
west. This westward expansion (2)_____ in the loss of their
land and the establishment of reservations. Now, people travel to Indian villages
and reservations to learn more about native cultures. Native Americans themselves
travel all over the country to participate in (3)_____, to meet
other tribes and to learn about their ancestry. Today it is only the
(4)_____ racist who thinks Native Americans were wild red-
skinned people who stood in the way of the expansion of the United States.

Thinking Together

*In "For My Indian Daughter," Sawaquat talks about a weekend that led to an awak-
ening of his cultural identity. Quickly list five cultural traditions that you would like to
pass down to your children so that they can preserve their ethnic identity. Then work
together in small groups to compare and discuss your lists.*

Writing about It

*Write one to two paragraphs on one of the following topics. Try to use some of the
vocabulary from this reading and from* **Focusing In**.

1. Write a letter from a resident of Harbor Springs to your local newspaper.
   Recount your observations of the incident on the beach between Sawaquat's
   family and the white man.

2. Briefly summarize two to three reasons why the people of Harbor Springs are
   unfriendly to the writer and his people. How does the author feel about their
   actions and opinions?

3. Explain what Sawaquat means when he says that "the moronic man on the
   beach today is blameless."

Reacting to the Reading

Given your own knowledge of and experience with prejudice, explain how you
would react to a racially charged incident like the one described in Sawaquat's story.

During the '90s,
there were an
estimated 2,000
powwows across
America and Canada
each year.

Wayne Reels, cultural
resources director for the
Pequots

■ There are many crosscultural and interracial families in the United States. Marcus Bleecker, a jazz musician, describes his own here.
■ What do you think some of the problems would be for a child growing up in a family with parents of different races? When you read the story, see if your ideas are confirmed.

My Father's Black Pride

Marcus Bleecker

from *The New York Times Magazine*

1   I am black. My mother is black. My father is white. This wouldn't necessarily be important, but we live in a country where conflict runs deep between blacks and whites. We live in a country where white male *slaveholders*[1] casually *disavowed*[2] the black children they had *sired*.[3] We live in a country where the worst of human traits—laziness, violence, and *irrationality*[4]—are seen as defining characteristics of those of African descent. This makes my being a mixed-race person whose ethnic identity is black somewhat more complicated. There is a *dissonance*[5] between who I say I am—a proud black man trying to do something positive with his life—and who society says I am. Yet I feel strong, and I embrace my black heritage. I've often reflected on how I learned to keep my positive self-image. The answer is, my white father.

2   With my olive-colored skin, hazel eyes and curly hair, I've been taken for Hispanic or Middle Eastern. In fact, in addition to being black, I am Jewish. And my father taught me to be proud of that heritage as well. When bullies at school demanded, "Are you black or white?" there was no confusion. When I ran home and asked my father, he said, "Tell them you are African-American." That was in the early 1970s and it was a term I wouldn't hear until the Afrocentric movement of the 1990s made it fashionable again.

3   It wasn't that my father wanted me to *deny*[6] my Jewish roots, it's just that he knew we live in a society where my African heritage would define me socially. He didn't want me to seem ashamed of my black roots. My father knew that love and hopes for an ideal world in the distant future would be no *panacea*[7] for the *bigotry*[8] and small-mindedness I would encounter in my lifetime. He didn't want me, my brother or my sister to be unprepared for racism.

4   And so, my father, a writer and avid reader, lined my shelves with books about black American culture, African culture and Jewish culture. He encouraged me to think, to come up with my own ideas. A simple

---

[1] *slaveholder* (n) owner of a person who works and has no freedom
[2] *disavow* (v) to reject, refuse, deny
[3] *sire* (v) to be the father of
[4] *irrationality* (n) lack of power of reason
[5] *dissonance* (n) conflict

[6] *deny* (v) to refuse to accept as true
[7] *panacea* (n) something claimed to cure an illness or problem
[8] *bigotry* (n) unreasonable but strong beliefs, usually about race or religion

question posed to him was sure to be followed by his search for a book on the subject, with articles and additional information to follow. In this way he gave me not only his opinion, but also the keys to how he arrived at that opinion. Knowing that I had those keys, too, he thought that I could evaluate his opinion and come up with my own. He encouraged me to determine what being black meant to me.

5   In the *predominantly*[9] white suburb near Princeton, NJ, where I grew up, my father knew that I needed to know black men. So when I started playing drums at age 14, my father took me to jazz clubs. He encouraged me to talk to the musicians and get their autographs. This introduction led to my decision to become a professional musician, and also filled my home with a black male presence. Jazz was more than a *genre*[10] of music; it instructed me in the cool posture of black men—Max Roach's *shades*,[11] Miles Davis's *scowl*[12] and his always stylish *threads*.[13] It also instructed me in a kind of heroism. These men were geniuses who created America's only enduring art form despite its best efforts to stifle and ignore them.

6   My father also hired James, a black 16-year-old, who became my favorite babysitter. My father gave me book knowledge and taught me to have an open mind; James showed me how to deal with people on a practical level. My father was gentle, but James taught me that as a black man, you have to be ungentle sometimes. You have to speak up for yourself. James never let me walk away from a *confrontation*[14] without speaking my mind.

7   During the summers, my parents sent me to my mother's family in Virginia. My cousins—especially Jeffrey, who is seven years older than I—helped me become a mature black man. Jeffrey taught me to treat women with respect, through his example as well as through his words. These are lessons my father had taught me

There has been a steady increase in interracial marriages in the United States since 1960.

also, but he hoped that my summer visits down South would reinforce those values by being transmitted by black men of my generation.

8   In college, I counseled children from mixed backgrounds. I could see the emptiness in some of the kids either who didn't have a black parent around—usually the father—or whose parents weren't in agreement about how much emphasis should be

---

⁹ *predominantly* (adv) mostly, mainly
¹⁰ *genre* (n) specific type of music, art, or literature
¹¹ *shades* (n) slang for sunglasses (Note: Roach and Davis were black jazz musicians.)

¹² *scowl* (n) frown; unhappy face
¹³ *threads* (n) slang for clothes
¹⁴ *confrontation* (n) fight or argument

put on black culture. Often these children would grow up in predominantly white environments with a negative view of their black fathers or of black culture in general. I realized how fortunate I was to have a father who encouraged me to develop as a black person while never making me feel that I was less his son because of my blackness.

9   In many ways what my father taught me about manhood was not related to color. He taught me that, ultimately, I determined through my behavior what a black man is. My father taught me to be a gentle man, to use my mind and not my fists. He taught me the value of education and encouraged me to ask questions. My father exposed me to black men who lived up to these universal ideals of manhood, and thereby emphasized that blacks shared in that tradition.

All these things have made me the man, the black man, I am today.

10   My father and I are now the closest we have ever been. Of course, there are race-related topics, things I feel, that he will never be able to understand. I know that there are probably people who meet my father and see just another white man. But I know that there are things he has learned from me and my brother that have given him an insight into black masculinity that most white men will never experience. In this way, we have taught each other. Our relationship *epitomizes*[15] a reality that is so rarely seen—a black man and a white man who are not *adversaries*.[16] Who are more than father and son. They are men who love each other very deeply.

Understanding the Reading: Identifying Facts and Details

A. *The most common types of questions are the five* **Wh–** *questions:* **who, what, where, when, why**. *See if you can write short answers to the five questions without looking back at the story. Then check your answers with a partner.*

1. *Who* was white in Marcus Bleecker's family?

2. *What* groups make up Bleecker's ethnic identity?

3. *Where* did Bleecker grow up?

4. *When* did Bleecker counsel children from mixed backgrounds?

5. *Why* did his father hire James as a babysitter?

---

[15] *epitomize* (v) to be typical of   [16] *adversary* (n) opponent or enemy

B. *The following sentences are **paraphrases**, or restatements, of information in the story. Work with a partner to identify the paragraphs in the reading that show the following points and fill in the paragraph numbers.*

_____ 1. Bleecker's father knew his children would face racism.

_____ 2. Today, Bleecker has positive self-esteem.

_____ 3. Bleecker is a jazz musician.

_____ 4. Books were an important means of learning about heritage in the Bleecker family.

_____ 5. Bleecker spent part of his childhood living among blacks.

Using the Vocabulary: Synonyms

A. *Test your knowledge of the new vocabulary words. Substitute a word from the list that is the closest in meaning to the word or phrase in parentheses in each sentence.*

adversary	dissonance	predominantly
bigotry	epitomized	scowl
confrontations	genre	shades
disavow	irrationality	threads

1. Ethnic groups from different eras often have a style of dress that characterizes them, such as the dark _____ (sunglasses) of black musicians in the 1950s and 1960s.

2. Some black Americans, Native Americans, and immigrants try to _____ (ignore) their heritage and native culture.

3. Jazz, a _____ (type) created by black musicians, was a major contribution to American music.

4. Unfortunately, the history of race relations in the United States has included many _____ (fights) between whites and blacks.

5. A person who is unhappy will walk around with a _____ (frown) instead of a smile.

> The great social adventure of America is no longer the conquest of the wilderness but the absorption of fifty different peoples.
>
> Walter Lippmann
> (1889–1974),
> U.S. journalist

B. *Now complete this paragraph with the correct forms of the words from the list in Exercise A (page 19) that best fit each sentence.*

Marcus Bleecker was lucky that he did not have to (1)_____ his culture. His mother and father (2)_____ the ideal understanding and sympathetic parents. In spite of their different backgrounds, there were few, if any, family (3)_____ over the way to raise the children. Even though Bleecker grew up in an area that was (4)_____ white, his parents tried to make sure their children understood their ethnic backgrounds and were prepared to face the (5)_____ they might encounter.

Thinking Together

Interview at least five members of your class to learn about their ethnic backgrounds. Ask each person a question about his or her heritage. Take notes. Share your information with the class to find out which student has the most diverse ancestry.

Writing about It

Write one to two paragraphs on one of the following topics. Try to use some of the vocabulary from this reading and from Focusing In.

1. Write a letter from Bleecker to his father, thanking him for his guidance.

2. Summarize four specific things Bleecker's parents did to help him understand and identify with all parts of his ethnicity.

3. Bleecker counsels children of mixed backgrounds. Write a paragraph presenting some of the advice he might give them.

Reacting to the Reading

Based on your observations, do you think that interracial marriages can be successful? Why or why not?

Keeping Track of Your Reading Rate

- "Reflecting on UCI's Diversity" is a report by Meghan Sweeney on a campus event to learn about other cultures represented by students in the United States.
- To establish your reading rate, when your instructor gives you the signal to begin, read the article at your normal speed and mark down the time as soon as you are done. Then answer the questions without looking back at the reading.

tip Confident readers are more efficient. Try not to pause often or reread phrases.

Looking back on a decade of cultural growth, last week's tenth annual University of California at Irvine [UCI] Rainbow Festival and Conference focused on "Reflecting on Our Faces and Dreams." "Rainbow Festival was created 10 years ago [in 1984] as a means to provide educational forums to increase the awareness of cultural diversity," said Corina Espinoza, chair of the conference. This year's festival featured workshops, seminars and speakers addressing the issues of diversity and multiculturalism. Ring Road of the UCI Student Center served as the location for displaying ethnic arts and crafts, performances by student clubs and organizations, and a variety of foods from different cultures.

Opening the two-day conference period was keynote speaker Audrey Yamagata-Noji, dean of student development at Rancho Santiago College in Santa Ana. She spoke on the theme of the festival at the Cross Cultural Center and on "recognizing the faces around us and realizing that all those faces have dreams," Espinoza said. The evening keynote speaker was Gregory Alan-Williams, Emmy award-winning actor and author of the book "Gathering Heroes: Reflections on Rage and Responsibility." He did not advocate diversity as being something new but "as American as apple pie."

Maceo Hernandez, referred to as the "Demon Drummer from East L.A.," along with John Esaki, put on a Japanese taiko drum presentation. . . . "You'd think that drumming with him would be intimidating, but taiko brings everybody together. You can bond with taiko," said Peggy Kamon, a senior English major. "It was kind of a thrill," added Miki Takushi. . . .

According to Espinoza, the planning committee for this year tried to schedule more events so that more people could attend at different times of the day. Three evening sessions of a workshop entitled "Walk in My Shoes" explored different cultural backgrounds and trying to be more sensitive to the way others feel. The session was located in the student dormitories. They also provided various afternoon performances at the cultural fair in the Ring Road so people could attend during the lunch hour.

In order to reach out to the surrounding community, a new evening cultural performance, "A Musical Mosaic," was presented in Crystal Cove Auditorium. This final performance featured the song and dance of different ethnic and cultural traditions, including the American Indian "Fancy Shawl" dance, the Hawaiian chants and hula of Na Opio Ka'aina, the songs of the Royal Scottish Country Dance Society, and the Filipino dance by Kababayan.

(400 words)   TIME _____

> The making of an
> American begins at
> the point where he
> himself rejects all
> other ties, any other
> history, and himself
> adopts the vesture of
> his adopted land.
>
> James Baldwin
> (1924–1987), U.S. author

Now mark these statements true (T) or false (F) without looking back at the reading.

_____ 1. This event took place at a high school campus.

_____ 2. UCI students come from many cultural backgrounds.

_____ 3. This was the tenth Rainbow Festival at UCI.

_____ 4. All of the festival events took place in the evening.

_____ 5. Hernandez and Esaki, two musicians from different cultures, performed together.

_____ 6. Only groups representing countries outside of the United States performed at the festival.

_____ 7. The festival included workshops, dancing, and music, but not food.

_____ 8. Students who were interviewed seemed to enjoy the conference and festival.

_____ 9. The school administration probably supports the need for cultural understanding among groups.

_____10. This festival is probably called Rainbow Festival because it is held on a bright sunny day.

Percent correct = _____ Words per minute (wpm) = _____

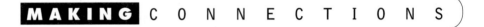

Responding to the Readings

Prepare short oral or written responses based on your personal experience and your reactions to the readings. Try to incorporate the information and the vocabulary you have learned in this chapter.

1. What hardships do immigrants face when they arrive in a new country? Are they similar to those of Native Americans and African Americans as expressed in the readings presented in this chapter?

2. Imagine you are an immigrant arriving at Ellis Island in the early 1900s. Describe the sights and sounds around you and your feelings and impressions.

3. Native Americans represent one of the racial minorities in the United States. Describe the racial minorities in your country.

4. Chuck Sambar changed his name from "Chakib" to "Chuck" when he arrived at Ellis Island. Lewis Sawaquat only recently gave up the name "Johnson" for the name that he had received in his naming ceremony. Have you ever gone

by another name? Would you ever change your name to fit in with your new surroundings?

5. Discuss your reaction to one of the quotes or facts in the margins of this chapter that you find most interesting or surprising.

Editing Your Work

A student wrote this paragraph without editing carefully for verb tense. When writing about earlier events, remember to check that all verbs related to the story you are telling are in the past. Correct the five verbs that should be changed to past tense.

This is about an Indian family. The parents decided to come to America with the intention of getting jobs and giving their children a better education. Before they came to America they had sold most of their property in their country. They thought they can earn three or four times more money than what they were earning in India. When they first arrived in America, they don't know anybody in the country. The family stayed in a hotel until they find a place to live. As soon as they move to an apartment, they started to apply for jobs that were related to their fields, but they didn't succeed. At first, they were unsuccessful because they don't speak English well and their degrees in engineering were not valid in the state they were living in. Their pride and self dignity were hurt and too many doors were closed to their success.

Writing an Essay

Choose one of the following topics and write an essay. As a prewriting activity, read over your shortwrites and notes for inspiration. Remember to review the brainstorming techniques on pages 262–263. In your essay, use the readings, factoids, quotes, class discussions, and personal experience to support your ideas. Try to use the vocabulary you have learned in this chapter. If you choose to write a research paper, make certain to cite your sources clearly.

1. In the voice of an elderly person in your family, relate your family's history for your descendants. Trace your family tree and tell about the important people, when they lived, and what they did. Tell about significant events in your family and in your country during your relatives' lifetimes. Make sure to give specific details on special celebrations, gatherings, and traditional ceremonies.

Here is not merely a nation, but a nation of nations.

Walt Whitman
(1819–1892), U.S. poet

> During the long voyage and the frightening five-hour trial at Ellis Island, we yearned to begin our new life in the new country. We pushed [the door open] and we inherited America.
>
> Shiao Chang,
> Chinese immigrant

2. If you are living in the United States, describe your journey to America in as much detail as possible. Tell about your decision to come, who and what you left behind, and what your arrival and first days were like. Give as much detail as possible so that your readers can imagine what you saw and how you felt at the time. You might also choose to write about someone in your family who has had this experience.

3. Discuss the problem of cultural conflicts. You might talk about immigrants adjusting to a new land, different generations within one culture with different ideas, racism, or intercultural marriages. Talk to friends and family to get ideas.

4. Write an essay on the values and traditions that are part of your culture that you feel would be important to pass on to future generations. Try to include details on holidays, celebrations, clothing, manners, language, and so on. Write about what immigrants can do to preserve their heritage while living in a new environment. What traditions and values are easiest to keep, and what ones should immigrants work hard not to lose?

5. Research the history of the immigration of people from your homeland to the United States. Find out if there was a particular time when people immigrated in great numbers and what caused them to leave home. What part of the United States did they immigrate to? What kinds of jobs were available for them? Was there ever a time when there was a quota against their immigration or rules regulating what they could do in the United States? How many immigrants from your country are living in the United States today? Summarize how your ethnic group has contributed to the diversity of this country.

Finding More Information

Magazines and Journals

American Heritage
Emerge
Native Peoples Magazine
Smithsonian
Yankee

Books

Angelou, Maya, *All God's Children Need Traveling Shoes*
Brown, Dee, *Bury My Heart at Wounded Knee*
Candelaria, Nash, *Memories of the Alhambra*
Haley, Alex, *Roots*
Reimers, David, *The Immigrant Experience*
Takaki, Ronald, *From Different Shores*
Terkel, Studs, *My American Century*

The World Wide Web

www.afroam.org—Afro-American newspapers
www.ellisisland.org—Ellis Island Immigration Museum
www.familytreemaker.com—Family Tree Maker Online
www.nativepeoples.com—Native Peoples Magazine
www.si.edu—The Smithsonian Institution
www.upapubs.com/guides/insa3.htm—Records of the Immigration and
    Naturalization Service

Movies and Videos

Dances with Wolves
El Norte
Far and Away
Green Card
Moscow on the Hudson
Roots

> Ultimately America's answer to the intolerant man is diversity, the very diversity which our heritage of religious freedom has inspired.
>
> Robert Kennedy
> (1925–1968),
> U.S. politician

CHAPTER 2

Changing the American Family

It is through our family that we pass down our culture—our language, traditions, beliefs, and customs. When many American families lived on farms far apart from one another, each family had to be self-sufficient and as a result was an independent unit. Large multigenerational families stayed on the same farm or in the same communities. Historical trends, such as westward expansion and the Industrial Revolution, enticed many Americans away from their extended families and the family farm to settle new territories or to work in the factories of big cities. Families in the urban areas started to decrease in size, and today the average American family consists of two adults and two children.

> Happy or unhappy, families are all mysterious. We have only to imagine how differently we would be described—and will be, after our deaths—by each of the family members who believe they know us.
>
> Gloria Steinem (1934–   ),
> U.S. feminist writer, editor

In the first reading in this chapter, Bernard Gavzer asks the question "What Is a Family?" because "the definition of family in America has been changing radically in the last few decades." One of the biggest changes in the American family has come with the increased involvement of fathers in raising children, as pointed out by Elizabeth Mehren in "It Takes a Strong Person to Survive Life on the Daddy Track." Because America is such a large country, efforts to keep family relationships strong often require a planned activity such as family reunions. Marcia Schnedler describes this American tradition in "Reunions Keep Families in Touch with Roots." Finally, adoption, and especially multicultural adoption, has changed the face of the American family. The last reading in the chapter was written by a young girl who grew up in a multicultural family.

How has the American family changed over the years? Discuss this question in small groups. Then talk about the picture on page 26 and answer the question: *Does this family look like the typical American family you usually think of?*

What Do You Think?

A **stereotype** is an oversimplified mental picture or opinion used by a person or a group to judge another. Working in small groups, discuss why you think these stereotypes about Americans have developed. How true do the members of your group think they are? Be prepared to share your opinions, reasons, and experiences with the class.

1. American families lack a sense of togetherness.
2. The elderly live in old folks' homes.
3. Parents expect their children to move out of the house when they are eighteen years old.
4. Most American marriages end in divorce.
5. Children do not treat their elders with respect.

Expand Your Word Power

See how fast your group can come up with the answers to these word puzzles. Then try to write one or two sentences using as many of these words as you can. Share your results with the class.

1. If *siblings* are brothers and sisters in one family, what is *sibling rivalry*?
2. If a *nuclear family* is a family of only two parents and their children living in one household, what is an *extended family*?
3. When are children in a family referred to as *half-brothers* and *half-sisters*?
4. If *adopting* a child means legally becoming his or her parent, will that child still be an *orphan*?

- Even though the composition of the family has changed dramatically over the years, Americans strongly believe in the safety, security, and autonomy of the family unit. Bernard Gavzer, a syndicated columnist, tries to define the word *family* by interviewing ordinary Americans.
- What do you think is the answer to the title question? As you read this article, think about the similarities and differences between families in your country and those in America.

What Is a Family?

Bernard Gavzer

from *Parade*

1 . . . The definition of family in America has been changing radically in the last few decades. For one thing, the traditional family—two parents, a father who works and a mother who raises her two or three children at home—is *waning*,[1] with a high divorce rate (nearly one in two marriages fails) *battering*[2] it even further. At the same time, one-parent families are becoming more common, whether by choice or circumstance.

2 We also are seeing more of those domestic setups that some say are families and that others *adamantly*[3] maintain aren't. Who is right? What is a "family" anyway? And what values should a family, any family, strive for?

3 Talk of the *demise*[4] of the American family is not new. "For more than 100 years—with the exception of the *baby boom*,[5] says Larry Burnpass, a University of Wisconsin demographer, "Western society has taken a course of increased emphasis on the individual and his own interest and well-being, and decreased emphasis on the family and family obligations." Yet there is a widespread feeling today that something is wrong. Experts cite grim statistics on divorce, teenage pregnancy, incest, single parents, unwed couples and abandonment.

A daughter greets her mother as she walks in from the office. Seventy-five percent of single mothers in the U.S. work outside the home.

---

[1] *wane* (v) to decline, go down
[2] *batter* (v) to hit repeatedly
[3] *adamantly* (adv) firmly

[4] *demise* (n) collapse, fall
[5] *baby boom* (n) period of rapid growth in U.S. birthrate following World War II

4   There is no single type of family that can be solely identified with these problems. Families of wealth, power and education are no more *immune*[6] from disruption than those of poverty. In recent years, for example, we have been treated to confessional books by the children of Ronald and Nancy Reagan, Joan Crawford, Lana Turner and Bing Crosby. They revealed lives of desperation and *dysfunction*.[7]

5   Strong families, however, have certain things in common: They are built out of two powerful commitments, say the experts. They are to nurture and protect the young while preparing them to join society; and to protect and support the well-being of the elderly.

6   These two goals are prized among people who differ in race, religion, wealth, heritage and culture. And they are shared by people whose lifestyles are both traditional and nontraditional, says Thomas F. Coleman, director of the nonprofit Spectrum Institute's Family Diversity Project in Los Angeles.

7   A strong family often starts with a strong marriage. Although marriage is no guarantee of a positive family environment, it is the first step to a strong family. What makes for a strong marriage? "There are two key *components*,[8]" explains Dr. Krister Stendahl, a theologian and professor of Christian studies at Brandeis University. "One is fidelity—a faithfulness and loyalty between man and wife. The other is mutuality—being equal, not using one another."

8   Don Cone, 71, and his wife, Doris, 70, of Baywood Park, Calif., may typify such a marriage in its most traditional sense. The Cones, who've been married for 50 years, first appeared in PARADE in 1955 as a typical middle-class couple with three children. Two of their children are married and have children of their own; one son is a retired Navy man. Don Cone sacrificed a possible career at the top *tier*[9] in the corporate world to build a strong family.

9   "It was clear in my company that if you were going to get ahead, you had to give your life to the company," says Cone, who was an engineer engaged in developing color TV. "But I put the Presbyterian Church and my work with the Boy Scouts and my family ahead of everything else."

10   Patricia Conway, 41, a teacher in Portland, Ore., and James Brunkow, 42, a chimney sweep, are not married. But they've been together for 11 years and have four children: Matthew, 10; Jacy, 8; Ian, 6; and Kelsey Rose, 3. Their family is the center of their life. Their huge kitchen table is crowded with children doing their homework or with everyone diving into huge meals. The family spends much time together. Yet Conway and Brunkow are not legally recognized as a family. The Census Bureau defines a "family" as those related by blood, marriage or adoption. Failing to meet that *criteria*,[10] unwed couples can run into complications, *ranging*[11] from getting health insurance to trying to file joint income-tax returns.

11   "Being married is not the issue," says Brunkow. "The commitment I make to Patricia and the kids is one I make freely. We are choosing to live in this fashion. Because we do it doesn't mean that we

---

6 *immune* (adj) unaffected, not susceptible
7 *dysfunction* (n) failure to work normally
8 *component* (n) part of a whole

9 *tier* (n) level, row
10 *criteria* (n pl.) standards of judgment
11 *range* (v) to extend

should be denied any of the benefits that normally exist between people who are married."

12 Dmitri Belser, 34, and Tom White, 37, who are homosexuals, call themselves a family too. Though the pair have taken upon themselves the responsibilities of a marriage and family, they also are unable to get the benefits of one, because the law does not recognize such unions as "marriages."

13 "We are a family," insists Belser. "We have two sons, Elliott, 7, and Sebastian, 3. The adoption decree names us both as parents, acknowledging the relationship. But the state won't recognize us as a couple, even though everything we have is held in common."

14 They were able to adopt their sons through networking. "We knew Elliott's mother from when she was in her second month, and we went through the entire pregnancy and delivery with her," says Belser. "We got Sebastian when he was 5 months old."

15 While, for some, a two-father household may seem like an extreme interpretation of "family," other changes in American society in the last few decades have been affecting the beliefs many Americans grew up with. Perhaps most powerful is the change in women's roles. This not only has affected thinking about how a woman should live her life but also has opened discussion about what a child needs from a parent—and from which parent.

16 The dual-income family is one in which both parents are working and probably spending less time with their kids. In 1960, just 20 percent of mothers with children under 6 were in the labor force; by last year, 58 percent of such women were working, mostly full-time.

17 "Increasingly, families rely on the woman's earnings," says Rep. Pat Schroeder (D., Colo.), who heads the House Select Committee on Children, Youth and Families. "That income can make a critical difference, enabling them to own a home, send a child to college or, in an increasing number of families, just get by."

18 "The important thing for working parents," says Dr. Martha Welch, a child psychiatrist, "is to convey to their children that the kids are their top priority." But it isn't always that simple. Jill Lawrence, an Associated Press writer, and her husband, John Martin, managing editor of *Governing* magazine, have had to figure out how to juggle[12] the interests and needs of their sons—Alex, 7, and Greg, 3—against the demands of their jobs and their commitment to their careers. They've arranged work schedules so that they are home in time to have meals with the boys and read to them before going to bed.

19 "As well as we do, money is still a problem," says Lawrence. "Even if it wasn't, I'd still want to work. I love being a mother, but I also love what I do."

20 Most single mothers have no choice: they must work to support their families. But while such families can be strong and stable, sharing the same goals and dreams for their children as two-parent families, they are particularly at risk.

21 One in four babies is now born to an unmarried mother (compared to one in 10 in 1970), and about half of all children today are expected to spend some part of their childhood in a single-parent family. The link between poverty and single

---

[12] *juggle* (v) to keep different objects (balls, plates, etc.) in the air simultaneously; to manage many tasks at one time

mothers is overwhelming. In 1990, 45 percent of all female-headed households with children aged 18 or younger fell below the poverty line, compared to just 8 percent of two-parent families.

22   Statistics show how quickly a broken family pushes women and children into poverty. One reason is nonpayment of child support. Of the 5 million women eligible for such support, only half reported receiving full payment, according to a 1990 Census Bureau study. To change that situation, pressure is building around the country to get divorced fathers to promptly and steadily pay *alimony*[13] and child support. Some experts say it might be time to make it more difficult to get divorces—especially in cases involving children. In addition, a variety of programs and organizations are committed to helping families at risk.

23   For single mothers, a workplace *sensitive*[14] to the needs of parents is important. "I found working mothers who say that they would never call in and tell the boss they had a sick child," says Representative Schroeder. "Instead, they would say their car had a radiator leak, and the boss could understand that."

24   Barbara Reisman, director of the Child Care Action Campaign, says: "There are 5,600 companies that provide some form of child-care benefit—such as helping to find such care, pay for it or provide it directly. There also are other companies that are family-friendly." This means they may offer *flex time*,[15] parental leave and other forms

of child care, but most of all, they recognize the value of enabling employees to balance family and work responsibilities.

25   Beth Munger, 30, of Portland, Oregon, is a young, married mother who resolved the work/daycare/home-leave problem by finding a job that lets the kids (Paul Eugene, 6, who attends kindergarten for half a day; Jeffrey, 4; and James, 2) stay with her most of the time. She works at Kids At Heart, a shop with environmentally *attuned*[16] toys and games. "They can show other kids how things work," says Beth. "I love having them with me."

26   Linda Walker has been a single mother 11 years. Her husband left when she was pregnant with twins. For two years, she lived in a shelter for the homeless on Chicago's South Side with her four children and two young relatives who are her dependents. "Being on *public assistance*[17] shamed me," she says. "I *resented*[18] the fact I didn't have the education that helps a person be independent."

27   Things changed for the better in October 1991, when she moved into *subsidized housing.*[19] She began working as a counselor for the homeless last July. Every day, Walker delivers the message of the need for education to her children—and her daughter, Lenora, seems to have received it. At age 13, she was recognized by the Chicago Department of Education as a *gifted*[20] child.

28   "I blanket them with love, but that doesn't do away with discipline," says Walker. "We are a family."

---

[13] *alimony* (n) money paid to a woman by her ex-husband
[14] *sensitive* (adj) receptive, understanding
[15] *flex time* (n) flexible hours at work
[16] *attuned* (adj) oriented
[17] *public assistance* (np) government aid/help

[18] *resent* (v) to feel angry or indignant at
[19] *subsidized housing* (np) housing that is paid for in part by the government
[20] *gifted* (adj) very intelligent, talented

> The percentage of American households in which children were being raised by grandparents rose between 1970 and 1997, from 3.8 to 5.5 percent.
>
> U.S. Census Bureau

Understanding the Reading: Recalling Facts and Charting Information

A. *First check your comprehension by circling the letter which best finishes the sentence. Compare your answers with a partner when you are finished.*

1. According to Larry Burnpass, Western society is placing more emphasis on
   a. the individual and his or her interests.
   b. the family and family obligations.
   c. education and entertainment.

2. Experts say strong families are built on
   a. wealth and education.
   b. powerful commitments.
   c. religious beliefs.

3. Gavzer says a strong family often starts with
   a. financial stability.
   b. a strong marriage.
   c. a well-educated couple.

4. The U.S. Census Bureau defines *family* as those related by
   a. traditional values.
   b. blood, marriage, and adoption.
   c. common customs and traditions.

5. Recently the most powerful change in American society has been
   a. the change in women's roles.
   b. the difference in a man's and a woman's earnings.
   c. the high cost of sending a child to college.

6. The article points out that most single mothers work because they
   a. love their jobs.
   b. want to avoid household responsibilities.
   c. have no choice but to work.

7. A broken family often pushes women and children into
   a. poverty.
   b. puberty.
   c. slavery.

8. Based on the example of Dmitri Belser and Tom White, homosexual couples

   a. are recognized as legally married.

   b. can adopt children together.

   c. can receive health and work benefits as a household.

9. According to the article, a family-friendly workplace offers

   a. flex time.

   b. parental leave and other forms of child care.

   c. both of the above.

10. Single mothers like Linda Walker also recognize that being financially indepen-dent requires

   a. a good attitude.

   b. a good education.

   c. extended family support.

B. *Charting information helps you remember it. Each of the families in the article had to deal with one of the following issues. The first has been identified for you. Write the names of the other families in the correct columns.*

Being Accepted by Others	Being Unmarried	Being a Single Parent	Juggling Work and Family
	Conway and Brunkow		

Using the Vocabulary: Antonyms

A. *Antonyms are words that have opposite meanings, such as "hot" and "cold" or "fast" and "slow." Work with a partner to test your knowledge of the vocabulary in this chapter by circling the antonym in the following groups of words.*

1. *adamantly*	firmly	weakly
2. *attuned to*	disconnected from	oriented toward
3. *batter*	hit	caress
4. *demise*	growth	collapse
5. *gifted*	talented	average
6. *immune to*	unaffected by	affected by
7. *resent*	dislike	appreciate
8. *sensitive*	unfeeling	understanding
9. *wane*	decline	increase

Although the teen pregnancy rate decreased steadily in the 1990s, almost 500,000 babies are born to teenage mothers in the United States annually.

National Center for Health Statistics

B. *Now fill in the blanks with the words that correctly complete the sentences.*

alimony   attuned   flex time   juggle   resent

Today, more and more single parents are required to (1)_____ careers and children. Everyone hopes the workplace will become more (2)_____ to employees' parental obligations. Children (3)_____ their parents for having to spend so much time at work. Employers should provide benefits such as on-site day care and (4)_____. Furthermore, divorced fathers should be required to pay (5)_____ and child support.

Reading Tables

Tables provide a summary of facts and statistics on a particular subject from which readers can draw conclusions. When you read a table, it is helpful to use a ruler to read across the columns to find the correct information.

With a partner, check the following table to see whether the statements that follow are true or false.

Families in the U.S.	1970	1997
Percentage of households with married couples and children under age 18	50	36
Percentage of single-parent families	6	13
Number of married adults	95 million	109.3 million
Median age for first marriage: men	23.2	27.1
Median age for first marriage: women	20.8	24.8
Number of unmarried-couple households	523,000	3.5 million
Number of never-married persons	21.4 million	45.9 million

Source: U.S. Census Bureau

Label each statement true (T) or false (F).

_____ 1. There was a decrease in the number of unmarried people living together between 1970 and 1997.

_____ 2. Men and women married at an older age in 1997 than in 1970.

_____ 3. The percentage of children being raised by single parents decreased between 1970 and 1997.

_____ 4. The number of people who chose not to marry almost doubled between 1970 and 1997.

_____ 5. There were more married adults living in the United States in 1997 than in 1970.

Thinking Together

Work in pairs or small groups. **Proverbs** *are short sayings that often tell universal truths, such as* All that glitters is not gold *or* Don't put all your eggs in one basket. *Discuss the meanings of the following proverbs related to parenting and children. What does each one mean? Which ones do you agree with? Disagree with? Are there similar proverbs or sayings in your culture? As a class, can you add any to the list?*

1. Silence is golden.
2. Children should be seen and not heard.
3. Spare the rod and spoil the child.
4. _____
5. _____

Writing about It

Write one to two paragraphs on one of the following topics. Try to use some of the vocabulary from this reading and from **Focusing In**.

1. How do you define the word *family?* Which of the families in the article best reflects your ideas and feelings?
2. Write a description of one of the families in this article from the point of view of one of the children.
3. Summarize some of the elements of strong American families that Gavzer presents.

Reacting to the Reading

Do you think governments should recognize all types of families, such as the non-traditional families described in this reading?

Parents bear the first and primary responsibility for their sons and daughters—to feed them, to sing them to sleep, to make countless daily decisions that determine whom they have the potential to become.

Hillary Rodham Clinton, U.S. first lady

■ In the 1950s the typical American husband went to work and the typical American wife stayed at home with the children. In the modern family described here by *Los Angeles Times* columnist Elizabeth Mehren, not only do both parents often work, but sometimes the father stays home to care for the children.

■ What do you think are some of the advantages and disadvantages of fathers staying at home while mothers work? Read the article to find out why "it takes a strong person to survive" as a stay-at-home dad.

It Takes a Strong Person to Survive Life on the Daddy Track

ELIZABETH MEHREN

FROM THE *LOS ANGELES TIMES*

1   In La Cienega Park on weekday mornings with baby Chelsea, a cooing infant in a ruffled bonnet and stroller, Marty Ross made a noble effort to connect with others in the same situation. But when the talk turned to husbands, things got ugly. . . .

2   "Yeah, I know, I mean sometimes my wife . . ." he would begin. At which point a pack of women with fury in their faces would descend on him.

3   "What do you mean, your *wife*?" "What do you know, you're a guy." "Get a job, what's wrong with you, anyway?" "Creep!" "Loser!"

4   Ross decided he needed to start hanging with the guys—other full-time, stay-at-home dads. But that turned out to be a great deal easier said than done. "I felt like I was in a *caste system*,[1]" said Ross, a 38-year-old musician and composer in Los Angeles whose wife, Doreen, is an executive in the entertainment industry. "There just wasn't anybody else."

5   In subscribing to a small bimonthly publication called *Full-Time Dads*, Ross, like others of his stay-at-home compatriots, has made his

A work-at-home dad keeps a watchful eye on his young son.

first feeble attempt—a baby step, you might call it—at reaching out to fellow househusbands. *At-Home Dad*, a quarterly newsletter with a circulation of 700, even carries a "network" page that resembles any magazine's or newspaper's personal ads. *Cyberspace pops*[2] can chat once a week in a cozy on-line group.

---

[1] *caste system* (np) social class based on family

[2] *cyberspace pops* (np) fathers who communicate over the Internet

What their efforts lack in numbers they make up for in serving as windows into the special challenge of stay-at-home fatherhood.

6   In San Diego, 33-year-old James Dicenzo found that as the full-time, stay-at-home father of 2-year-old Lauren, and now of 4-week-old Gabriel as well, he was viewed less as a *pariah*[3] than as a curiosity.

7   "It was like, 'You cook and clean? You care for the kids? I want one of those too!'" said Dicenzo, who left a 15-year career in social services to stay home and raise his children while his wife, Leslie, worked as an electronics engineer.

8   James Levine, head of the Fatherhood Project at the Work and Families Institute in New York, noted that not all at-home dads are "role reversal fathers in the stereotype created by the movie *Mr. Mom*." Many such families are made up of split-shift workers, Levine has found, where a father—a firefighter or police officer at night, for example—may care for children during the day while a wife is at work, or vice versa. At-home dadhood, said Levine, who has been studying the *phenomenon*[4] for 20 years, has now reached a "critical mass," where "while it is unusual still, it is no longer considered freakish."

9   Census Bureau figures show that in 1993, the most recent year for which there is data, about 9.9 million children under 5—or about 16% of all preschoolers—were cared for full time by their fathers while their mothers worked outside the home.

10   Readily and loudly, many of these dads admit to a nagging sense of isolation. They feel lonely, alienated from a culture that barely acknowledges their existence—never mind offering them any *shred*[5] of respect.

11   They are viewed not only with suspicion, but also with the almost inevitable assumption that they are simultaneously unemployed and unemployable—a double whammy for all but the most secure of work-focused male egos. When Dicenzo got playful with a telephone surveyor recently, for instance, and described his occupation as "domestic god," the poll-ster—with not a trace of *drollery*[6] in his own voice—replied, "that would be 'unemployed.'"

12   Family members are often *perplexed*[7] when a man opts to stay home to raise children. "So you'll do this for a few months and then you'll go back to work, right?" is the usual refrain from in-laws and grandparents.

13   Friends puzzle too. Stay-at-home fathers point out that whereas a woman may leave one set of coworkers behind when she moves from a career outside the home to full-time mothering, she soon finds another set of coworkers in the form of other mothers. Men say it is far more difficult to connect with a male peer group.

14   Stephen Harris, 36, contends that "there are enough out there doing it that need the validation" that comes with *camaraderie*.[8] As editor and publisher of *Full-Time Dads* (circulation 350), produced in his Cumberland, Maine, home, Harris hears the complaints and concerns of men who are forging the trail of full-time fatherhood.

15   Often they coincide with his own experiences since making the decision seven years ago to stay home with the kids while his wife went off to work as the editor of a computer service newsletter.

16   Before 7-year-old Ben and Robin, 4, were born, Harris had been a cook, a photographer and a catalogue designer for Brookstone, a *purveyor of yuppie playthings*[9]. As Harris reasoned, "Some people have vacation homes or drive big cars. Our luxury was for one of us to stay home."

17   Letting out a *self-effacing*[10] laugh, he explained, "We have chosen to *eschew*[11] having anything nice around the house in order to have our kids raised by one of their parents."

18   While his sons John, 3, and David, 3 months, take their daily three-hour naps, 38-year-old Peter Baylies publishes *At-Home Dad* from his home in North Andover, Mass.

19   Laid off three years ago from his job as a software engineer, Baylies, who had earlier worked as a newspaper photographer, first thought of putting out a publication for David Letterman fans. When he learned that such a newsletter already existed, he launched what

---

[3] *pariah* (n) outcast
[4] *phenomenon* (n) a fact or event that can be scientifically studied and described
[5] *shred* (n) scrap, bit
[6] *drollery* (n) humor, wit
[7] *perplexed* (adj) confused, mystified
[8] *camaraderie* (n) companionship
[9] *purveyor of yuppie playthings* (np) supplier of items that young urban professionals like to buy
[10] *self-effacing* (adj) not attracting attention, modest
[11] *eschew* (v) to avoid

he initially envisioned as a small circular.

20   Over and over, Baylies said, readers and contributors write in with common theses and questions. Some dads wonder how to have a home business while also caring for the kids. Others ask how to react when they go to the grocery store with their children during the day and people say, "Baby-sitting today?" Or there is the knotty playground issue, where mothers see a lone man and assume he is an ax murderer on *parole*.[12]

21   But isolation is the major *lament*.[13] "Men don't reach out for support the way women do," Baylies said. "They kind of secretly wait for support, hoping someone will call them up and say 'come on over.' But they have a hard time making that call themselves. It's like the guy who won't stop for directions, even when he's completely lost. They think they can do it by themselves."

22   Virtually the same issues arise each Monday at 7 P.M. PDT when Baylies, Harris and several dozen other dads—and even, on occasion, moms—gather around their computer screens for a nationwide "chat" about stay-at-home fathering. The hour-long electronic conversation is carried via America Online and is the brainchild of David Boylan of Chicago, an actor who gave up all work that required him to be away from home during the day when daughter Caitlin was born eight years ago.

23   "A woman with a baby is instantly considered a primary caregiver—while a man is considered a baby-sitter or laid off," Boylan said. Like many men who stay home with their kids, Boylan's choice was influenced by the fact that his wife, Mary, had the better job.

24   As a news writer and producer for CBS-TV in Chicago, Mary Boylan earned consistently more money than her husband. Her job also came with a strong benefits package, another important consideration for a family that grew to include Patrick, 5.

25   Once he started his on-line salon two years ago, "Boom! I started getting all this response," Boylan said. "We get intense," he said, zeroing in on such difficult and disturbing problems as how an at-home dad reacted when a mentally ill woman struck his child at a playground. But there is also electronic *fluff*,[14] Boylan said, recalling one earth-shattering discussion about sporting equipment.

26   In California, Ross said his computer dated from the Stone Age and thus precluded on-line dialogue. But Rick Garrett of Rancho Santa Margarita said he recently acquired on-line services and was looking forward to diving into the stay-at-home dads' group.

27   As an elementary school teacher married to a physical therapist with a packed professional schedule, Garrett defines himself as a part-time stay-at-home dad. Garrett said he reads at-home fathering publications for the information, the recipes and the humor. One recent cartoon depicted a boy standing at the laundry room door while his father struggles with a bundle of linens. "Come quick, everyone!" the boy is shouting, "Dad's going to try to fold the fitted sheets again!"

28   But real-life, full-time fathering has more than enough laughs to go around, the dads maintain. On the rare occasions when they do go out together, Jim and Leslie Dicenzo take their children to a baby-sitter—an older woman they have known for years—who "just thinks it's a riot that I'm home with the kids," Jim Dicenzo said. "She thinks it's hysterical. She just laughs and laughs and laughs."

29   Peter and Susan Baylies have learned to chuckle over the different standards of cleanliness that seem to come with the turf of gender.

30   "After about three months [of at-home fathering], my wife said, 'so when are you going to clean the bathroom?'" Baylies reported. "I'm like, 'What? It looks OK to me.' But I don't notice dirt unless you can grow a garden in it."

---

[12] *parole* (n) early release from jail for good behavior
[13] *lament* (n) complaint, moan, wail

[14] *fluff* (n) trivia, unimportant information

Understanding the Reading: Recalling Facts and Discussing Details

Discuss these questions with a partner.

1. According to the article, what reasons do fathers like James Dicenzo, Stephen Harris, and David Boylan give for staying at home?

2. What are some of the reasons a father might want to join Marty Ross's "cyber-space pops" group?

3. According to the author, what are some of the reactions people have when these fathers tell them they are stay-at-home dads?

4. What Internet provider do you have to subscribe to in order to talk with fathers like Baylies, Harris, and Boylan online? What day and time do they meet in cyberspace?

5. Give the former occupation of three of the men who are now stay-at-home dads. Do you think it was easy for these men to give up their jobs?

Using the Vocabulary: Synonyms and Antonyms

A. *Test your understanding of the vocabulary by identifying the word pairs on the chart as* **S** *(synonyms—similar in meaning) or* **A** *(antonyms—different in meaning).*

Column A	Column B	S (Synonym) / A (Antonym)
suspicion	trust	*A*
nagging	annoying	
respect	admiration	
acknowledge	ignore	
inevitable	unavoidable	
unemployed	working	
ego	self	

B. *Now fill in the blanks with the correct form of the appropriate words from column A. Then compare your answers to paragraphs 10 and 11 in the article.*

Readily and loudly, many of these dads admit to a (1)_____ sense of isolation. They feel lonely, alienated from a culture that barely

(2)_____ their existence—never mind offering them any shred of

(3)_____. They are viewed not only with (4)_____,

but also with the almost (5)_____ assumption that they are simul-

taneously (6)_____ and unemployable—a double whammy for all

but the most secure of work-focused male egos.

C. *In this paragraph from* Redbook *magazine (1985) Margaret Mead, a famous anthropologist, writes her opinions on family. Fill in the blanks with the correct choice of words.*

relate   sufficient   useful   willingly   wives

"What the world needs is not romantic lovers who are (1)_____ unto themselves, but husbands and (2)_____ who live in communities, (3)_____ to other people, carry on (4)_____ work, and (5)_____ give time and attention to their children."

Thinking Together

What types of duties/chores around the house do men and women have in your country? Who is primarily responsible for the care of children? Fill in the chart. Then compare your chart and discuss your answers in a small group.

Duties/ Chores	Fathers			Mothers		
	Always Do	Sometimes Do	Never Do	Always Do	Sometimes Do	Never Do

Writing about It

*Write one to two paragraphs on one of the following topics. Try to use some of the vocabulary from this reading and from **Focusing In**.*

1. Describe some of the activities in a day in the life of one of the stay-at-home dads in Mehren's article.

2. Summarize several reasons why some of the fathers in the article have decided to stay at home to raise their children.

3. Write a response to someone who makes comments such as these that the women made to Marty Ross in the park: "What do you mean, your *wife*?" "What do you know, you're a guy." "Get a job, what's wrong with you, anyway?" "Creep!" "Loser!"

Reacting to the Reading

What is your opinion about Marty Ross and other stay-at-home dads? Do you think it's possible for your own family to one day be in such a position? Why or why not?

- Since the United States is such a large country and work and school often require people to move away from their birthplace, family unity is hard to maintain. Holidays such as Thanksgiving and Christmas bring most families together on a regular basis, but when multigenerational families whose members live far apart want to reconnect, they schedule special activities such as the one Marcia Schnedler describes in this reading.
- Do extended families generally live in the same areas in your country, or do they need to schedule family gatherings? Have you ever been to a family reunion? As you read this article, think of some of the benefits of this tradition.

Reunions Keep Families in Touch with Roots

MARCIA SCHNEDLER

FROM THE *SALT LAKE TRIBUNE*

1   Philadelphian Sheila Linton and family members were visiting relatives in Newport News, Va., during the summer of 1977, when someone mentioned a family backyard picnic over in Portsmouth. "We all decided to go, and I met all those other wonderful family members for the first time," Linton says. "To be polite, my mother's cousin, Ernestine, casually commented, 'We should do this again. You should come to Philadelphia next year.'"

2   The next February, the Virginians called, asking where and when the *get-together* would be. They were planning to charter a bus and bring 48 people. The Philadelphians panicked. Then they started planning, and an annual reunion was born. They found a hotel where the visitors could stay. Somebody knew a *caterer*.[1] Others found a spot for a Saturday afternoon picnic and organized the recreational activities and a Saturday night *banquet*[2] and dance. Everyone had such a grand time that the family decided to make it an annual event.

The Harmon family brings generations together for a reunion every five years.

3   They're among a *whopping*[3] 45 percent of African-American travelers who attend at least one family reunion a year, according to a 1993 study by the Travel Industry Association of America (TIAA). That's a significantly higher percentage than for white travelers, the TIAA says.

4   Family reunions are an almost uniquely American phenomenon. U.S. families often *scatter* more than those in other countries, and when they do, they're farther apart than they would be in the Ivory Coast or Italy, for example. Overall, 7 million Americans attend 200,000

---

[1] *caterer* (n) one who prepares/serves special meals for parties or weddings

[2] *banquet* (n) formal dinner for many people

[3] *whopping* (adj) very large, extraordinary

family reunions a year, says Edith Wagner, publisher of the quarterly *Reunions* magazine. Some have been held for more than 100 years.

5   For most African-American families, however, reunions are a relatively recent development. Many were inspired by the 1977 TV series based on Alex Haley's book, *Roots*. "It has become such a popular idea among African-American families that it's a movement," says Ione Vargus, retired dean of Temple University's School of Social Administration and director of the African-American Family Reunion Institute in Philadelphia. The institute is a resource for reunion organizers and people tracing their family roots. Vargus sees more first-time African-American reunions every year.

6   For U.S. family reunions, relatives in their 50s and 60s, usually women, are the primary organizers and regular *attendees*[4] of the get-togethers, Wagner says. The senior members of African-American families are honored at reunions as elders, while younger men and women more often take the lead in organizing the event. Often, teen-agers and young adults are given active roles in the planning.

7   African-American reunions frequently get large turnouts, too. An average U.S. reunion draws 35 to 40, but many black families attract hundreds. But the 1978 get-together of the Bullock family, to which Linton belongs, began without a mailing list or family tree.

8   While her relatives began plans for the *impromptu*[5] reunion in Philadelphia, Linton, then in her mid-20s, volunteered to develop the invitation list. Beginning with her mother's eight brothers and sisters and their 25 children, she easily gathered 300 names and addresses. Other family members provided additional names. From that *evolved* a family tree with more than 750 entries, leading back to her mother's grandfather, George Bullock Sr., born into slavery in Edgecomb County, N.C., in 1858. He married Sally Jones and brought up 13 sons and daughters as well as a nephew. An average of 200 of Bullock's descendants attend the annual reunion each July.

9   As many as 700 family members have attended the Gaither-Janes reunion. The family reaches back to three Gaither brothers born in Virginia between 1809 and 1820, and to Cato Janes, born in Barbados in 1802. The two families moved to Liberty Hill, S.C., and *intermarried*,[6] says Warren Gaither, 60, from Detroit.

10   Reunions can last anywhere from one day to one week, but three- or four-day weekend events are common among African-Americans. The Gaither-Janes family, for example, holds its reunion each July 4th weekend. Some families travel to locations like theme parks. Others use state park lodges, church retreats or conference centers. A reunion may be held in conjunction with a church homecoming. An increasing number of hotels, resorts and cruise ships actively seek reunion business.

11   The Bullock and Gaither-Janes families rotate their sites among cities or regions where large numbers of family members have settled. Each branch takes its turn planning and hosting the event. Wagner notes that African-American reunions tend to be highly structured and packed with activities. "They're pushing the reunion envelope," she says, "always looking for and developing new ideas."

12   The Bullock and Gaither-Janes families begin with a Friday night event such as a reception or talent show. Saturdays often include such activities as picnics or *excursions* to sightsee, shop or golf. Reunions at or near the family *homestead*[7] may visit the family *cemetery*,[8] former *plantation*[9] or other site important in the family history.

13   Educational programs are often included. Vargus' first reunion had workshops exploring what it means to be a black family and whether the family's background affects members' everyday lives, she says at the African-American Family Reunion Institute. Bullock family teens organized an essay contest.

14   The Gaither-Janes reunions include *seminars* led by family members and guest speakers. "We've had classes on community development, intergenerational living, teen pregnancy and other issues," Gaither says. "We want to give everyone something substantial and to create *activism*.[10]" Sunday morning worship services, often led by a family member, are followed by a business meeting.

---

[4] *attendee* (n) person who goes to a gathering or meeting
[5] *impromptu* (adj) unplanned; spontaneous
[6] *intermarry* (v) to marry into another race or religion
[7] *homestead* (n) house and land

[8] *cemetery* (n) burial place
[9] *plantation* (n) large farm usually in the old South, often worked by slaves
[10] *activism* (n) desire for active participation

15   "As reunions continue, families begin to think about things they can do to help the family," Vargus says. They may raise money for scholarships, invest in the family's homestead or home community, donate to charitable projects, or establish family credit unions or other programs to help one another economically, Vargus says. Fund-raising events during the year assure all family members can afford to attend.

16   The main event is a Saturday night banquet and dance, during which family elders are honored, achievements and graduations are recognized and traditions are passed on. "We sing the Negro National Anthem, then memorialize our elders in a candlelight service," Linton says. "A huge white candle represents George and Sally Bullock. Fourteen *flanking*[11] candles include two in red for their two children still living. A 15th candle is for all the *deceased*[12] family members. We honor the two living elders, and since about 1989, the next generation of elders, including my mother."

17   Such *rituals*[13] reinforce family traditions and bonds. "After *emancipation*,[14] black people *reconstituted*[15] their family structures," Vargus says. "Black families are reaching back to their heritage to ensure that the *crucial*[15] function of the extended family is revived through family reunions."

18   During reunions, Gaither has seen the extended family operating much as it would if everyone attending lived in the same small town: teens talk out problems with older relatives or friends; kids hero-worship a family member who is a Chicago Bulls coach, and seek advice from another who is a university president. "There's a wonderful *chill that comes over you*[17] during a reunion," Linton says, "a beautiful feeling that you belong to this group, have the same blood. It's *intangible*,[18] but it's who you are."

Understanding the Reading: Scanning for Facts

Remember that to **scan** *is to look for a specific piece of information. This reading technique is especially useful when looking for a date or a number. Scan the article to find the following information.*

- the title of Haley's book televised in 1977 _____
- the family that had a get-together in 1978 _____
- the man who had 13 sons and daughters _____
- the words that TIAA are an abbreviation for _____
- the place in which Cato Janes was born in 1802 _____
- the number of Americans who attend 200,000 reunions a year _____
- the event that happens every July 4th weekend _____

> 'Tis a shame that your Family is an Honor to you! You ought to be an Honor to your Family!
>
> Benjamin Franklin, U.S. statesman, *Poor Richard's Almanac,* 1750

---

[11] *flanking* (adj) on the side of
[12] *deceased* (adj) dead
[13] *ritual* (n) ceremony
[14] *emancipation* (n) freedom from slavery

[15] *reconstitute* (v) to reform; to reestablish
[16] *crucial* (adj) very important
[17] *chill that comes over you* (idiom) exciting feeling
[18] *intangible* (adj) not visible or touchable

Using the Vocabulary: Vocabulary in Context

Thanksgiving, on the third Thursday in November, is the holiday known for family reunions in the United States. The day before Thanksgiving is the busiest travel day of the year.

A. *It is often easy to figure out the meanings of new words in a reading because they are part of complete sentences and paragraphs that provide clues. From this* **context,** *a reader can figure out the part of speech of each word and fit the word into the general meaning of the sentence. Use the context to identify each of these italicized words as an adjective* (**A**)*, noun* (**N**)*, or verb* (**V**).

_____ 1. Somebody knew a *caterer*.

_____ 2. . . . plans for the *impromptu* reunion . . .

_____ 3. . . . black people *reconstituted* their family structures . . .

_____ 4. . . . for all the *deceased* family members.

_____ 5. The two families moved to Liberty Hill, S.C., and *intermarried* . . .

_____ 6. Family reunions are an almost uniquely American *phenomenon*.

B. *You will notice that five of the new words that are italicized in the text are not defined in the glossary at the bottom of the page. Now that you have read this article on reunions, read the sentences that contain the following words. Use your knowledge of the topic and of grammar to help you identify the parts of speech (* **N**/*noun,* **V**/*verb,* **A**/*adjective) and define the words; sometimes a synonym for the word is right in the text. Then write a sentence with each one.*

Word	Part of Speech	Definition	Sentence
get-together (par. 2)			
scatter (par. 4)			
evolve (par. 8)			
excursion (par. 12)			
seminar (par. 14)			

C. *Now use the words from the chart to complete the sentences in this paragraph. Change forms when necessary.*

Because the families in the United States are (1)_____ all over the country, many families plan special (2)_____ or family reunions. Reunions may have started with the simple idea of getting the family together to share a picnic, but they have (3)_____ to include elaborate activities such as (4)_____ to historical places and (5)_____ on family history.

Thinking Together

In a small group plan a weekend of activities for a family reunion. Make a list of the things each person should do to prepare for the big event.

Writing about It

*Write one to two paragraphs on one of the following topics. Try to use some of the vocabulary from this reading and from **Focusing In**.*

1. Imagine you are a member of one of the families Schnedler describes. Write a short letter to members of your family whom you haven't seen for a long time. In the letter invite them to a family reunion that you are planning. Give details about the reunion.

2. Write a report for your local newspaper on a Gaither-Janes family reunion.

3. Write a summary of the reasons reunions are popular among American families.

Reacting to the Reading

Does this article convince you that American families are close-knit and that the younger generations appreciate their elders and their family traditions? Why or why not?

Keeping Track of Your Reading Rate

tip Take a moment to think about what you already know about adoption. Anticipating what you will be reading about helps you to read faster and understand more.

- "Is That Your REAL Brother?" is a story written by Kaitlyn Kerry about being adopted and growing up in a multicultural family.
- When your instructor gives you the signal to begin, read the story and mark down the time as soon as you are done. Then answer the questions without looking back at the reading.

I think that being adopted is a lot like being left-handed. You just don't notice it unless someone else points it out. . . . I was constantly hearing the comment, "Jason's not really your brother, is he?" Not being the particularly shy and reclusive type, I would often times meet a comment like that with raised eyebrows, and a, "No, Jason comes from Mars, and I was born right here on the planet Earth."

My brother, Jason, and I were both adopted. Jason was born in Michigan, and I was born in Korea. Together with my parents we made a family. A Real family. I can't say that I am really offended when people see our family together and inquire about it. Education has done a lot to promote the idea that families are made in many ways. Still, there are times when I wish that it were not so obvious that we are different. . . .

According to the U.S. State Department, Americans adopted 15,744 children from foreign countries in 1998.

My parents, especially my mom, did a wonderful job of explaining to us about adoption and about how families are made in different ways. I really felt special more than I did *different*. We lived in a large city, and through my parents' adoption agency, my parents were able to locate other parents who had adopted from Korea. When I was young, my mom made a real effort to get together with two of these families for dinners and picnics. . . .

It wasn't until I was in my teens that I really started to realize that I come from another country, another culture, that given different circumstances, my life would be completely and totally different. . . .

I felt different for the first time; I felt unsure about who I was and had a hard time resolving that. At first I denied my heritage; I wanted to be like everyone else. Fortunately for me, I have the most wonderful parents in the world! They stood by me and when I finally was ready to explore my feelings and needs, they were there to guide and share with me. From one extreme, I went to the other, and immersed myself in learning about my Korean heritage, and the history of my birth-country. Slowly I moved towards the middle ground, and am now happily at peace with who I am. I want to say, however, that having a supportive and loving family was key in reaching the place that I now am.

(400 words)   TIME: _____

Now mark these statements true (**T**) *or false* (**F**) *without looking back at the reading.*

_____ 1. The Kerrys have adopted more than one child.

_____ 2. Jason Kerry was born in Mars, Michigan.

_____ 3. The author, Kaitlyn Kerry, is a shy girl.

_____ 4. Kaitlyn has always wanted to learn more about her native culture.

_____ 5. Kaitlyn's parents were very supportive.

_____ 6. Kaitlyn does not know any other children that have been adopted.

_____ 7. Even though people learn about nontraditional families, they often ask Kaitlyn about hers.

_____ 8. The author is probably about thirteen years old.

_____ 9. Kaitlyn probably thinks multicultural adoptions are OK.

_____10. People probably ask "Is that your REAL brother?" because Jason and Kaitlyn look different.

Percent correct = _____   wpm = _____

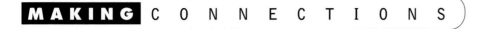

MAKING C O N N E C T I O N S

Responding to the Readings

Prepare short oral or written responses based on your personal experience and your reactions to the readings. Try to incorporate the information and the vocabulary you have learned in this chapter.

1. Assuming you want to have children, what type of role do you want to play as a father/mother in your future family?

2. How do you think the institution of family will change in your country and/or in the United States during the next century?

3. Write about a family gathering such as a reunion that takes place in your country.

4. According to "What Is a Family?" by Bernard Gavzer, some people choose not to marry, and others can't marry legally. What types of nontraditional families are you aware of in your country? Are these families' lifestyles accepted or resented?

5. What are some of the advantages/disadvantages of cross-cultural adoptions and marriages?

6. What kind of relationship do you have with your parents?

7. Discuss your reaction to one of the quotes or facts in the margins of this chapter that you found surprising or interesting.

Editing Your Work

*A student wrote this paragraph without editing carefully for subject-verb agreement. When writing in the present tense, all verbs with the subjects "he," "she," or "it" must have an **S** ending; however, verbs with the subjects "I," "you," "we," "they" do not. Edit this paragraph by checking the verbs. Insert the missing **S** endings and delete those that are incorrect; remember the verb "be" is irregular. (10 errors)*

> In *Parade,* the article by Gavzer state that traditional American families often includes "two parents, a father who works, and a mother who raise her two or three children at home." This is also true for traditional Japanese families. Japanese men want their wives to stay at home and take care of their children while they are out working very hard to support their families. Therefore it can be said that families in America and Japan bases their belief of a traditional family on the same points. But I also found some differences. Americans seem to date more people before

> Discipline is the symbol of caring to a child. He needs guidance. If there is love, there is no such thing as being too tough with a child. . . . If you have never been hated by your child, you have never been a parent.
>
> Bette Davis, U.S. actress, in the 1962 movie *The Lonely Life*

> If you bungle raising your children, I don't think whatever else you do well matters very much.
>
> Jacqueline Kennedy
> Onassis (1929–1994),
> U.S. first lady

marriage than Japanese people does. Although an American experience many dates, this do not make it any easier to marry the right person. Everybody have a hard time picking the right person to be their husband or wife. In Japan there is many networks that can arrange marriages for men and women. When the right person is found, the marriage follow.

Writing an Essay

Choose one of the following topics and write an essay. As a prewriting activity, read over your shortwrites and journal writings for inspiration. Remember to review the brainstorming techniques on pages 262–263. In your essay, use the readings, factoids, quotes, class discussions, and personal experience to support your ideas. Try to use the vocabulary you have learned in this chapter. If you choose to write a research paper, make certain to cite your sources clearly.

1. In this chapter you have seen some views of the American family. Compare and contrast the American family with the families in your culture. Describe the roles of mothers and fathers. Do nuclear or extended families live together? Are the families similar or different in the ways couples meet and marry and the ways children are raised?

2. A family is the place where culture, customs, and tradition are passed on. In the reading "Reunions Keep Families in Touch with Roots," Ione Vargus said, "Black families are reaching back to their heritage to ensure that the crucial function of the extended family is revived through family reunions." Discuss the ways in which a family preserves and passes down its heritage. Use the readings and your own personal experience in your discussion.

3. The article "It Takes a Strong Person to Survive Life on the Daddy Track" presents the new role of the father in America. Write an article on the changing role of fathers. Is this role changing only in the United States., or do you see this change in your own country as well? Make sure to discuss the fathers' participation in child-rearing, cooking, and housework, and the ways fathers balance this with their jobs outside of the home. Use the readings and your own family experience to support your ideas.

4. Write a description of the ideal family. Where would it live? How many members would it have? Who would live together and until what point? How would the chores of the home be divided? How would the parents and children communicate with one another? How would the family work together as a unit? How does your current family compare to the ideal one you have created?

5. Is the institution of the family in danger? Will it be possible to maintain strong family unity in the 21st century? What problems might prevent the family from surviving and maintaining strong ties? Think about the problems raised by the

demands on parents of a competitive job market, the problem of overpopulation, the migration of family members to different cities, states, and countries, and the influences of popular culture as you analyze the problem.

6. Research trends and regulations regarding cross-cultural adoption. Can anyone adopt a child from a foreign country or one of a different race or ethnic background? What countries do American families adopt children from most often? What policies do different countries have regarding adoption by parents from other countries or ethnic groups? What are some of the advantages and disadvantages for the child? What adjustments would both parents and child have to make? If you know any families in this situation, be sure to include them.

Finding More Information

Magazines and Journals

Child Magazine
Family Life
Parent Magazine
Parenting
Working Mothers

Books

Adamec and Pierce, *The Encyclopedia of Adoption*
Clinton, Hillary Rodham, *It Takes a Village*
Cosby, Bill, *Fatherhood*
Davis, J. Keyser, *Becoming the Parent You Want to Be*
Hochshild, Arlie, *The Time Bind*
Thornton, Yvonne, *The Ditchdigger's Daughters*

Movies and Videos

A Home of Our Own
Little Women
Marvin's Room
Mr. Mom
My Family/Mi Familia

The World Wide Web

divorce-online.com—Divorce Online
rainbowkids.com—an online international adoption publication
www.cwla.org—The Child Welfare League of America
www.fathers.com—National Center for Fathering
www.frca.org—Family Resource Coalition of America

> How could youth better learn to live than by at once trying the experiment of living?
>
> Henry David Thoreau (1817–1862), U.S. philosopher

Leveling the Playing Field

Professional sports is a big business in America. Fans pay as much as $500 for a floor-seat ticket at a basketball game or a ring-side seat at a boxing match. Athletes often become celebrities who go on to endorse products for companies, such as Nike shoes, Wheaties cereal, and Hanes underwear. Because of this, the sports industry is criticized for giving athletes extraordinarily high salaries. On a more positive note, many games bring in thousands of dollars to support charities and school programs. The youth of America are also inspired by coaches and athletes to be the best that they can be. American sports keep alive the belief that with hard work and perseverance the underdog can win. A popular statement by Yogi Berra (a famous former Yankee baseball player)—"It's not over 'til it's over"—reflects this American optimism. Americans also believe in a level playing field where the competition must be fair and the rules equal for everyone. Consequently we have the saying that "it isn't if you win or lose, it's how you play the game."

> It is the ceremony of innocence that the fans pay to see—not the game or the match or the bout, but the ritual portrayal of a world in which time stops and all hope remains plausible, in which everybody present can recover the blameless expectations of a child, where the forces of light always triumph over the powers of darkness.
>
> Lewis H. Lapham (1935–), U.S. essayist

Whereas most sports were formerly reserved for men, since the 1970s women have had the opportunity to participate on school athletic teams and as a result have gone on to compete and play in professional sports such as tennis, basketball, golf, and baseball. This has increased Americans' interest in sports, as Mike Tharp points out in "Ready, Set, Go. Why We Love Our Games." An example of how much Americans love their games is exemplified in the passage from *Baseball's All-Star Game* by Jeff Lenburg. Because of the enthusiasm for running, the Boston Athletic Association (BAA) has to limit the number of participants in its 26.2-mile race, the Boston Marathon, that attracts more than a million spectators each year. This national event is described in the BAA publication *The Race through History*, which is excerpted here. Finally, the last reading in the chapter on the Special Olympics shows how Americans try to provide the opportunity for everyone to participate in sports.

Why are sports and athletes such a big part of American culture? Discuss this question in small groups. Then talk about the picture on page 50 and answer the question: *Is it common to see people with disabilities playing sports?*

Are You a Sports Fan-atic?

Test your knowledge of sports facts. Try to answer the questions. Then compare your answers in your group.

1. What is considered the national sport in the United States?
2. What competitive sports take place on U.S. beaches?
3. What is the American game of soccer called in other countries?
4. In what professional team sport have women excelled?
5. Who funds the training of Olympic athletes in the United States?
6. How much physical education do American students receive?
7. What is A.Y.S.O.?
8. How many people run in the New York marathon every year?
9. What sport is typically associated with retired people?
10. How many players are on an American football team?

Test Your Word Power

Take this vocabulary quiz. Then compare your answers with a partner.

_____ 1. fan (n)
_____ 2. jock (n)
_____ 3. stadium (n)
_____ 4. champ (n)
_____ 5. coach (n)
_____ 6. spectator (n)
_____ 7. team (n)
_____ 8. slam-dunk (n)
_____ 9. amateur (n)
_____ 10. pro (n)

a. slang for "athlete"
b. an observer of an event
c. admirer
d. sports trainer
e. two or more people working together, especially in sports
f. playing field surrounded by seats
g. a professional, especially a professional athlete
h. short for "champion"; winner of a contest
i. in basketball, to shoot the ball in the basket from above; a sure thing
j. a nonprofessional

■ In this article, sports writer Mike Tharp analyzes Americans' love of athletics, both as participants and as spectators. Sports are even an important part of the public education system. There are physical education (P.E.) classes during school hours, and school teams compete as part of extracurricular activities.

■ Do parents spend hours volunteering as coaches for their children's athletic teams in your country? As you read this article, compare the interest in sports described here to that in your country.

Ready, Set, Go.
Why We Love Our Games

Mike Tharp

from *U.S. News and World Report*

1   . . . The *quadrennial*[1] reminder of swifter, higher, stronger human performance—and global hopes—returns to American soil this month, as the Summer Olympics open in Atlanta. It's fitting that the United States hosts the last games of the 20th century, because few other societies have been as *obsessed*[2] with sports and their attendant lifestyle as this one. A new *poll*[3] conducted by *U.S. News* and Bozell Worldwide on Americans' attitudes toward sports and the Olympics shows that we *overwhelmingly*[4] appreciate sports in our culture. The survey shows that Americans think spectator sports have a positive *impact*[5] on society, that competitive sports help children learn valuable life lessons and that those *virtues*[6] translate into other advantages in many areas of adults' lives. "Across the board, Americans find benefits from sports and exercise," argues pollster Marcela Berland of KRC Research, the polling arm of Bozell

Worldwide. "But their judgment about the virtues of sports extends well beyond *fitness*[7] and fun."

Society's metaphor

2   The love of athletics has now become deeply rooted in national life. Says John Walsh, senior vice president and executive editor of the sports cable network ESPN, "Sports have moved from being a subculture to becoming a major force in America's social and cultural landscape." The idiom of sports is the way that many Americans feel most engaged—and comfortable—talking about racial issues, standards of excellence, comparative worth, even right and wrong. And the passion over sports issues can *rival*[8] the intensity of political debates. Americans are sharply divided about the purpose and role of the Olympic Games in the *U.S. News*/Bozell survey: Fifty-one percent say the Olympics should

---

[1] *quadrennial* (adj) happening every four years
[2] *obsessed* (adj) controlled by an idea
[3] *poll* (n) survey of a group's opinion
[4] *overwhelmingly* (adv) to an extreme degree
[5] *impact* (n) effect or impression
[6] *virtue* (n) special quality; moral goodness
[7] *fitness* (n) physical condition
[8] *rival* (v) to be as good as or similar to

be open to all athletes (amateurs and pros), while 46 percent say only amateurs should be allowed to participate. In the cold war era, global political *hostilities*[9] shaped the public's appreciation for the games. Today Americans are almost evenly divided about the meaning of the competition: Forty-nine percent think the competition is among individuals; 47 percent view it as competition among nations. Because many feel that nationalism still *infuses*[10] the games, about two thirds of the respondents think American Olympians should get direct government aid, something that's not available to them now.

3   In unusual ways, sports have turned a mirror on ourselves. Our language reflects their impact, from "three strikes" laws in criminal sentencing to "level playing fields" in trade to "slam-dunks" in business deals. Our fashion is transformed by baseball caps, basketball sneakers and football jerseys. Our audiovisual tastes are shaped by all-sports radio and TV, sports-specific magazines and Internet-linked scoreboards. Our pocketbooks are opened to buy billions of dollars in sports *gear*,[11] tickets for sports contests, *wagers*[12] (legal and otherwise) on the contests, team accessories, *memorabilia*[13] shows and adult fantasy camps. Says Phil Knight, chairman and chief executive of Nike, "Sports and music have become the universal languages. . . ."

Good for what ails

4   As the *millennium*[14] approaches, however, there's growing evidence of a flip side: that sports have an ever greater influence on American society. The *U.S. News*/Bozell poll, for example, reveals that Americans strongly believe the lessons of sports contribute positively to other life *realms*.[15] An amazing 91 percent think sports participation helps people get along with those from different racial or ethnic groups; 84 percent think sports involvement helps people in the business world; 77 percent think sports help people be better parents, and 68 percent think sports help people get along better with people of the opposite sex.

5   Nowhere is this influence more felt in the United States than through women's and girls' increasing participation and interest in sports. Among the nearly 11,000 athletes at Atlanta, just under 4,000 of them will be female, a record total. And it is a virtual certainty that the nation's female Olympians will do better overall in their competitions than will U.S. men. Women are now besting world records held by men 10 and 15 years ago, and an astonishing 66 percent of Americans believe the day is coming when top female athletes will beat top males at the highest competitive levels.

6   The same growth of female sports participation has occurred in colleges and high schools. In 1971–72, about 30,000 women participated in college sports. By 1994–95, that number had soared to more than 110,000. During the same period, the number of female high school athletes jumped from about 300,000 to more than 2 million—about 1 in every 3 girls, according to the Women's Sports Foundation. (Boys' high school participation rates have remained steady. About 50 percent of high school boys take part in sports, totaling about 3.5 million participants most years.)

---

[9] *hostility* (n) hatred; anger
[10] *infuse* (v) to fill or permeate
[11] *gear* (n) equipment
[12] *wager* (n) bet

[13] *memorabilia* (n) things that remind people of the past
[14] *millennium* (n) period of 1,000 years
[15] *realm* (n) general field

This player on the Pittsford Sutherland High School girls soccer team is one of more than 2 million girls who participate on high school sports teams.

7   The *impetus*[16] for such explosive growth was Title IX of the Education Amendments. Passed in 1972, the law guaranteed equal access and opportunity for women in college sports. . . . In the *U.S. News*/Bozell survey, though, three quarters of respondents said they think that even in 1996 girls do not have the same opportunity as boys to take part in competitive sports.

New generation

8   Some Americans already prefer a women's game. Legendary UCLA men's basketball coach John Wooden admires the advances of women's basketball in the past 20 years. "I feel that the best pure basketball is now being played, below the rim, with *finesse*[17] and beauty, by the very best women's teams," says Wooden, now retired. The men's game "has become too individualistic and focused on showmanship."

9   More and more girls are beginning their athletic careers at the same age as boys—and with the same intensity. One main reason is grass-roots encouragement, starting with the family. Donna Lopiano, Women's Sports Foundation executive director, suggests that a new generation has arisen that is highly supportive of girls in sports. As the T-shirt on one father's chest at a recent soccer tournament for 10-year-old girls put it: "I don't have a life—My daughter plays soccer."

10   . . . So powerful are the joy of sports, the *allure*[18] of athletic contests and the marketing of sports *prowess*,[19] that a significant, madly attached segment of the population has formed itself into a "jock culture." Those inside it adore sports and think the country reaps splendid rewards from athletic competition; those outside it have significantly less respect for the role of sports in American society. According to the *U.S. News*/Bozell poll, this "jockocracy" constitutes about a quarter to a third of the adult population and is composed of people who say they play sports at least a couple of times a week or those who watch sports contests on television a number of times per week. Those who exercise a great deal are not necessarily in this culture, which centers much more on those who play or watch competitive sports.

11   How is this culture distinctive? Its members are much more likely than "nonjocks" to have had positive experiences with sports while growing up; to think pro athletes deserve a lot of respect; to believe that athletic participation helps a person succeed in business, get along with those from other racial or ethnic groups and be a good

---

[16] *impetus* (n) encouragement needed to do something
[17] *finesse* (n) fine skill

[18] *allure* (n) attractiveness
[19] *prowess* (n) fighting ability in battle or sports; skill

parent. And the 1 in 10 Americans who says he had awful experiences with sports during his childhood continues to be affected by those events. The majority are women, and they are twice as likely to feel that sports have a negative impact on society, much more *inclined*[20] to think kids learn destructive win-at-any-cost lessons from sports, and less supportive of the idea of giving government aid to U.S. Olympic athletes.

12   Maybe Americans *vest*[21] too much of their lives and their energies in sports and the spectacle they provide. Maybe, though, the majority have it right. They're not saying that athletic competition is the sum of all that's good in American society. They're more likely saying that sports have been good to them and sports heroes represent some of the best of who we are and what we cherish. Sports at their best can be bigger than the problems that swirl around them—the drug *scandals*,[22] cheating incidents, college recruiting abuses, evidence of commercialism and greed, lingering gender and racial unfairness and even the false gods they promote. They can enlarge a person's life, invigorate it, provide instruction, inspiration, *diversion*[23] and delight like few other things.

Understanding the Reading: Identifying Information

*First, test your memory to see if you think the following information was in this article. Indicate your answer by writing **Y** for "yes" or **N** for "no" in the first column of the chart. Then **skim**, or glance quickly over, the article to see if you can find the information you labeled **Y**. Circle the phrase and complete the third column. Compare your answers with a partner to see if you missed anything.*

Y/N	Information	Phrase/Fact in Text and Paragraph Number
	1. The number of people surveyed in the *U.S. News* poll.	
	2. Most Americans in the *U.S. News* poll believed the government should support Olympic athletes financially.	
	3. The name of the law that opened up sports for women in college.	
	4. The author concludes that Americans believe sports figures are heroes.	
	5. Most Americans polled had bad experiences with sports as children.	

(chart continued on next page)

---

[20] *incline* (v) to bend toward; to tilt at an angle;
   to be inclined to—to be likely to
[21] *vest* (v) to give power to

[22] *scandal* (n) embarrassing behavior
[23] *diversion* (n) break from normal activity; entertainment

According to Nielsen Media Research, auto racing is the fastest-growing spectator sport in America today.

Y/N	Information	Phrase/Fact in Text and Paragraph Number
	6. More than one-third of the athletes at the 1996 Olympics in Atlanta were women.	
	7. Sports influence language and fashion.	
	8. Americans in the 1996 poll believed girls and boys had the same opportunities to participate in sports.	
	9. The majority of Americans interviewed participated in sports at least twice a week.	
	10. Most people in the survey believed sports had a good influence on American life.	

Using the Vocabulary: Compound Words

Languages are constantly changing and adding new words. **Compound words** are made up of two words. They may be written as one word *(half + time = halftime)*, hyphenated *(all + star = all-star)*, or written separately as a phrase *(home + run = home run)*.

A. *There are many compound words in "Ready, Set, Go. Why We Love Our Games." This chart has a list of some that are written as only one word. Scan the article to find the complete words. Underline, highlight, or circle them. Then complete the chart and add a definition for each one. Compare your chart with a partner.*

Compound Words	Definitions	Compound Words	Definitions
life _____	way of living	score _____	
_____ wide		_____ books	
net _____		_____ wise	
_____ ball		chair _____	
_____ ball		out _____	
_____ ball			

B. *Now fill in the blanks with the words from the chart that correctly complete these sentences.*

According to Mike Tharp, Americans are very sportsminded people. In other words, sports are part of the American (1)_____. Some favorite sports include (2)_____, (3)_____, and (4)_____. Although most Americans are merely spectators and nonjocks, almost every Saturday and Sunday there is at least one major sporting event on a television (5)_____. However, there are also many active participants, such as the more than 2 million female high school athletes mentioned in the reading.

Thinking Together

Write down the three most popular sports in your country in order of their popularity. Your teacher will conduct a survey by polling the class and writing the results on the board. Which sport is the most popular around the world, according to the results of your survey?

Writing about It

Write one to two paragraphs on one of the following topics. Try to use some of the vocabulary from this reading and from **Focusing In**.

1. Explain some of the important results of the *U.S. News*/Bozell poll on sports and what they showed about Americans.

2. Describe the changes that took place in sports participation in 1972 and what caused them.

3. Discuss the great influence of sports on American culture and provide details from the reading.

Reacting to the Reading

Do you think that boys and girls should be allowed to compete on the same sports teams? Why or why not?

In October 1996 the American Basketball League, founded by and for female athletes, was formed. In the summer of 1997 the Women's National Basketball Association (W.N.B.A.) began.

Roger Maris, the New York Yankee baseball player, held the title for most home runs hit in one season—61 home runs in 1961—until 1998, when Mark McGwire hit 70 and Sammy Sosa hit 66.

■ In the spirit of competition, America has two major political parties, Democratic and Republican, and two major baseball leagues, the National League and the American League. These two leagues play separately from April until October, when the best teams from each league play against each other in the World Series. Since baseball is considered America's national sport, there are hundreds of books on the subject, including Jeff Lenburg's *Baseball's All-Star Game*.

■ Before you read this excerpt from the book, discuss the game of baseball with your class. As you read, find out what other time the National League plays against the American League, and what makes that game so "democratic." Why do you think this game is called the All-Star Game?

Baseball's All-Star Game: A Game by Game Guide

JEFF LENBURG

1   Baseball's "dream game," better known as the All-Star Game, has been a favorite now of baseball fans for more than fifty glorious years. Originally intended as "a one-game *promotion*[1]" to *pit*[2] players from both leagues in a mid-season exhibition, perhaps nobody ever dreamed it would turn into such an annual *spectacle*.[3]

2   The All-Star Game was the brainchild of a gentleman by the name of F. C. Lane, who, in 1910, first proposed the idea of sponsoring an interleague contest. Until now, Lane has never received appropriate credit for his actions, but his entire plan was made public in an article he *penned*[4] for *Baseball Magazine* in 1915.

3   Lane's concept varied slightly from the one being utilized today, however. His dream was for the players from both leagues—the National (NL) and the American (AL)—to team up against each other in a series of seven consecutive games, à la the World Series, to crown a champion of this annual competition. Unfortunately, Lane's unique proposal was shot down by the commissioner and baseball owners, who feared that players' salaries were much too high then to make the games profitable.

4   While Lane regrettably abandoned his dream game, in 1933, Arch Ward, sports editor of the *Chicago Tribune*, made the game a reality. With salaries now severely *trimmed back*[5] after the *Great Depression*,[6] the owners found

---

[1] *promotion* (n) making known to the public; advertising
[2] *pit* (v) to match or set against
[3] *spectacle* (n) public performance; a strange or amazing sight
[4] *pen* (v) to write
[5] *trim back* (vp) to reduce; to cut back
[6] *Great Depression* (proper n) a long period of economic slowdown in the United States during the 1930s

Close plays at home plate bring baseball fans to their feet.

Ward's *revamped*[7] proposal more to their liking. The contest would be held to one game—billed as "The Game of the Century"—and would be scheduled as a special event in *conjunction*[8] with the Chicago Century of Progress Exposition which Ward had been organizing to celebrate the city's 100th anniversary.

5   Ward did have his share of obstacles to *hurdle*[9] in pushing through the idea, however. Commissioner Kenesaw Mountain Landis played an important role in breaking the *stalemate*[10] that brought about the first midsummer contest. The owners wanted the *Tribune* to guarantee both leagues against any losses if, for some reason, the contest was postponed for rain or because of some unforeseeable circumstance. Landis worked on the owners' behalf in negotiating such a clause with the *Tribune*.

6   Another catch-all which concerned the owners was whether such a contest would bring about a *rash of*[11] injuries to key players and *jeopardize*[12] *pennant*[13] hopes for their teams. This time, Ward stepped in to make a counter proposal: The contest would be "a one-year spectacular" (he used the word long before it came into general use as a noun) and the gate receipts would be earmarked for a retired players' fund.

7   Ward was in from then on, and Chicago's Comiskey Park became the site of the *inaugural*[14] game on July 6, 1933. Players were selected to team rosters by fan voting (Babe Ruth polled just over 100,000 votes, a far cry from the million-plus votes some players receive today), while the choice of man-

---

[7] ***revamp*** (v) to redo; to change completely
[8] ***conjunction*** (n) connection
[9] ***hurdle*** (v) to jump over
[10] ***stalemate*** (n) situation in which no action can be taken; a deadlock
[11] ***a rash of*** (idiom) a sudden increase in number of
[12] ***jeopardize*** (v) to put in danger
[13] ***pennant*** (n) victory flag; in baseball, the championship of the league
[14] ***inaugural*** (adj) first; initial

A ball player's got to be kept hungry to become a big leaguer. That's why no boy from a rich family ever made the big leagues.

Joe Dimaggio (1914–1999), U.S. baseball player

> Whoever wants to know the heart and mind of America had better learn baseball, the rules and realities of the game.
>
> Jacques Barzun (1907–),
> U.S. scholar

agers was almost automatic. (A number of Chicago newspapers published *ballots*[15] for fans to mail in, with popular voting acting as an advisory to manager selections.) John McGraw, the recently retired manager of the New York Giants, and Connie Mack, still the manager of the Philadelphia Athletics, were named to *pilot*[16] the two teams in their first interleague confrontation.

8 Even though the event was scheduled during the bottom of the Depression and four months after President Franklin D. Roosevelt took office, 47,595 screaming fans jammed inside Comiskey Park for this special interleague affair. The atmosphere was all that Ward had imagined, too. Fans *gawked*[17] at "all the talent collected on the field," and the excitement of the day helped spread baseball fever throughout the Windy City that much more.

9 Babe Ruth headed the list of noted All-Stars, and his *clutch home run*[18]—the first in All-Star game history—led the Americans to a 4–2 victory over the Nationals. This seemingly uneventful game created so much interest among the baseball communities of America—and surprisingly, the owners—that it became an annual fixture. Each year the commissioner's office alternated between American and National league ballparks to offer fans in various cities a chance to cheer on their favorites.

10 Year by year, the games have been dramatic and eventful. . . . Fan voting has played an important and often controversial role since the method was revised in 1934. Also, the size of each team has increased throughout the years, from 20 players in 1934 to 25 in 1939 to 39 in 1982. From 1935 through 1946, managers from each league selected players from both All-Star squads and used their own *discretion*,[19] of course. New York Yankees manager Joe McCarthy still holds the record for having the most opportunities to pick starting lineups; he piloted a record seven American League teams.

11 All-Star voting also went through another major *overhaul*[20] from 1947 through 1957, when fans again elected the star players with the Associated Press tabulating the results. But when Cincinnati fans *overzealously*[21] *stuffed the ballot boxes*[22] in 1957, Commissioner Ford Frick returned the voting chores back to the players, managers, and coaches the

---

[15] *ballot* (n) paper used for writing down a secret vote
[16] *pilot* (v) to guide
[17] *gawk* (v) to stare at in a rude manner
[18] *clutch home run* (np) a hit over the wall that scores the game-winning run in a baseball game
[19] *discretion* (n) caution; choice
[20] *overhaul* (n) complete change
[21] *overzealously* (adv) with too much enthusiasm
[22] *stuff the ballot box* (idiom) to influence an election by voting more than once for the same candidate

following year. This method of voter polling was finally changed in 1969—using the same process fans use today—when Commissioner Bowie Kuhn returned voting to the fans. Since then, over 71 million fans participate annually in All-Star voting, which is a far cry from 1960 when only two million votes were counted.

12 Ward's midsummer classic experienced only two other interruptions. In 1945, during World War II, President Roosevelt ordered that no game be played, and from 1959 through 1962 the event was expanded to two contests a year for the purpose of raising more money for the players' *retirement fund*.[23] In 1963 the extra game was *abolished*[24] when it was agreed that one interleague *match*[25] a year was enough.

13 Today, however, baseball fans just can't seem to get enough.

Understanding the Reading: Identifying Topics

Each paragraph in a reading usually has its own **topic**, or theme, that relates to the theme of the whole article or essay. To find the topic, ask the question *What is this paragraph about?* The main idea of this chapter from Lenburg's book is that since 1910, many men have contributed to the development of the All-Star Game as it evolved into a popular yearly baseball event.

Match the paragraph number with the phrase which best states the topic of the paragraph.

_f_ par. 1   a the first game atmosphere

____ par. 2   b. solutions to problems

____ par. 3   c. the inaugural game

____ par. 4   d. picking current teams

____ par. 5   e. the revised plan for a game at an exposition

____ par. 6   f. an annual favorite for more than fifty years

____ par. 7   g. the results of the first game

____ par. 8   h. specific plans and promises

____ par. 9   i. the first plan fails

____ par. 10   j. the originator of the idea

____ par. 11   k. picking the teams through 1946

____ par. 12   l. changes in the All-Star schedule

· **H I N T** ·

As you use items in a matching exercise, cross them out to eliminate the need to read all choices.

---

[23] *retirement fund* (np) money set aside for old age after one is no longer working
[24] *abolish* (v) to put an end to; to do away with
[25] *match* (n) contest or game

In 1993, Jim Abbott, a baseball pitcher born without a right hand, pitched a no-hitter for the N.Y. Yankees and inspired people with disabilities everywhere.

Using the Vocabulary: Suffixes

*A. Common **suffixes**, or word endings, which change verbs into nouns in English are -**ment**, -**ion**, and -**er**. Fill in the second column with the noun form(s) of the verbs in column one (most of the nouns appeared in this article).*

Verb	Noun
1. play	1. *player*
2. commission	2.
3. commit	3.
4. retire	4.
5. interrupt	5.
6. manage	6. a. b.
7. promote	7. a. b. *promoter*
8. excite	8.
9. exhibit	9.
10. own	10.

In paragraph 6, the author mentions that Ward used the word *spectacular* as a noun long before it became a noun. What part of speech was *spectacular,* as indicated by the ending -***ar***? _____

B. Write two sentences with the word "spectacular" using it as a different part of speech in each.

_____

_____

C. Fill in the blanks with the correct noun or verb form from the chart in Exercise A. Make any necessary changes in tense and number.

There are two leagues in professional baseball, the American League and the National League. A (1)_____ governs the leagues. One person, or sometimes a family, (2)_____ each team. Each baseball team has nine (3)_____ on the field during a game, and each team has its

own coaches and a (4)_____. Players are usually between the
ages of 20 and 35, and most (5)_____ by the time they are 40.
Baseball games last about two hours. While many think there is not much
(6)_____ during a game, the real fans love sitting in the sun, eating hot dogs, and watching their favorite team during the lazy days of summer.

Reading Tables

Information is often summarized in a chart or a table. When you read a table, it is helpful to use a ruler to guide your eyes across and down the correct rows and columns.

Work with a partner. Use this chart to find the information and fill in the blanks.

ALL-STAR BASEBALL GAMES, 1980–1999

Year	Site	AL score	NL score	Year	Site	AL score	NL score
1980	Dodger Stadium Los Angeles, CA	2	4	1990	Wrigley Field Chicago, IL	2	0
1981	Municipal Stadium Cleveland, OH	4	5	1991	SkyDome Toronto, Canada	4	2
1982	Olympic Stadium Montreal, Canada	1	4	1992	Jack Murphy Stadium San Diego, CA	13	6
1983	Comiskey Park Chicago, IL	13	3	1993	Camden Yards Baltimore, MD	9	3
1984	Candlestick Park San Francisco, CA	1	3	1994	Three Rivers Stadium Pittsburgh, PA	7	8
1985	H. Humphrey Metrodome Minneapolis, MN	1	6	1995	The Ballpark Arlington, TX	2	3
1986	Astrodome Houston, TX	3	2	1996	Veterans Stadium Philadelphia, PA	0	6
1987	Oakland-Alameda County Stadium, Oakland, CA	0	2	1997	Jacobs Field Cleveland, OH	3	1
1988	Riverfront Stadium Cincinnati, OH	2	1	1998	Coors Field Denver, CO	13	8
1989	Anaheim Stadium Anaheim, CA	5	3	1999	Fenway Park Boston, MA		

During World War II, a women's professional baseball league was created to keep the national sport alive while men were at war. It wasn't until 1994 that a women's professional baseball team reappeared.

_____ 1. The year the All-Star game took place in Minneapolis.

_____ 2. The number of years the All-Star game was in Texas between 1980 and 1999.

_____ 3. The number of times the American League won the game during the 1980s.

_____ 4. The state in which the most All-Star games took place between 1980 and 1999.

_____ 5. The highest number of total runs scored in a game in the 1990s.

American Mark Spitz won seven gold medals in swimming in 1972, the most ever won by an Olympic athlete.

Thinking Together

Work in groups of four. Each person writes down a description of the action and play-ers in a sport without naming the sport and reads the descriptions aloud. See if the members of the group can guess the sports that have been described.

Writing about It

Write one to two paragraphs on one of the following topics. Try to use some of the vocabulary from this reading and from **Focusing In**.

1. Discuss the two aspects of the All-Star Game that involve the fans and make the game "democratic."

2. Summarize the development of the All-Star Game.

3. Write a letter from a baseball fan to a friend about seeing an All-Star Game.

Reacting to the Reading

In baseball, fans vote for the players in the All-Star Game. Do you think that fans are capable of judging the best-qualified players for an all-star team? Why or why not?

- Although running is an individual sport, there are many organized competitions and fundraisers that bring runners together from different backgrounds and for different causes. One of these events, the Boston Marathon, is described in a brochure published by the Boston Athletic Association.
- Are there any sporting events like the Boston Marathon in your country that involve a whole city or area? Read this description to find out how this famous race has developed and changed over time.

The Race through History

BOSTON ATHLETIC ASSOCIATION

1. the Boston Athletic Association

Established in 1887, the Boston Athletic Association (B.A.A.) is a non-profit organization committed to encouraging and promoting fitness through athletics. The B.A.A. currently supports several active local *charities*[1] and a competitive running club and is involved with the *orchestration*[2] of several far-reaching community-wide efforts. However, its primary *endeavor*[3] is staging the world's oldest and most *prestigious*[4] annual *marathon*,[5] the B.A.A. Boston Marathon. Since 1897, the B.A.A. has been the sole *caretaker*[6] of this true sporting classic. The majority of the U.S. team at the first modern Olympic Games, held in Athens in 1896, was comprised of B.A.A. members. Inspired by the Games' marathon, the B.A.A. decided to have a marathon race of its own. On April 19, 1897, fifteen men started the inaugural B.A.A. Marathon, whose finish coincided with the Annual Athletic Games of the B.A.A.

2. the 100th anniversary exhibit of the Boston Marathon

On April 15, 1996, the B.A.A. and the world of athletics celebrate a *milestone*[7] in sports history—the 100th Running of the Boston Marathon. The celebration activities include a historical exhibit, entitled "The Race Through History." The exhibit not only pays *tribute*[8] to the people and

---

[1] *charity* (n) organization that helps people in need
[2] *orchestration* (n) organization; arrangement
[3] *endeavor* (n) task; effort
[4] *prestigious* (adj) admirable; famous
[5] *marathon* (n) foot race of 26.2 miles
[6] *caretaker* (n) one who takes care of
[7] *milestone* (n) important achievement or event
[8] *tribute* (n) praise; honor; admiration

More than 10,000 volunteers help make sure the Boston Marathon runs smoothly each year.

Boston Athletic Association

> The 100th anniversary of the Boston Marathon, the world's oldest and most prestigious race, brought more than 38,000 runners and $10 million to the state of Massachusetts.

events which have helped shape the race but also recognizes the eight cities and towns along the famous 26.2-mile route. . . . The B.A.A. has two goals for the exhibit: (1) to educate the citizens of the marathon communities—especially our youth—on its rich tradition; and (2) to highlight and develop an appreciation for the continuity and importance of the race within the communities.

3. _____

   . . . The 1896 Olympic marathon distance of 24.8 miles was based on the distance run, according to famous Greek legend, in which the Greek foot-soldier Pheidippides was sent from the plains of Marathon to Athens with the news of the astounding victory over a superior Persian army. Exhausted as he approached the leaders of the City of Athens, he *staggered*[9] and gasped, "Rejoice! We conquer!" and then collapsed. In the twelve track and field events at the first modern Olympic Games in Athens, Greece, in 1896, B.A.A. members took home six gold medals. Greek shepherd Spiridon Loues won the first modern Olympic marathon.

4. _____

   . . . The marathon distance was based on the Greek legend which covered a distance from Marathon to Athens in Greece, but the length changed as a result of the 1908 Olympic Games in London. That year, King Edward VII and Queen Alexandra wanted the race to begin at Windsor Castle outside the city so that the Royal family could view the start. The distance between the castle and the Olympic Stadium in London proved to be 26 miles. Organizers added extra yards to the finish around a track, 385 to be exact, so the runners could finish in front of the King and Queen's royal box. Every Olympic marathon run since the 1908 Games has been a distance of 26 miles, 385 yards.

5. _____

   Who has won the Boston Marathon more times than anybody else? Bill Rodgers? Guess again. Clarence H. DeMar, of Melrose, Massachusetts. DeMar won the 15th Boston Marathon in 1911 with a time of 2 hours, 21 minutes and 39 seconds. Eleven years later, in 1922, he won again. With five more wins in 1923, 1924, 1927, 1928, and 1930, DeMar holds the record of seven wins that may never be broken. Commonly known as Clarence DeMar(velous) and Mr. DeMar(athon), he won his last Boston Marathon at 41 years old. In dominating the road racing world for nearly half a century and representing the U.S. on three Olympic teams, DeMar

---

[9] *stagger* (v) to walk or run with unsteady movements

Participants in the Boston Marathon run a grueling 26-mile, 385-yard race.

was an attraction to spectators whenever he appeared in his nearly 1000 career races.

6. _____

Today, many of the world's best runners are full-time professional athletes, but it wasn't always that way. Through most of Boston Marathon history, the top runners were amateurs who worked long days at *mills*,[10] shops and factories and had to fit in training before and after work. One such worker was 1917 Boston Marathon champion: Bill Kennedy, a *journeyman*[11] bricklayer. Kennedy also fit into the era where annual participation in the Boston Marathon became popular. In fact, he ran 20 out of 26 races between 1916 and 1941. . . .

7. _____

Roberta Gibb was the first woman to run the full Boston Marathon. Gibb, who did not run with an official race number during any of the three years (1966–68) that she was the first female finisher, hid in the bushes near the

---

[10] *mill* (n) a factory where cloth is woven, grain is ground, or metal is made
[11] *journeyman* (n) worker whose work is acceptable but not superior

Because it was believed that running would make women sick, women were not allowed to run in the Boston Marathon until 1972.

start until the race began. When the A.A.U. permitted its *sanctioned*[12] marathons (including Boston) to allow women entry in the fall of 1971, Nina Kuscsik's 1972 B.A.A. victory the following spring made her the first official champion. Eight women started that race and all eight finished.

8. _____

The greatest period of growth for the B.A.A. and its Boston Marathon has been during the last twenty years. In the early 1970's, the Association introduced qualifying standards, resulting in increased interest and the race that "local heroes" *aspired*[13] to run. The running *boom*[14] in the U.S. followed with Boston at its center. Bill Rodgers' reign (champion in 1975, 1978–80), the strong community support, and the long-term involvement by John Hancock Financial Services into the next millennium ensured that the Boston Marathon will remain one of running's *marquee events.*[15]

9. _____

Four-time Boston Marathon champion and Massachusetts resident Bill Rodgers became the people's choice as the symbol of distance running in the U.S. after his 1975 victory when he wore a hand-painted shirt with "BOSTON" on its front. That year, he became the first to run under two hours and ten minutes (2:09:55) at Boston, setting a course and American record in the process. Rodgers also won the New York City Marathon four times.

10. _____

In the same year of Rodgers' epic American run, Bob Hall, of Massachusetts, became the first athlete to officially complete the Boston course in a wheelchair. With a time of 2 hours, 58 minutes, he collected on a promise by then Race Director Will Cloney that if he finished in less than three hours he would receive an official B.A.A. Finisher's Certificate. Thus, the Boston Marathon became the world's first major marathon to allow wheelchair racers to compete. Americans Jean Driscoll (six victories; five world records) and Jim Knaub (five inspirational victories; four world records) helped to further establish and popularize the division.

11. *retaining the traditions of the marathon* _____

The B.A.A. Marathon remains a race of tradition and prestige for its participants, spectators and the citizens of the communities through which the course lies. . . . The Boston Marathon continues to evolve, but some traditions will always remain as they have for a century. On a spectacular

> Athletes have studied how to leap and how to survive the leap some of the time and return to the ground.
>
> Harold Brodkey
> (1930–1996), U.S. author

---

[12] *sanctioned* (adj) formally approved
[13] *aspire* (v) to desire strongly
[14] *boom* (n) time of rapid growth
[15] *marquee event* (np) well-publicized, attention-getting performance or act

Patriots' Day each April, both the marathon champions and the race community graciously celebrate victory, pausing to acknowledge and *reciprocate*[16] each other's support and *embrace*.[17]

> The New York Marathon has so many applicants that a lottery is used to limit the number of runners to 20,000 from the United States and 10,000 from other countries.

Understanding the Reading: Identifying Topics

There is a line above each paragraph in the reading from The Race through History. *Go back and skim each paragraph. Then write the topic of each paragraph on the line. The topic may be an event, the name of a person, or a stage in the history of the marathon. Some of the topics have already been added.*

Using the Vocabulary: Word Forms

As you found in the previous reading, **suffixes** can change the forms of words. For example, many adjectives end in suffixes such as *-al*, *-ive*, *-ous*, and *-ar*. Adverbs usually end in *-ly*, but there are a few adjectives with this ending. Do you know what they are? List them here:

A. *Fill in the chart with the adjective forms of the verbs and nouns listed. All the adjectives can be found in the reading.*

Verbs	Nouns	Adjectives
act	action	
compete	competition/competitor	
inaugurate	inauguration	
inspire	inspiration	
populate	population	
locate	location	
profess	profession	
officiate	office	
	spectacle/spectator	
	miracle	
	fame	

---

[16] *reciprocate* (v) to give equally in return for something you have received

[17] *embrace* (n) hug

Just do it.

B. *Now complete the sentences below with the correct form of the words in the chart in Exercise A.*

The stories of (1)_____ runners such as Carl Lewis and Bobbi Gibb (2)_____ athletes all over the world, but one of the most remarkable is the story of Wilma Rudolph. Born in 1940 in Clarksville, Tennessee, Wilma Rudolph was stricken with scarlet fever and pneumonia when she was only four years old. With her left leg paralyzed, her doctors' diagnosis was that she would never walk again. But Wilma's (3)_____ spirit proved them wrong. By the time she was a teenager, she had managed to make a (4)_____ recovery. Then, as (5)_____ lined the track at the 1960 Olympics, the girl with the once-paralyzed leg won three gold medals in track, the first American woman to ever win so many gold medals. Wilma Rudolph had become the greatest runner in the world.

Thinking Together

Work in small groups and discuss the sports you are familiar with, including those mentioned in this chapter. See if you can fill in the circles with at least one sport that has the indicated number of players on a team. You can use sports from any country, but be prepared to explain those that your classmates are not familiar with.

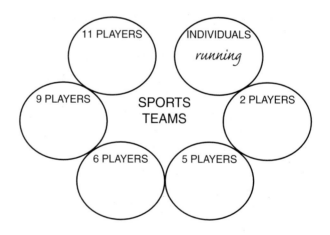

Writing about It

Write one to two paragraphs on one of the following topics. Try to use some of the vocabulary from this reading and from **Focusing In**.

1. Summarize some of the changes that have taken place during the history of the marathon.

2. Describe some of the important past participants in the Boston Marathon.

3. Write a letter to the local Boston newspaper arguing for or against the participation of women and wheelchair athletes in the Boston Marathon.

Reacting to the Reading

In 1975, the first wheelchair athlete competed in the Boston Marathon. Do you think that it is fair and safe for people with disabilities to compete in athletic events? Why or why not?

Keeping Track of Your Reading Rate

- Sports have been opened up to people with disabilities and the mentally retarded in the United States. The following is a description of Special Olympics from the Special Olympics International homepage on the World Wide Web.

- When your instructor gives you the signal to begin, read the story at a quick pace and mark down the time as soon as you are done. Then answer the questions without looking back at the reading.

tip When you read, try to concentrate on the task at hand. Blocking out distractions and unrelated thoughts helps you to focus.

The Special Olympics Oath is: *Let me win. But if I cannot win, let me be brave in the attempt.* Our mission is to provide year-round sports training and athletic competition in a variety of Olympic-type sports for individuals with mental retardation by giving them continuing opportunities to develop physical fitness, demonstrate courage, experience joy, and participate in a sharing of gifts, skills, and friendship with their families, other Special Olympics athletes, and the community.

The benefits of participation in Special Olympics for people with mental retardation include improved physical fitness and motor skills, greater self-confidence, a more positive self-image, friendships, and increased family support. Special Olympics athletes carry these benefits with them into their daily lives at home, in the classroom, on the job, and in the community. Families who participate become stronger as they learn greater appreciation of their athletes' talents. Community volunteers find out what good friends the athletes can be. And everyone learns more about the capabilities of people with mental retardation.

Special Olympics believes that competition among those of equal abilities is the best way to test its athletes' skills, measure their progress, and inspire them to grow. Special Olympics believes that its program of sports training and competition helps people with mental retardation become physically fit and grow mentally, socially, and spiritually. . . .

Special Olympics began in 1968 when Eunice Kennedy Shriver organized the First International Special Olympics Games at Soldier Field, Chicago, Illinois, USA. The concept was born in the early 1960s when Mrs. Shriver started a day camp for people with mental retardation. She saw that people with mental retardation were far more capable in sports and physical activities than many experts thought. Since 1968, millions of children and adults with mental retardation have participated in Special Olympics. . . .

Special Olympics provides year-round training and competition in 22 official sports. More than 140,000 qualified coaches train Special Olympics athletes. . . . Special Olympics competitions are patterned after the Olympic Games. More than 15,000 games, meets, and tournaments in both summer and winter sports are held worldwide each year. World Games for selected representatives of all programs are held every two years, alternating between summer and winter. More than 500,000 volunteers organize and run local Special Olympics programs, serving as coaches, Games officials, drivers, and in many other capacities. Anyone can learn how to participate through the many training programs Special Olympics offers for coaches, officials, and volunteers.

(400 words)   TIME _____

*Now mark these statements true (**T**) or false (**F**) without looking back at the reading.*

_____ 1. The founder of Special Olympics was Eunice Kennedy Shriver.

_____ 2. Special Olympics offers training in about ten sports.

_____ 3. Before Special Olympics, experts believed the mentally retarded could be good athletes.

_____ 4. Special Olympics started in the United States but has spread to other countries.

_____ 5. Special Olympics has volunteers who serve as coaches, drivers, and officials.

_____ 6. Special Olympics provides only summer programs.

_____ 7. Families of the mentally retarded athletes are encouraged to participate in the program.

_____ 8. Special Olympics improves only the physical development of the mentally retarded.

_____ 9. Only child athletes participate in Special Olympics.

_____10. Special Olympics will train new coaches and volunteers.

Percent correct = _____   wpm = _____

Michael Jordan, possibly the most famous athlete in the world, earned as much as $38 million per year, while the average salary for a full professor at Havard University has not even come close to a quarter of a million dollars.

MAKING C O N N E C T I O N S

Responding to the Readings

Prepare short oral or written responses based on your personal experience and your reactions to the readings. Try to incorporate the information and the vocabulary you have learned in this chapter.

1. Are athletes important figures in your country? Are there any All-Star competitions?

2. Write about your favorite sport and your participation in it.

3. What athletes do you admire most? Why?

4. Is participation in sporting events open to women and people with disabilities in your country?

5. Are physical education and sports teams a part of school activities in your country? Do you think they should be?

6. Discuss your reaction to one of the quotes or facts in the margins of this chapter that you find most interesting or surprising.

In a 1996 Gallup survey, 82 percent of Americans believed Special Olympics sports programs should be available to all school-aged athletes through a combination of schools, social service agencies, and private community efforts.

Editing Your Work

*A student wrote this paragraph without editing carefully for singular and plural forms. Remember that an **S** is required on all plural count nouns, but it is not used on adjectives or on noncount nouns. The following paragraph has five **S**s that are incorrect and should be omitted. It is also missing five **S**s that are needed on plural nouns. Correct all ten errors.*

> I enjoy playing soccer. Soccer is a very healthy sports. The players have to run most of the times. Their eye always concentrate on the ball. In this game, the players get tired very quickly. In a competitions, the players must wear uniform to identify their teams. Usually they wear soccer shoe that have sharps edges. These edge help the players run. They wear short and T-shirts with numbers on them. Each players has his name on his shirt to identify him to his coach.

> The American Youth Soccer Organization, run by parent volunteers around the country, had 625,000 players nationwide in 1999; 39% were girls.
>
> *Soccer Now*

Writing an Essay

Choose one of the following topics and write an essay. As a prewriting activity, read over your shortwrites and notes for inspiration. Remember to review the brainstorming techniques on pages 262–263. In your essay, use the readings, factoids, quotes, class discussions, and personal experience to support your ideas. Try to use the vocabulary you have learned in this chapter. If you choose to write a research paper, make certain to cite your sources clearly.

1. American parents encourage their children to join athletic teams because they believe participating in sports helps teach children to work hard, persevere despite the odds, and live a healthy and balanced life. Describe a sport you have played. Did it involve a lot of training and hard work? Did you have a special coach or athletic hero who inspired you to excel? What were the advantages and disadvantages of your participation?

2. Do you believe "winning is everything," or is it the experience that is the most important? Describe an athletic activity you have participated in that involved competition. Was it an individual or a team sport? Provide details about the sport and the competition. Did you enjoy competing? Write about what you learned about the sport and about yourself from this experience.

3. The Olympic Games provide an opportunity for athletes from all over the world to compete against one another. How does your country participate in these games? Does your government support the training of Olympic athletes? What types of teams does your country send? At which sport is your country most successful? Are the games broadcast on television or radio? Have the Olympics ever been held in your country?

4. In the United States, sports influence many aspects of people's lives. Businesspeople meet on the golf course; children learn sports in school and play team sports on weekends. Some television and radio stations are devoted entirely to sports coverage. There are sports bars and restaurants where fans congregate to watch games together. Compare and contrast this level of interest with the involvement of sports in the lives of people in other nations. Are Americans unusual in their enthusiasm for sports?

5. Research any sport. Find out about how it started and where, and how it has developed over time. Include details on its participants, the games and tournaments followers can participate in or watch, and where it is most popular. What kind of success, financial and otherwise, can winners hope to achieve?

Finding More Information

Magazines and Journals

Field and Stream
Inside Sports
Running
The Sporting News
Sports Illustrated

Books

Kinsella, W. P., *Shoeless Joe*
Krugel, M., *Jordan: The Man, His Words, His Life*
Mantle, Mickey, *My Favorite Summer*
Novak, Michael, *The Joy of Sports*
Onard, Michael, *Dreaming of Heroes: American Sports Fiction*
Ward, G. and K. Burn, *Baseball*

The World Wide Web

www.baa.org—the Boston Athletic Association
www.cnnsi.com—CNN and Sports Illustrated
www.espn.go.com—ESPN Sports
www.majorleaguebaseball.com—Major League Baseball
www.specialolympics.org—the Special Olympics

Movies and Videos

Hoop Dreams
A League of Their Own
The Mighty Ducks
The Natural
Rocky
Rudy

> I'm not out there sweating for three hours every day just to find out what it feels like to sweat.
>
> Michael Jordan (1963–),
> U.S. basketball superstar

Staying Healthy and Fit

Foreigners have conflicting images of American health. Are Americans beautiful people with perfect teeth and bodies sculpted by plastic surgeons or are they overweight couch potatoes who smoke too much and rarely exercise? Both images are probably true. America is a youth-oriented culture, so a youthful appearance is highly valued. A large health and fitness industry has been created as Americans try to stay physically fit and build perfect bodies. However, many Americans, thinking they can get away with anything, eat what they want, when they want, and end up with health problems that require treatment.

> When we are young, we think we are invincible. When we are older, we think we can't change our behavior. Our health destiny is in our own hands.
>
> Donna Shalala, U.S. Secretary of Health and Human Services, 1997

Medical care in the United States is private, and there is a great deal of competition among health providers. Americans can choose an old-fashioned family doctor or a high-tech specialist. Treatments range from conventional antibiotics to alternative herbal medicines. However, critics complain that the wealthy receive the best care and can choose from a multitude of specialists, while the poor are sometimes turned away from public hospitals except in emergency cases. Meanwhile, government officials, trying to solve the issue of health coverage for all Americans, argue over private versus universal medical care.

The articles in this chapter pertain to health care and fitness. The first reading, "Body Ritual among the Nacirema" by Horace Miner, is an anthropological study of a culture that readers might recognize because of its obsession with the body. Debate over health treatments is the focus of Doris Williams' article "Alternative Medicine Is Natural and Gives Patients More Freedom." In spite of all of their apparent concern, Americans are still out of shape according to the former U.S. Surgeon General, C. Everett Koop. His plan to "shape up America" is included in this chapter. As fitness becomes a goal for more citizens, they sign up for all types of exercise programs including yoga, aerobics and martial arts. This fitness phenomenon is the theme of the last reading by Dennis Fiely, "Martial Arts Festival Will Share Stage at Arnold Fitness Weekend."

Are Americans as healthy as they could or should be? Discuss this question in small groups. Then talk about the picture on page 76 and answer this question: *What popular American fitness activity are these people getting ready for?*

What Do You Think?

Why do you think the following stereotypes about Americans developed? How true do the members of your group think they are? Be prepared to share your opinions, reasons, and experiences with the class.

1. Most Americans are overweight.
2. Americans spend millions of dollars trying to keep fit.
3. Americans eat fast food every day.
4. Americans are obsessed with cleanliness.
5. Americans are more concerned about their physical appearance than their health.

Test Your Word Power

Take this vocabulary quiz. Then compare your answers with a partner.

____ 1 fit (adj)	a. treatment for mental or physical problems
____ 2. pharmacy (n)	
____ 3. obese (adj)	b. in good physical condition
____ 4. diet (n)	c. very fat
____ 5. hygiene (n)	d. drugstore
____ 6. disorder (n)	e. rules for healthy living; cleanliness
____ 7. vegetarian (n)	f. person who does not eat meat
____ 8. therapy (n)	g. to write a medical order
____ 9. to work out (vp)	h. sickness or disturbance (of the mind or body)
____10. to prescribe (v)	i. to do physical activities to strengthen the body
	j. weight loss program; a food plan

Health is a state of
complete physical,
mental and social
well-being, and not
merely the absence of
disease or infirmity.

Constitution of the World
Health Organization

■ Horace Miner, an anthropologist, pokes fun at the culture and customs of people from a particular country. The author describes the body rituals or special health routines that they practice.

■ While this passage may seem difficult at first, understanding each word is not necessary. First read it through once to grasp the overall meaning and tone. Try to figure out what group of people the author is referring to. Then reread the article to better appreciate its hidden meanings and humor. What Nacirema rituals do you find most amusing?

Body Ritual among the Nacirema

HORACE MINER

from *American Anthropologist*

1   The anthropologist has become so familiar with the diversity of ways in which different peoples behave in similar situations that he *is not apt to*[1] be surprised by even the most exotic customs. In fact, if all of the logically possible combinations of behavior have not been found somewhere in the world, he is apt to suspect that they must be present in some yet undescribed tribe. This point has, in fact, been expressed with respect to clan organization by Murdock. In this light, the magical beliefs and practices of the Nacirema present such unusual aspects that it seems desirable to describe them as an example of the extremes to which human behavior can go.

2   Professor Linton first brought the ritual of the Nacirema to the attention of anthropologists twenty years ago, but the culture of this people is still very poorly understood. They are a North American group living in the territory between the Canadian Cree, the Yaqui and Tarahunnare of Mexico, and the Carib and Arawak of the Antilles. Little is known of their origin, although tradition states that they came from the east. According to Nacirema mythology, their nation was originated by a culture hero, Notgnihsaw, who is otherwise known for two great feats of strength—the throwing of a piece of wampum across the river Pa-To-Mac and the chopping down of a cherry tree in which the Spirit of Truth resided.

3   Nacirema culture is characterized by a highly developed market economy which has evolved in a rich natural habitat. While much of the people's time is devoted to economic pursuits, a large part of the fruits of these labors and a considerable portion of the day are spent in ritual activity. The focus of this activity is the human body, the appearance and health of which loom as a dominant concern in the *ethos*[2] of the people. While such

---

[1] *to be apt to* (vp) to be likely to do something
[2] *ethos* (n) belief system

a concern is certainly not unusual, its ceremonial aspects and associated philosophy are unique.

4   The fundamental belief underlying the whole system appears to be that the human body is ugly and that its natural tendency is to *debility*[3] and disease. *Incarcerated*[4] in such a body, man's only hope is to *avert*[5] these characteristics through the use of the powerful influences of ritual and ceremony. Every household has one or more shrines devoted to this purpose. The more powerful individuals in the society have several shrines in their houses and, in fact, the *opulence*[6] of a house is often referred to in terms of the number of such ritual centers it possesses. . . .

5   The *focal point*[7] of the shrine is a box or chest which is built into the wall. In this chest are kept the many charms and magical potions without which no native believes he could live. These preparations are secured from a variety of specialized practitioners. The most powerful of these are the medicine men, whose assistance must be rewarded with *substantial*[8] gifts. However, the medicine men do not provide the *curative*[9] potions for their clients, but decide what the ingredients should be and then write them down in an ancient and secret language. This writing is understood only by the medicine men and by the herbalists who, for another gift, provide the required charm. . . .

6   Beneath the charm-box is a small *font.*[10] Each day every member of the family, in succession, enters the shrine room, bows his head before the charm-box, mingles different sorts of holy water in the font, and proceeds with a brief rite of *ablution.*[11] The holy waters are secured from the Water Temple of the community, where the priests conduct elaborate ceremonies to make the liquid ritually pure.

7   In the *hierarchy*[12] of magical practitioners, and below the medicine men in prestige are specialists whose *designation*[13] is best translated "holy-mouth-men." The Nacirema have an almost pathological horror of and fascination with the mouth, the condition of which is believed to have a supernatural influence on all social relationships. Were it not for the rituals of the mouth, they believe that their teeth could fall out, their gums bleed, their jaws shrink, their friends desert them, and their lovers reject them. . . .

---

[3] *debility* (n) weakness
[4] *incarcerated* (adj) in jail or prison
[5] *avert* (v) to avoid or prevent from happening
[6] *opulence* (n) great wealth and luxury
[7] *focal point* (n) something on which attention is focused
[8] *substantial* (adj) large, considerable
[9] *curative* (adj) able to heal or make well
[10] *font* (n) basin; bowl for holy water
[11] *ablution* (n) washing of the body
[12] *hierarchy* (n) organization from higher to lower by rank, social status, or function
[13] *designation* (n) official name

Almost half of the Americans (48%) responding to a *Parade* survey in 1997 reported they were taking a prescription drug.

8   The daily body ritual performed by everyone includes a mouth-rite. Despite the fact that these people are so *punctilious*[14] about care of the mouth, this rite involves a practice which strikes the uninitiated stranger as *revolting*.[15] It was reported to me that the ritual consists of inserting a small bundle of hog hairs into the mouth, along with certain magical powders, and then moving the bundle in a highly formalized series of gestures.

A "holy-mouth-woman" demonstrates her augers, awls, probes, and prods.

9   In addition to the private mouth-rite, the people seek out a holy-mouth-man once or twice a year. These practitioners have an impressive set of paraphernalia, consisting of a variety of augers, awls, probes, and prods. The use of these objects in the *exorcism*[16] of the evils of the mouth involves almost unbelievable ritual torture of the client. The holy mouth-man opens the client's mouth and, using the above mentioned tools, enlarges any holes which decay may have created in the teeth. Magical materials are put into these holes. If there are no naturally occurring holes in the teeth, large sections of one or more teeth are *gouged out*[17] so that the *supernatural*[18] substance can be applied. In the client's view, the purpose of these ministrations is to arrest decay and to draw friends. The extremely sacred and traditional character of the rite is evident in the fact that the natives return to the holy-mouth-men year after year, despite the fact that their teeth continue to decay. . . .

10   The medicine men have an *imposing*[19] temple, or *latipso,* in every community of any size. The more elaborate ceremonies required to treat very sick patients can only be performed at this temple. These ceremonies involve a permanent group of vestal maidens who move *sedately*[20] about the temple chambers in distinctive costume and headdress.

11   The *latipso* ceremonies are so harsh that it is phenomenal that a fair proportion of the really sick natives who enter the temple ever recover. Small children whose *indoctrination*[21] is still incomplete have been known

---

[14] *punctilious* (adj) very concerned about details
[15] *revolting* (adj) disgusting
[16] *exorcism* (n) removal of evil from a person
[17] *gouge out* (vp) to press, shape, or force out
[18] *supernatural* (adj) beyond nature, spiritual; not explained by science or natural laws
[19] *imposing* (adj) having a strong or powerful effect; grand
[20] *sedately* (adv) calmly
[21] *indoctrination* (n) teaching in order to enforce beliefs

to resist attempts to take them to the temple because "that is where you go to die." Despite this fact, sick adults are not only willing but eager to undergo the protracted ritual purification if they can afford to do so. No matter how ill the *supplicant*[22] or how grave the emergency, the guardians of many temples will not admit a client if he cannot give a rich gift to the custodian. . . .

12 There remains one other kind of practitioner, known as a listener. This witchdoctor has the power to exorcise the devils that lodge in the heads of people who have been bewitched. The Nacirema believe that parents bewitch their own children. Mothers are particularly suspected of putting a *curse*[23] on children while teaching them the secret body rituals. The counter-magic of the witch doctor is unusual in its lack of ritual. The patient simply tells the listener all his troubles and fears, beginning with the earliest difficulties he can remember. The memory displayed by the Nacirema in these exorcism sessions is truly remarkable. . . .

13 In conclusion, mention must be made of certain practices which have their base in native *esthetics*[24] but which depend upon the *pervasive aversion*[25] to the natural body and its functions. There are ritual fasts to make fat people thin and ceremonial feasts to make thin people fat. Still other rites are used to make women's breasts larger if they are small, and smaller if they are large. . . .

14 Our review of the ritual life of the Nacirema has certainly shown them to be a magic-ridden people. It is hard to understand how they have managed to exist so long under the burdens which they have imposed upon themselves. But even such exotic customs as these take on real meaning when they are viewed with the insight provided by Malinowski when he wrote: "Looking from far and above, from our high places of safety in the developed civilization, it is easy to see all the *crudity*[26] and irrelevance of magic. But without its power and guidance early man could not have mastered his practical difficulties as he has done, nor could man have advanced to the higher stages of civilization."

> Two-thirds of Americans surveyed in 1997 said they were in "excellent" or "good" health, but one in five reported being afraid to go to the doctor.
>
> *Parade*

Understanding the Reading: Reviewing Topics and Identifying Terms

A. *Write the overall topic of this article on the line below. Remember that to find the topic, you should ask the question,* What is this reading about?

---

[22] *supplicant* (n) person who begs for help
[23] *curse* (n) something that causes harm
[24] *esthetics* (n) ideas about beauty
[25] *pervasive aversion* (np) widespread hatred or dislike
[26] *crudity* (n) roughness; primitiveness

> He had had much experience of physicians, and said, "the only way to keep your health is to eat what you don't want, drink what you don't like, and do what you'd druther not."
>
> Mark Twain (1835–1910), U.S. author

B. *The author uses special phrases to describe common items and activities, so understanding his message involves decoding certain words and phrases. Work with a partner to match the expressions on the left with their definitions on the right.*

_____ 1. Nacirema

_____ 2. Notgnihsaw

_____ 3. wampum

_____ 4. shrines/ritual centers

_____ 5. chest/charm-box

_____ 6. medicine men

_____ 7. font

_____ 8. holy-mouth-men

_____ 9. curative magical potions

_____10. small bundle of hog hairs

_____11. certain magical powders

_____12. witch doctor

_____13. latipso temple

_____14. vestal maidens

_____15. ritual fasts

a. sink

b. doctors

c. nurses

d. hospital

e. prescription drugs

f. toothpaste

g. psychiatrist/psychologist

h. dentists

i. Washington (George)

j. money

k. diets

l. bathrooms

m. medicine cabinets

n. toothbrush

o. American

Using the Vocabulary: Dictionary Skills

Knowing how to use a dictionary when you need one is an important reading skill. The following exercise uses vocabulary from the article and pages from the *Longman Dictionary of Contemporary English.*

A. *First, alphabetize the following words from the reading:*

practice   paraphernalia   protracted   practitioner

pathological   prestige   phenomenal   pathology

purification   pathologist

1. _____

2. _____

3. _____

4. _____

5. _____

6. _____

7. _____

8. _____

9. _____

10. _____

par·a·mount /ˈpærə,maunt/ *adj* more important than anything else: *The needs of the customer should be paramount.*

par·a·noid /ˈpærə,nɔɪd/ *adj* **1** DISAPPROVING extremely worried because you believe that you cannot trust other people: *Ever since her keys were stolen she's been paranoid about going into the house alone.* **2** suffering from a mental illness that makes you believe that other people are trying to harm you –paranoia /,pærəˈnɔɪə/ *n* [U]

par·a·pher·na·lia /,pærəfəˈneɪlyə, fəˈneɪl-/ *n* [U] a lot of small things that belong to someone or that are used for a particular activity: *photographic paraphernalia*

par·a·phrase /ˈpærə,freɪz/ *v* [T] to express what someone has written or said in a way that is shorter or easier to understand: *Write a paragraph that paraphrases the story.*–paraphrase *n*

path /pæθ/ *n* **1** a track that people walk along over an area of ground: *a path through the woods* **2** a way that allows you to move forward through something: *The police cleared a path through the crowd.* **3** the direction or line along which someone or something moves: *The storm destroyed everything in its path.*

pa·thet·ic /pəˈθɛtɪk/ *adj* **1** making you feel pity or sympathy: *the pathetic sight of starving children* **2** very bad, useless, weak: *Vicky made a pathetic attempt to apologize.* –pathetically *adv*

path·o·log·i·cal /,pæθəˈlɑdʒɪkəl/ *adj* **1** pathological behavior or feelings are unreasonable, impossible to control, and caused by a mental illness: *a pathological liar* **2** TECHNICAL relating to the causes and effects of disease: *a pathological condition*

pa·thol·o·gy /pəˈθɑlədʒi, pæ-/ *n* [U] the study of the causes and effects of diseases –pathologist *n*

pa·thos /ˈpeɪθɑus, θɑs, ˈpæ-/ *n* [U] LITERARY the quality that a person or a situation has that makes you feel pity and sadness

phase² *v* [T]

phase sth ↔ in *phr v* [T] to introduce something gradually: *New rules about claiming overtime will be phased in over the next two months.* **phase sth ↔ out** *phr v* [T] to gradually stop using or providing something: *Leaded gas was phased out in the 1970s.*

Ph.D. /,pi eɪtʃ ˈdi/ *n* Doctor of Philosophy; the highest university degree that can be earned, or someone who has this degree

pheas·ant /ˈfɛzənt/ *n* a large colorful bird with a long tail, that is hunted for food and sport, or the meat from this bird

phe·nom·e·nal /fɪˈnɑmənl/ *adj* very unusual and impressive: *We have a phenomenal view of the harbor at night from here.* –phenomenally *adv*

phe·nom·e·non /fɪˈnɑmənɑn, -,nɑn/ *n* **1** *plural* **phenomena** something that happens or exists in society, science, or nature that is unusual or difficult to understand: *Homelessness is not a new phenomenon.* **2** *plural* **phenomenons** a person or thing that has a rare ability or quality: *Gillespie called him one of the phenomenons of our century.*

prac·ti·ca·ble /ˈpræktɪkəbəl/ *adj* FORMAL able to be used successfully in a particular situation: *a practicable idea*

prac·ti·cal /ˈpræktɪkəl/ *adj* **1** relating to real situations and events rather than ideas: *Do you have a lot of practical experience as a mechanic?/ I deal with practical matters, like finding people places to stay.* **2** sensible and likely to succeed or be effective: *We have to be practical and not spend so much money. / Is that a practical solution to the problem?* **3** designed to be useful, or to be suitable for a particular purpose: *She gives practical gifts, such as clothes. / a practical car for a family* **4 for all practical purposes** used in order to describe what the real situation is, although it might seem to be different: *For all practical purposes, the election is over.* (=we already know who the winner is)

prac·ti·cal·i·ty /,præktɪˈkæləti/ *n* **1 practicalities** [*plural*] the real facts of a situation, rather than ideas about how it might be: *We have to think about practicalities, like how long it will take, and how much it will cost.* **2** [U] how sensible and suitable an idea is: *It's a nice idea, but I'm not sure about the practicality of it.*

practical joke /,...ˈ./ *n* a trick that is intended to surprise someone and make other people laugh

prac·ti·cal·ly /ˈpræktɪkli/ *adv* **1** SPOKEN almost: *Practically everyone was there. / She practically jumped out of her chair.* **2** in a sensible way: *Vasko just doesn't think practically.*

prac·tice¹ /ˈpræktɪs/ *n*
1 >SKILL< [U] **a)** regular activity that you do in order to improve a skill or ability: *It takes a lot of practice to be a good piano player.* **b)** the period of time in which you do this: *We have football practice tonight.*
2 >STH THAT IS USUALLY DONE< [C,U] **a)** something that people do often and in a particular way: *unsafe sexual practices* **b)** something that people do in a particular way because it is usually done that way in their religion, society, organization, etc.; CUSTOM: *the practice of kissing someone as a greeting / It's standard/normal practice to do the payroll in this way.*
3 in practice used in order to describe what the real situation is rather than what seems to be true: *Annette is the head of the company, but in practice Sue runs everything.*
4 >DOCTOR/LAWYER< the work of a doctor or lawyer, or the place where s/he works: *She has a successful medical/legal practice.*
5 be out of practice to be unable to do something well because you have not done it for a long time: *I'd like to sing with you, but I'm really out of practice.*
6 put sth into practice to start using an idea, plan, method, etc. instead of just thinking about it or studying it: *Now's your chance to put the skills you've learned into practice.*

practice² *v* **1** [I,T] to do an activity regularly to improve your skill or ability: *Gail practices the piano more than an hour every day.* **2** [I,T] to work as a doctor or lawyer: *Bill is practicing law/medicine in Ohio now.* **3** [T] to do an activi

ty as a habit, or to live according to the rules of a religion: *The posters encourage young people to practice safe sex.*

prac·ticed /ˈpræktɪst/ *adj* good at doing something because you have done it many times before: *a practiced pilot*

prac·tic·ing /ˈpræktɪsɪŋ/ *adj* **1 a practicing doctor/lawyer/architect etc.** someone who has trained as a doctor, lawyer, etc., and who still works as one **2 a practicing Catholic/Jew/Muslim, etc.** someone who obeys the rules of a particular religion

prac·ti·tion·er /prækˈtɪʃənɚ/ *n* FORMAL someone who is trained to do a particular type of work that involves a lot of skill: *a tax practitioner / Dr. Reynolds is a family/general practitioner.* (=a doctor who treats general medical problems)

prag·mat·ic /prægˈmætɪk/ *adj* dealing with problems in a sensible and practical way rather than following a set of ideas that are considered correct: *The diet gives you pragmatic suggestions for eating healthily.*

pres·sur·ized /ˈprɛʃə,raɪzd/ *adj* in an aircraft that is pressurized, the air pressure inside it is similar to the pressure on the ground

pres·tige /prɛˈstiʒ, -ˈstidʒ/ *n* [U] the respect or admiration that someone or something receives, usually as a result of success, high quality, etc.: *Being a doctor has a certain amount of prestige.* –prestige *adj*: *a prestige automobile* (=one that a rich person drives)

pres·tig·ious /prɛˈstɪdʒəs, -ˈsti-/ *adj* admired or respected as one of the best and most important: *a prestigious award for writers*

pro·ton /ˈproutɑn/ *n* TECHNICAL a part of an atom that has a positive electrical charge

pro·to·type /ˈproutə,taɪp/ *n* a model of a new car, machine, etc., used in order to test the design before it is produced

pro·tract·ed /prouˈtræktɪd, prə-/ *adj* continuing for a long time, usually longer than necessary: *a messy protracted divorce* –protraction /prouˈtrækʃən, prə-/ *n* [U]

pro·trac·tor /prouˈtræktɚ, prə-/ *n* a flat tool shaped like a half circle, used for measuring and drawing angles

pro·trude /prouˈtrud/ *v* [I] FORMAL to stick out from somewhere: *a rock protruding from the water* –protruding *adj* –protrusion /prouˈtruʒən/ *n* [C,U]

pur·ga·to·ry /ˈpɚgə,tori/ *n* [U] a place where, according to Roman Catholic beliefs, the souls of dead people must suffer for the bad things they have done, until they are good enough to enter heaven

purge /pɚdʒ/ *v* [T] **1** to force your opponents to leave an organization or place, often by using violence: *The army was purged of anyone the government considered dangerous.* **2** TECHNICAL to get rid of something bad that is in your body, or of bad feelings –purge *n*

pu·ri·fy /ˈpyurə,faɪ/ *v* [T] to remove the dirty or unwanted parts from something: *The water should be purified before drinking.* –purification /,pyurəfəˈkeɪʃən/ *n* [U]

pur·ist /ˈpyurɪst/ *n* someone who has very strict ideas about what is right or correct in a particular subject

In 1997, 54 percent of Americans were wearing eyeglasses or contact lenses.

B. *The numbered sentences in this exercise come from the article "Body Ritual among the Nacirema." For each underlined word, look up the definitions on the dictionary page provided. Be sure to pay careful attention to the context of each sample sentence. Use the dictionary to complete the statements and answer the questions about the words. Then write a sentence of your own when indicated.*

Example

These preparations are secured from a variety of specialized <u>practitioners</u>.

    a. The word <u>practitioner</u> means a person who does skilled work.

    b. The word <u>practitioner</u> is a noun (part of speech).

    c. Sentence: *He is a legal practitioner.*

1. In the hierarchy of magical practitioners, and below the medicine men in <u>prestige</u>, are specialists whose designation is best translated "holy-mouth-men."

    a. The word <u>prestige</u> means _____

    b. Its adjective form is _____

    c. What symbol indicates that <u>prestige</u> is a noncount noun?

    _____

    d. Sentence: _____

2. The Nacirema have an almost <u>pathological</u> horror of and fascination with the mouth, the condition of which is believed to have a supernatural influence on all social relationships.

    a. The word <u>pathological</u> means _____

    b. Its part of speech is _____

    c. Its noun form is _____

    d. In the alphabetical list below, the word <u>pathological</u> has been omitted. Indicate where it belongs by writing in the correct space.

    _____

    pathogen

    _____

    pathologist

    _____

    pathos

    _____

3. Despite the fact that these people are so punctilious about care of the mouth, this rite involves a <u>practice</u> which strikes the uninitiated stranger as revolting.

    a. There are many definitions for the word <u>practice</u>. In this sentence, is <u>practice</u> a noun, a verb, or an adjective? _____

    b. What is the verb form of the word <u>practice</u>? _____

    c. Sentence: _____

4. These practitioners have an impressive set of <u>paraphernalia</u>.

   a. Is <u>paraphernalia</u> a count or noncount noun? _____

   b. What <u>paraphernalia</u> do you keep in your medicine cabinet?

   _____

   c. Sentence: _____

5. The latipso ceremonies are so harsh that it is <u>phenomenal</u> that a fair proportion of the really sick natives who enter the temple ever recover.

   a. The word <u>phenomenal</u> means _____

   b. Its noun form is _____

   c. The plural noun form is _____

   d. Sentence: _____

6. Despite this fact, sick adults are not only willing but eager to undergo the <u>protracted</u> ritual <u>purification</u> if they can afford to do so.

   a. The word <u>protracted</u> is what part of speech? _____

   b. On which syllable is the stress placed in the adjective <u>protracted</u>?

   _____

   c. What does <u>protracted</u> mean? _____

   d. The definition of <u>purification</u> is _____

   e. What verb is it derived from? _____

Thinking Together

Horace Miner describes the action of brushing one's teeth, yet he never uses any of the words we usually associate with this ritual such as "teeth," "toothbrush," or "toothpaste." The tone of his report is humorous because his observations are written like a true anthropological study. With a partner or in a small group, write a similar paragraph that describes a common everyday routine that people do; do not use the actual words. Like Miner, you can disguise the words by spelling them backwards or by using hyphens to change them. Share your paragraphs with your classmates.

Writing about It

*Write one to two paragraphs on one of the following topics. Try to use some of the vocabulary from this reading and from **Focusing In**.*

1. Discuss the ways Miner tries to fool his readers into thinking they are reading about an unknown culture. Give examples from the text.

2. Choose one of the rituals and describe it using everyday American English.

3. Miner uses humor in this passage. Write a paragraph about some of the descriptions that you found to be the most humorous.

In 1997, Utah had the lowest percentage of smokers (13%) in the United States. The highest was in Kentucky, where 27 percent of people smoked.

University of California at Berkeley Wellness Letter

Reacting to the Reading

Miner states that "our review of the ritual life of the Nacirema has certainly shown them to be a magic-ridden people." Do you think of the American people as being "magic-ridden"? Why or why not?

- As scientists and healthcare professionals debate complex medical issues, many of them are beginning to recognize that conventional medicine does not always offer the best treatment for a variety of ailments. The author of the following article, Doris Williams, thinks alternative medicine "gives patients more freedom." Why do you think she believes this?
- While reading this article, think about the two types of healthcare systems. Which one are you most familiar with? Do you think you could ever consider choosing a different type from the one you are used to?

Alternative Medicine Is Natural and Gives Patients More Freedom

DORIS WILLIAMS

FROM THE *SALT LAKE TRIBUNE*

1   There is an important concern that must not be passed over in the *intensifying*[1] debate of healthcare reform. This concern is the need we have as citizens to preserve and expand our right to choose not only our doctors, but the method by which our health care is delivered.

2   There are two systems of health care in our country today. The first is conventional Western medicine, with its well-known web of preferred and secondary providers, insurance forms, expensive drugs and testing, limited office hours and access to information.

3   The other, less well-known, but gaining in acceptance, is the *domain*[2] of alternative medicine, which includes a diversity of practitioners and specialties such as *homeopathy*,[3] *acupuncture*,[4] herbal medicine, energy medicine and naturopathic medicine, to name just a few.

4   The world of Western medicine, with which most of us are familiar, is the world of the American Medical Association, which is filled with doctors schooled in the treatment of disease. Most of the doctors are in specialized practice. This world is supported at every turn by the multi-billion-dollar *pharmaceutical*[5] industry. It is this practice of medicine that has brought about many modern-day miracles and is unsurpassed when we need surgery, emergency or trauma care. However, it leaves much to be desired when we are faced with a chronic *degenerative*[6] disease such as cancer,

---

[1] *intensifying* (adj) getting stronger, increasing in strength
[2] *domain* (n) world, realm
[3] *homeopathy* (n) system of medicine based on developing the body's natural immunities

[4] *acupuncture* (n) part of Chinese medicine that treats diseases and pain by putting needles into the body
[5] *pharmaceutical* (adj) having to do with the study, making, and selling of medicine and drugs

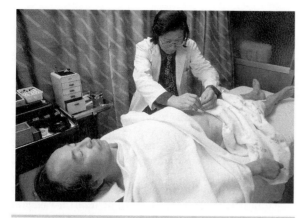

An increasing number of Americans are visiting acupuncturists who place needles in the body to treat disease.

heart disease, rheumatoid arthritis or diabetes. Even common ailments such as asthma, *gastrointestinal*[7] disorders and headaches are slow to respond to its therapy.

5 Alternative therapies have established their own record of successful treatment of most of the medical conditions that continue to afflict much of the population. But these therapies are largely ignored, even *suppressed,*[8] by the dominant system of medical care in our country today. Our government continues to pass over their well-established procedures in favor of pouring federal funds into "more research" and programs, granting only a *trickle*[9] to expand our knowledge about our alternative choices. These choices are also based on science, but many are natural therapies, as opposed to those that are drug-based.

6 My personal experience with medicine has been weighted heavily on the *allopathic*[10] side of the scale. I have been a practicing registered nurse for 21 years. My first experience with homeopathy came early this year.

7 Recently I had a return of a formerly diagnosed *hiatal hernia.*[11] My doctor prescribed a new (and very expensive) medication along with some familiar advice about living with a hiatal hernia. The medication helped some, but with increasing stress, the symptoms returned. About six weeks later, when it was time to renew my expensive prescription, I decided to be treated with homeopathy.

8 I was beginning to experience difficulty in swallowing food, so I was drinking more liquids in place of solids. The day before my appointment I could hardly swallow anything but liquids. The doctor took an extensive health history and prescribed a remedy, which he placed under my tongue. I was in for a real surprise. Within the hour, I was swallowing normally, and I continue to experience no difficulty at the present time. The remedies used in homeopathy are generally *dilutions*[12] of natural substances from plants, minerals and animals and have none of the side effects of a drug.

9 I am convinced that the success of the treatment depends upon the skill of the doctor or health professional in finding the appropriate remedy to stimulate the *immune system*[13] of the patient toward health. Although homeopathy is an integral part of the healthcare delivery system in England and is used by hundreds of millions of people worldwide, there are only an estimated 3,000 medical doctors and licensed healthcare providers who practice homeopathy in the United States at the present time.

10 In spite of this fact, the World Health Organization has cited homeopathy as one of the systems of traditional medicine that should be *integrated*[14] worldwide with conventional medicine in order to provide adequate global health by the year 2000. Although my own experience with alternative medicine is limited to homeopathy, I have talked to others who have had similar positive experiences in this realm of medicine. My concerns are about the need to recognize and acknowledge the healing that many of these therapies provide, at considerably less risk and cost.

---

[6] *degenerative* (adj) deteriorating, declining in functional activity

[7] *gastrointestinal* (adj) affecting the stomach and intestines

[8] *suppress* (v) to conceal or keep from being seen or heard

[9] *trickle* (n) thin stream

[10] *allopathic* (adj) relating to treatment of disease with drugs such as antibiotics

[11] *hiatal hernia* (n) tear or opening in the muscles of the abdomen

[12] *dilution* (n) weakening of the strength of a liquid

[13] *immune system* (n) the body's own defenses

[14] *integrate* (v) to put different groups together

11   I recently purchased a book which was compiled by Burton Goldberg and 350 consulting physicians. It is called *Alternative Medicine.* I quote: "Their alternatives are *sound*,[15] based on science, and really work. Many are natural, as opposed to drug-based therapies. . . . Because it emphasizes prevention and goes after causes rather than symptoms, it doesn't trap people on the merry-go-round that begins with one drug, and ends up requiring them to take others to compensate for the side-effects each one causes."

12   Many alternative methods work by assisting your own body to heal itself instead of introducing strong drugs. You probably know someone who has had the experience of getting rid of one illness, only to come down with another from the procedure used by the doctor. . . . " Too many mainstream doctors today become so specialized, they treat the body parts and forget they are treating a whole human being. Disease usually appears as a local symptom, but it is always related to the entire system; so you have to treat the whole person to cure the disease, not just the symptom."

13   Goldberg further documents the fact that state medical boards have *censured*[16] and *revoked*[17] the licenses of *conscientious*[18] physicians who practice alternative medicine simply because their treatments are not conventional and do not conform to the "accepted standards of care," despite the fact that many of these treatments work. I hope that we will write letters or otherwise let our congressional and senate representatives, both on the local and national level, know that we want to have freedom of choice regarding healthcare providers. We need to work to overcome the refusal of insurance companies to pay for established alternative treatments. I know that money drives the systems of our country, be they political, legal, corporate or health. I repeat a statement by Benjamin Rush, M.D., physician to George Washington and a signer of the Declaration of Independence as quoted by Goldberg: "Unless we put medical freedom into the Constitution, the time will come when medicine will organize into an undercover dictatorship. . . . All such laws are un-American and *despotic*[19] and have no place in a republic. . . . The Constitution of this republic should make special privileges for medical freedom as well as religious freedom.". . . We need to speak up for the allocation of a fair share of the healthcare research dollar to investigate and test alternative therapies and educate our citizens accordingly.

Understanding the Reading: Annotating and Listing Information

If this reading were part of a class in health education, it would be a good idea to **annotate**, or mark, it so that information could be found more easily when studying for a test. Each reader develops his or her own system for annotating a text. It might include circling key words and underlining definitions or important phrases. Many students like to write a phrase or key word in the margin to show what the paragraph is about and what information can be found in it. Other students like to list information on index cards, which is also a good study technique.

---

[15] *sound* (adj) learned or known from study and experience
[16] *censure* (v) to disapprove of officially
[17] *revoke* (v) to take something back, such as a right or a favor; to cancel

[18] *conscientious* (adj) careful about doing things
[19] *despotic* (adj) harsh, tyrannical

A. *Skim the reading to find two systems of health care in our country. List the two systems here:*

1. _____

2. _____

B. *Find and list some specialties in alternative medicine:*

1. _____

2. _____

3. _____

4. _____

C. *Circle the degenerative diseases that are described in the article. List them here:*

1. _____

2. _____

3. _____

4. _____

D. *Underline the definition of the remedies used in homeopathy. What are the dilutions of natural substances that are generally used? Write them here:*

1. _____

2. _____

3. _____

E. *Cite two reasons why we should speak up for a fair share of health care money. Highlight them in the text.*

1. _____

2. _____

> Through the Nutritional Labeling and Education Act, the U.S. Food and Drug Administration (FDA) regulates the contents of foods, drugs, and some nutritional supplements and how they are advertised.

Using the Vocabulary: Prefixes and the Roots of Words

The meaning of a word can often be figured out by examining its roots and prefixes. The **root** is the part of a word on which other words are based, often derived from other languages (*bio* is a Latin root meaning "life"). A **prefix** is a letter or letters added to the beginning of a word that can change its meaning (*sure/unsure*).

The number of patient visits to practitioners of "alternative" medicine in the United States now outstrips consultations with traditional physicians.

Annals of Internal Medicine, 1997

Prefix/Root	Meaning	Examples
alter-	other	alternative
-arth-	joint	arthritis
-gastro-	stomach	gastrointestinal
intro-	inwardly, within	introduce
-neuro-	nerves	neurology
-pathy-	suffering, disease	pathological
-pharmaco-	drug	pharmaceutical
pre-	before	prescribe
pro-	forward	procedures

A. *Circle the correct phrase for each of the underlined vocabulary words.*

1. The doctor told her the <u>prognosis</u> for her disease was uncertain.

    a. treatment

    b. outcome

    c. cause

2. He had suffered from <u>neuralgia</u> when he was old.

    a. pain radiating from the heart

    b. pain radiating from the kidneys

    c. pain radiating from the nerves

3. The aspiring doctor decided to specialize in <u>gastroenterology</u>.

    a. the study of the structure and diseases of the digestive system

    b. a style of cooking

    c. a symptom of certain stomach ailments

4. Scientists at the Centers for Disease Control in Atlanta trace the <u>pathology</u> of contagious diseases.

    a. science of paths and roadways

    b. study of the origin, nature, and course of disease

    c. criteria for natural cures

5. She agreed to marry him after long <u>introspection</u>.

    a. easy maneuver

    b. wise manipulation

    c. careful thought

6. The <u>pharmacist</u> sold the medicine to the sick customer.

    a. a person who fills prescriptions

    b. a person who makes predictions

    c. a person who orders subscriptions

7. The patient's <u>preoperative</u> condition was stable, so the surgery

    a. went ahead as planned.

    b. was canceled.

8. Physical therapists often have to help tennis players who suffer from <u>arthropathy</u>.

    a. a disease of the nervous system

    b. a disease of the joints

    c. a disease of the heart

9. She changed her mind while driving, so she chose an <u>alternate</u> route to the hospital.

    a. obscure

    b. optimum

    c. different

B. *Now fill in the blanks with the appropriate words from the chart on page 90.*

More and more healthcare professionals are realizing the importance of (1)_____ medicine. This includes homeopathic remedies such as herbal medicine and natural (2)_____ such as acupuncture. In some cases it is preferred over conventional medicine, which typically requires drugs that are manufactured by (3)_____ companies. Conservative doctors continue to (4)_____ more traditional treatments for diseases such as cancer, (5)_____, and diabetes.

Reading Graphs

Data can be represented in graphs or in tables. In a **bar graph**, vertical or horizontal bars are used to visually display information. To understand a bar graph, it is important to read the title, the labels on the sides (or axes), and the key. Be sure to pay attention to the type of numerical information provided (i.e., number of thousands, percentages, total number). You may sometimes have to use a ruler to measure the bars.

California had 5,988 registered acupuncturists in 1996.

Forbes, "California Dreamin"

Study the bar graph with a partner and answer the questions.

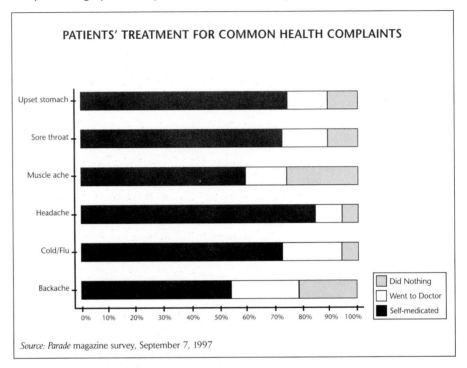

PATIENTS' TREATMENT FOR COMMON HEALTH COMPLAINTS

Source: Parade magazine survey, September 7, 1997

1. What are the three categories of patients that the graph describes?
2. For which ailment did the highest percentage of the patients self-medicate?
3. Approximately what percentage of people went to the doctor when suffering from a muscle ache?
4. Which complaint did most people ignore?
5. Did more people go to the doctor for sore throats or for upset stomachs?

Thinking Together

In a small group, make a list of three common ailments. Then analyze how you think they would be treated by conventional and alternative medicine.

Writing about It

*Write one to two paragraphs on one of the following topics. Try to use some of the vocabulary from this reading and from **Focusing In**.*

1. Do you think that alternative medicine will eventually become more accepted in the United States? Support your opinion with information from the article.
2. Compare and contrast alternative and conventional approaches to the healing of some common ailments using examples of treatments from "Alternative Medicine Is Natural and Gives Patients More Freedom."

Our growing softness, our increasing lack of physical fitness, is a menace to our society.

John F. Kennedy
(1917–1963), U.S. president

3. The author suggests writing a letter to Congress in support of freedom of medical choice. Write a letter using his suggestions.

Reacting to the Reading

Many insurance companies in the United States do not cover the cost of homeopathic treatments such as acupuncture or herbal medicines. Using some of the information in the article on alternative medicine, write a letter to a member of Congress expressing your belief that Americans deserve more "freedom of choice regarding healthcare providers."

Between 1990 and 1997, visits to alternative practitioners jumped by about 47 percent. The two most commonly used alternative therapies were relaxation techniques and herbal medicines.

Journal of the American Medical Association

- Each American president appoints a U.S. Surgeon General to oversee health issues. Started by Dr. C. Everett Koop (U.S. Surgeon General, 1981–1989), Shape Up America! is a high-profile national *initiative*[1] to promote healthy weight and increased physical activity in the United States.
- Read this series of articles by the Shape Up America! organization to find out why such a nationwide program is necessary. Do you think this problem exists in other countries as well?

Shape Up America!

SHAPE UP AMERICA! ORGANIZATION

Dr. C. Everett Koop Launches a New "Crusade" to *Combat Obesity* in America

1   Washington, D.C.; December 6, 1994—At a White House ceremony on the importance of physical activity and healthy weight hosted by First Lady Hillary Rodham Clinton, Dr. C. Everett Koop, the former U.S. Surgeon General, launched *Shape Up America!,* his new "great *crusade*[2]" to place healthy weight and physical activity high on the national *agenda*.[3]

2   The new report—Weighing In For America's Health: Elevating Healthy Weight and Physical Activity as a National Priority—declaring obesity as a public health crisis, will serve as the foundation for *Shape Up America!* The new report estimates that approximately 58 million American adults are

---

[1] *initiative* (n) first step
[2] *crusade* (n) organized effort to reach an ideal goal
[3] *agenda* (n) list of topics to talk about or do

obese or overweight. The obesity rates in the U.S. are already among the highest in the world and continue to rise among adults from 25 percent in 1980 to 34 percent today. Further, childhood obesity rates have increased substantially since 1980 with 21 percent of all 12 to 19 year olds—one in five teens—now significantly overweight. Compared to the population at large, minority populations are particularly at risk for being overweight or obese. And since being overweight is directly linked to a number of disabling and life threatening diseases—diabetes, hypertension, heart disease, and some forms of cancer—it is likely that the disease rates related to obesity will also rise.

3   "After smoking, which causes an estimated 500,000 deaths annually, obesity-related conditions are the second leading cause of death in the U.S., resulting in about 300,000 lives lost each year," Dr. Koop explained. Furthermore, obesity-related diseases cost the U.S. economy more than $100 billion annually. "Creating a public policy agenda that elevates healthy weight and physical activity as *priority*[4] concerns must occur as a first step in combating the obesity *epidemic*[5] in America. The changes *advocated*[6] through the *Shape Up America!* initiative will serve as a *catalyst*[7] for action that will make a difference in the lives of many Americans," concludes Dr. Koop.

> In 1998, 28.2 percent of American men and 23.1 percent of American women admitted smoking cigarettes every day.
>
> American Heart Association

So How Did We Get into Such Bad Shape?

4   Despite the fitness craze of the 80s, we're *plumping up*[8] for these simple reasons: We eat too much; we eat the wrong foods; we exercise too little; and our portions, both at home and when eating out, are too big. The fact is, our typical diet is a recipe for risk: high fat, high calories, and low fiber—all piled too high on the plate.

5   Life in the fast lane—past the fast-food window—has *detoured*[9] many of us off the road to good health. We drive everywhere. We rush all the time; we eat standing up—and then go on our hurried, unhealthy ways.

6   Besides this, we've become a push-button society—pressing, clicking, tapping away—erasing the need for any body movement. Everywhere you look buttons do it all: from the PC to the elevator, from the microwave to the *remote control*.[10] Think about it: modern technology has robbed us of what little effort we once exerted to crank up the car window. With each flick of a switch, our American lifestyle becomes more *sedentary*.[11]

---

[4] *priority* (n) of the most importance
[5] *epidemic* (n) disease that spreads quickly
[6] *advocate* (v) to propose or support an idea
[7] *catalyst* (n) person, idea, or chemical that causes important changes
[8] *plump up* (vp) to gain weight
[9] *detour* (v) to move away from the planned direction
[10] *remote control* (n) device used to change channels from a distance
[11] *sedentary* (adj) related to sitting; without physical activity

Outdated Beliefs Are Keeping Americans from Shaping Up

7   Washington, D.C.; June 1, 1995—Surrender your remote control, get on your feet, and think of small ways to get your body moving! This simple advice from Dr. C. Everett Koop, the former U.S. Surgeon General, is based on a new attitude that any bodily movement—such as walking or taking the stairs—counts in terms of achieving and maintaining a healthy weight.

8   But a new consumer poll commissioned by Dr. Koop's *Shape Up America!* campaign finds that the American public isn't getting the message. Rather, the survey reveals that many Americans

Snacking while watching TV contributes to America's childhood obesity rate.

are "couch potatoes" because of an outdated view about the *perceived*[12] time *commitment*[13] and intensity of exercise needed to achieve significant health benefits.

9   "Today, the biggest challenge isn't convincing Americans about the value of exercise; it's letting people know that physical activity is something everyone can do. We've got to get the message out loud and clear that moving more throughout the day is all that is required to start shaping up," said Dr. Koop.

10   Moderate levels of activity associated with a number of activities that may not raise a sweat, such as walking, dancing, vacuuming and gardening, all count towards the 30 minute minimum recommended daily activity. "Many people think they need to have sweat running down their brow and be out of breath in order to get health benefits. These individuals have turned physical activity into a grim experience rather than the pleasant part of everyday life that it should be," said James M. Rippe, M.D., Associate Professor of Medicine at Tufts University and a member of the *Shape Up America!* scientific advisory committee.

11   Adults are not the only ones who need to increase their physical activity levels. Childhood obesity rates are also on the rise. "There needs to be a renewed sense of *urgency*[14] on the part of parents about the importance of physical activity to their children's development and better health," Dr. Koop said.

12   "The goal is to end the confusion about physical activity by letting people know that to be less sedentary doesn't mean you have to exercise

---

[12] *perceived* (adj) understood
[13] *commitment* (n) promise
[14] *urgency* (n) strong need

Thirty-two percent of Americans reported they ate out frequently in 1997.

American Dietetic Association

strenuously.[15] It just means moving more. Based on what we know, everyone can find some time to include more activity in their day. The key is to think of small ways to get the body moving, which will add up to big *dividends*[16] in terms of better health," Dr. Koop concluded.

Understanding the Reading: Annotating and Listing Information

Review the tips on annotating and listing information on page 88. An important part of annotating also includes finding and marking the **main idea**, or central thought, of a text.

A. *The main idea of the two press releases in Shape Up America! are clearly stated. The main idea of the first is stated in the heading on page 93. The two sentences in paragraph nine on page 95 state the main idea of the second. Highlight or circle these.*

B. *Skim the reading for the rates of obesity in the United States. Circle the term "obesity rates." Then list the obesity rates in 1994 for:*

1. adults _____

2. children age 12 to 19 _____

C. *In the same paragraph, find the phrase "disabling and life-threatening diseases" and circle it. Then list four life-threatening diseases brought on by obesity.*

1. _____
2. _____
3. _____
4. _____

D. *Skim the reading for the paragraph on the costs in lives and medical care caused by obesity. Label the paragraph in the margin with the phrase "costs of obesity" and list the two major costs.*

1. _____
2. _____

E. *In the margin, mark paragraphs 4–6 with a phrase such as "causes for increase in obesity in America" or "reasons for plumping up." Then list three causes for the increase in obesity in America.*

1. _____

Only 39 percent of Americans surveyed in 1997 reported they were doing all they could to achieve a healthful diet, down from 44 percent in 1991.

American Dietetic Association

---

[15] *strenuously* (adv) with great effort
[16] *dividend* (n) benefit or advantage

2. _____

3. _____

F. *Skim the reading for the list of daily activities that count as exercise. Label the paragraph "daily exercise." Then list three everyday activities that count toward the recommended 30 minutes of exercise per day.*

1. _____

2. _____

3. _____

Using the Vocabulary: Classifying Words

A. *To **classify** is to organize into groups based on relationships. Classify the following words by labeling them **F** (physically fit) or **O** (out-of-shape).*

_____ 1. obesity   _____ 7. shape up

_____ 2. aerobics   _____ 8. plump up

_____ 3. sedentary   _____ 9. exercise

_____ 4. health   _____10. overweight

_____ 5. hypertension   _____11. physical activity

_____ 6. diet   _____12. disease

B. *Now complete this paragraph using words from Exercise A.*

According to many national studies, Americans are in poor physical condition. Some suffer from (1)_____, which is to say that they are very overweight. Even though the image is that many Americans are always on a (2)_____ and spend a lot of time in health clubs where they (3)_____ to keep their beautiful bodies, this is not true. This image comes from the stars of Hollywood. In fact, according to Dr. Koop, most Americans are (4)_____ and don't get enough exercise. As a result, their (5)_____ suffers.

Thinking Together

Dr. Koop has developed the "Physical Activity IQ" test on page 98. Take the test and then interview a partner to see what his or her "Physical Activity IQ" is. Compare your answers to the answers on page 276, and discuss the ones you missed. Which of you had the higher score? Take a class survey to see how much students know about physical fitness.

In 1998, the top killers of Americans were heart disease and cancer.

National Center for Health Statistics

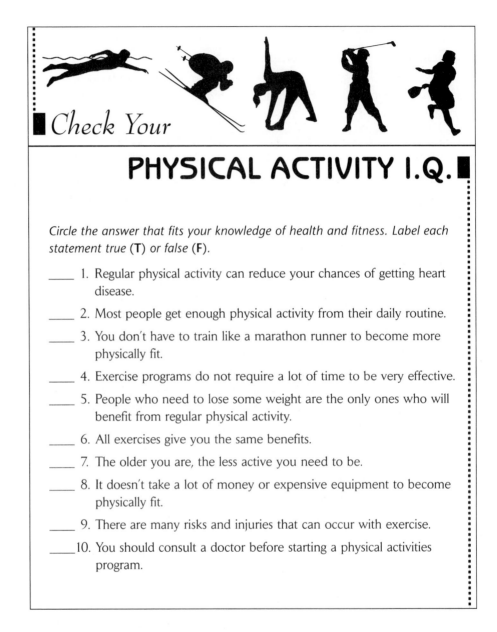

Check Your
PHYSICAL ACTIVITY I.Q.

Circle the answer that fits your knowledge of health and fitness. Label each statement true (T) or false (F).

_____ 1. Regular physical activity can reduce your chances of getting heart disease.

_____ 2. Most people get enough physical activity from their daily routine.

_____ 3. You don't have to train like a marathon runner to become more physically fit.

_____ 4. Exercise programs do not require a lot of time to be very effective.

_____ 5. People who need to lose some weight are the only ones who will benefit from regular physical activity.

_____ 6. All exercises give you the same benefits.

_____ 7. The older you are, the less active you need to be.

_____ 8. It doesn't take a lot of money or expensive equipment to become physically fit.

_____ 9. There are many risks and injuries that can occur with exercise.

_____10. You should consult a doctor before starting a physical activities program.

Writing about It

*Write one to two paragraphs on one of the following topics. Try to use some of the vocabulary from this reading and from **Focusing In**.*

1. Explain why obesity is a problem in America today.

2. Use some of the information in the article to assess whether you would be a good candidate for the *Shape Up America!* program.

3. Summarize some of the simple things people can do to stay in shape.

Reacting to the Reading

The article provides many reasons why Americans are not in shape. Why do you think Americans do not pay attention to the warnings from Dr. Koop?

Keeping Track of Your Reading Rate

- This is an article by Dennis Fiely which appeared in the *Columbus Dispatch*. It describes an interesting combination of fitness activities planned for an event organized by the actor Arnold Schwarzenegger.
- When your instructor gives you the signal to begin, read the article at a quick pace and mark down the time as soon as you are done. Then answer the questions without looking back at the reading.

tip When you read this passage, try to concentrate on important words such as nouns, verbs, numbers, and dates. This will help you skip over unimportant words and read more quickly.

As part of his three kung fu residencies at the Shaolin Temple in central China, Jeff Naayers of Reynoldsburg punched trees with his fists "until the bark came off," crawled shirtless on snowy mountain steps and had walnuts cracked on his head. Naayers, who earned the honorary title "sifu" for his accomplishments, will need to call on all of his training to win the $10,000 grand prize during the Martial Arts Festival at the 1997 Arnold Fitness Weekend, Feb. 28–March 2, in Veterans Memorial auditorium. Introduced to the body-building event in 1996, the martial arts rise in prominence this year with a junior-senior tournament, a national championship karate fight and a five-person demonstration team competition.

"This will be the biggest martial arts program ever held in Columbus," said Doug Grant, martial arts chairman for the '97 Arnold Fitness Weekend. . . .

The teams will display judo, jujitsu, tae kwon do, karate, kung fu, kick boxing and western boxing, which Grant, a retired Worthington police officer, described as "the oldest martial art." The variety is significant, Naayers said. "The martial arts historically have been separated," he said. "There has been so much ego involved and so much dissension that people are fed up with it. With all styles welcome, this is allowing us to bring them together again."

Actor Arnold Schwarzenegger enthusiastically embraces the martial arts component in the fitness weekend that bears his name. "Both of his daughters are taking karate lessons three times a week," Grant said. "He recognizes the fact that the martial arts instill discipline, self-confidence and respect for others."

. . . Naayers will take about 30 students from his studio to compete in the junior karate tournament, which will award trophies to all competitors. "We're most excited about bringing the kids and their families to this tournament," he said. "It will offer the children an opportunity to see their futures in martial arts." His demonstration team has entertained audiences at Epcot Center at Walt Disney World and Universal Studios Florida. Naayers also teaches a tai chi course at Ohio State University.

> Modern bodybuilding is ritual, religion, sport, art, and science, awash in chemistry and mathematics. Defying nature, it surpasses it.
>
> Camille Paglia (1947–),
> U.S. author

"My passion as an earthly being is to use the martial arts to promote good fellowship and health," he said. About 15 million Americans participate in martial arts training.

"It is taking the place of parenting in some cases," Naayers said. "Parents send their children to me for the discipline and moral values that the martial arts can give."

(400 words)   TIME _____

*Now mark these statements true (**T**) or false (**F**) without looking back at the reading.*

_____ 1. Jeff Naayers is a martial arts expert and teacher.

_____ 2. Naayers once studied martial arts in residence in Japan.

_____ 3. Arnold Schwarzenegger is a martial arts teacher.

_____ 4. The event planned in this article is called the Martial Arts Weekend.

_____ 5. Schwarzenegger's daughters are studying tae kwan do.

_____ 6. The people mentioned here study martial arts for health and discipline.

_____ 7. The Grand Prize for the martial arts competition is going to be more than $1,000.

_____ 8. Fewer than 1 million Americans study martial arts.

_____ 9. According to Grant, one of the oldest forms of martial arts is western boxing.

_____10. Naayers teaches martial arts to both adults and children.

Percent correct = _____   wpm = _____

MAKING C O N N E C T I O N S

Responding to the Readings

Prepare short oral or written responses based on your personal experience and your reactions to the readings. Try to incorporate the information and the vocabulary you have learned in this chapter.

1. Write a letter of advice to a friend who needs to "shape up."

2. Describe what you eat on a typical day.

3. Analyze some of the differences and similarities in the attitudes people have toward diet and fitness in your country and in the United States.

4. Write an activity you do on a regular basis that keeps you in shape physically.

5. Stress causes many health-related problems in the United States. How do you relieve stress in your life?

6. Describe some of the differences and similarities between the way common illnesses are treated in your country and in the United States. Which is most common in your country, alternative or conventional medicine?

7. Discuss your reaction to one of the quotes or facts in the margins of the chapter that you find most interesting or surprising.

Editing Your Work

A student wrote this paragraph without editing carefully for **parallelism**. *When writing a series of verbs, adjectives, adverbs, or nouns in one sentence, all of these words must be in parallel, or the same, form. For example: The woman is* kind, intelligent, *and* rich. *Edit this student paragraph by finding the five errors in parallelism and correcting them.*

Self-improvement can be accomplished through physically, mental and educational activities. According to the reading topic, Americans who never exercised in the past are now on the streets jogging, swimming, dance and practicing martial arts to improve their physical fitness and reducing their stress. Others improve themselves by meditating quietly in their homes or return to school to qualify for better jobs. In a nation where the rhythms of life are at a fast pace, people are seeking ways to find peaceful, traquility, and most of all, a sense of accomplishment in their lives.

Writing an Essay

Choose one of the following topics and write an essay. As a prewriting activity, read over your shortwrites and notes for inspiration. Remember to review the brainstorming techniques on pages 262–263. In your essay, use the readings, factoids, quotes, class discussions, and personal experience to support your ideas. Try to use the vocabulary you have learned in this chapter. If you choose to write a research paper, make certain to cite your sources clearly.

1. Compare and contrast the state of health and fitness in your country with that of the United States, based on your experience and what you have learned from the readings in this chapter. Analyze the leading health problems and diseases. Talk about exercise, eating habits and diet, and weight. Use facts and figures when possible, but avoid making overgeneralizations.

In 1998, the life expectancy for a baby born in 1996 was 76.1 years.

Department of Health and Human Services

> There is a strong relationship between socio-economic status and health in the United States for every race and ethnic group studied.
>
> Donna Shalala, U.S. secretary of Health and Human Services

2. Write an essay that pokes fun at your country's approach to health, diet, and fitness in the style of Horace Miner. Use some of Miner's techniques to disguise your facts and make your essay more interesting. Look over **Understanding the Reading** on pages 81–82 to see how Miner manipulated words and expressions.

3. Compare and contrast conventional/traditional medicine and alternative medicine. What types of diseases are most commonly treated with drugs? When do people tend to try alternative methods? Discuss the increasing popularity of alternative medicine as presented in the reading on pages 86–88. Which of these two treatments is most popular in your country?

4. Write a "shape-up" program for your country. In your proposal discuss the problems and the solutions. Use the article from *Shape Up America!* as a model to help you develop the ideas in your essay.

5. Describe your own physical condition and what you do to keep fit. Discuss the kinds of food you eat, the sports you play, the types of exercise you do, and the ways you relieve stress. If you have ever been in a different physical condition, discuss what you did to change it. What could you do to improve your physical condition now?

6. Write a research paper on a specific area of health that interests you (obesity, cancer, diabetes, vitamin deficiency, stress, etc.). Go to the library to get information on your topic. Make sure to cover all aspects of this health issue including causes, symptoms, treatments, and cures. Try to find some statistics to support your findings. If you or someone you know has personal knowledge in this health area, make sure to describe it.

Finding More Information

Magazines and Journals

Journal of the American Medical Association
Living Healthy
Natural Health
Prevention
Psychology Today
Running

Books

Grisham, John, *The Rain Maker*
Levinson, David, *Health and Illness: A Cross-Cultural Encyclopedia*
Nath, Shambhu, *Stress Management through Yoga and Meditation*
Terrence, Felix M., *Physical Fitness as a Way of Life*
Weil, Andrew, *Health and Healing*

The World Wide Web

ahf.org—American Health Foundation
shapeup.org—Shape Up America! organization
www.healthfinder.com—Healthfinder Healthy People 2010
www.hhs.gov—U.S. Department of Health and Human Services
www.phys.com—PHYS. in Fitness and in Health

Movies and Videos

And the Band Played On
Awakenings
Lorenzo's Oil
The Other Side of the Mountain
Outbreak
Patch Adams

> The true aim of medicine is not to make men virtuous; it is to safeguard and rescue them from the consequences of their vices.
>
> H. L. Mencken
> (1880–1956),
> U.S. journalist

Keeping the Beat

Music gives us insight into the culture and history of a country because it encompasses many different types of songs that help explain people's hopes, frustrations, and experiences. The love of folk music goes back to colonial times when Americans celebrated their freedom in song. It is a reflection of the democratic principle "by and for the people." Its lyrics tell the story of the American people and where they came from, what they did, and how they struggled. Folk music's form evolved from European music. Country and western music descends directly from folk songs. Jazz, an authentically American genre, includes blues, ragtime, swing, and Dixieland, as well as more contemporary progressive forms. Blues had its roots in slavery—from the rhythms of Africa, the spirituals of gospel music, and the laments of harsh life in the fields. Rock music is a blend of jazz, blues, country and western, and gospel music.

> Nothing separates the generations more than music. By the time a child is eight or nine, he has developed a passion for his own music that is even stronger than his passions for procrastination and weird clothes.
>
> Bill Cosby (1937–), U.S. comedian and actor

In this chapter, Mercedes Hardey's article, "Folk Music in America," traces the evolution of this genre and its influence on contemporary singers. The influence of both folk music and blues on the atmosphere of two cities can be seen in the article by Dan McGraw, "True Blues and Country." Music has always been the focus of American television shows, such as the variety shows of Ed Sullivan in the 1950s and 1960s and later shows such *as American Bandstand* and *Soul Train*. Today, however, there are television stations dedicated entirely to music and dance, including The Nashville Network (TNN), Music Television (MTV), and Black Entertainment Television (BET). Alan Bunce describes the most successful of these in his article "MTV—Tomorrow the World?" The last reading, about the ballet dancer and arts educator Jacques d'Amboise, shows how music and dance can touch people by bringing out their creative talents.

Is music really a universal language? Discuss this question in small groups. Then talk about the picture on page 104 and answer the question: *What kind of music are these people listening to?*

Can You Hear the Beat?

Work with a partner to answer these questions on American music and dance.

1. What do the initials MTV stand for?
2. What music idol lived in Graceland?
3. Can you name two or three famous American folksingers?
4. What music genre is authentically American?
5. What are some of the awards given to American musicians?
6. What is the French word that English uses for a classical dance style?
7. What happened in the town of Woodstock in 1969?
8. What is the term used for music that is unique to a country's heritage?
9. What instruments are many children taught to play in elementary schools?
10. What is America's national anthem?

Test Your Word Power

Take this vocabulary quiz. Then compare your answers with a partner.

_____ 1. jazz (n)

_____ 2. blues (n)

_____ 3. ballet (n)

_____ 4. video (n)

_____ 5. rap (n)

_____ 6. entertainment (n)

_____ 7. network (n)

_____ 8. audience (n)

_____ 9. beat (n)

_____ 10. the media (n pl.)

a. system of communication lines or stations

b. people who gather to listen to or watch an event

c. television or videotape pictures

d. slow jazz music form about sad feelings

e. combination of newspaper, magazine, television, and radio

f. dance telling a story with movements, not words; usually done on the toes

g. American popular music ranging from slow blues to fast Dixieland

h. amusement

i. street music form in which words are said, not sung, to a strong beat

j. tempo, rhythm

> It is only in his music, which Americans are able to admire because a protective sentimentality limits their understanding of it, that the Negro in America has been able to tell his story.
>
> James Baldwin
> (1924–1987), U.S. author

- In this article, folksinger Mercedes Hardey traces the historical and cultural development of American folk music. Reminding us that "each song is like a thread of fabric woven into American history," she points out how the people who settled this country influenced this unique music.

- What types of folk music do you have in your homeland? What groups had the greatest influence on this music? Are any of the influences similar to the ones Hardey presents?

Folk Music in America

MERCEDES HARDEY

1   Our folk songs are one of our most precious national resources. When one looks at the resource bank of American folk music, each song is like a thread of fabric woven into American history. In its short lifespan, our nation has produced folk songs that reflect its struggles, *aspirations,*[1] major events, and changing moods, morals, and manners. More than any other nation, America has had the fertile soil from which "music by and for the people" could grow. This new land, full of natural resources and untainted by centuries of political *toil*[2] and oppression, lay ready for the people of the world with the necessary courage and *initiative*[3] to carve a new beginning out of it for themselves.

2   In addition to its material wealth, America also offered the possibility of freedom of expression and the pursuit of happiness. Within that framework, people not only had a natural arena for singing, but more important, they could sing as much as they wanted, and in an *unrestrained*[4] manner. Because of these things, American folk music is plentiful, diverse, and unique. There are songs of pioneers, cowboys, gold miners, slaves, and a host of songs contributed by our transplanted European nationals. Therefore, the rich variety of all these contributing factors make the study of American folk music a fascinating subject!

3   American folk music was strongly influenced by the music of the Anglo-Saxons [early English ancestors] and by the contributions of the European nationals who emigrated to our shores during the nineteenth century. Each group of settlers to America tenaciously held on to their way of life and to the culture into which they were born. Survival was the foremost concern in the early years, so settlers surrounded themselves with familiar things from home, such as food, music, and religious customs. They

---

[1] *aspiration* (n) strong desire; great ambition
[2] *toil* (n) struggle; hard work
[3] *initiative* (n) first step, usually showing strength
[4] *unrestrained* (adj) moving freely

performed the songs of their native lands as often as they could, singing them as they worked, played, and prayed. As their physical survival became easier, they preserved the best rituals and recipes from their homeland and gradually blended them with traditions from their new environment. When people took their favorite songs from their country of origin and adapted them to fit their life in this new land of *peril,*[5] promise, and progress, the resulting music became American "by adoption."

4   With this in mind, it shouldn't be surprising to learn that our favorite American standards like "Yankee Doodle" and "On Top of Old Smoky" are really American by adoption and adaptation. This blending and shaping, where the most pleasing songs are made the property of the adopting group, is what we folklorists and historians call the "folk process."

5   Folk songs tell us about human experiences and for this reason we have many kinds. There are work songs, love songs, cradle songs, drinking songs, war songs, play songs, and protest songs, just to name a few. In most cases the creator of the song was forgotten, but the song was remembered by someone and passed on. Sometimes there were additions to the lyrics or modifications to the music. These changes could be small: a single word or a few notes of the melody. Or they could be big: new verses if there was some gossip worth repeating or even a completely new melody if the song was transported to a new region. As a result, what has come down to us are songs that have evolved over generations as hundreds of different people have had a turn at singing them. And even today, though both traditional and modern music is written out and delivered via concerts, TV, and recordings, there still remain songs passed down from singer to singer as in the past.

6   Prior to the Revolutionary War, the major musical influence in the colonies had been from the Pilgrims, a group of Anglo-Saxon immigrants who had separated from the Church of England so that they could worship in their own way. They brought along their collection of music called psalms, sung out of a special hymnbook called a Psalter. They were a deeply religious, hard-working and pious people. They believed that singing was a way of worshipping their God, so they sang at every opportunity. However, they also believed that musical instruments detracted from true worship, so when they sang they did so without accompaniment of any kind.

7   The early colonists were also intrigued by Native American music, but soon came to the conclusion that it sounded very different, and there-

> **Folk songs:**
> - represent the musical expressions of ordinary people;
> - are usually the product of an unknown person or group;
> - have lyrics that reflect common speech patterns of a region;
> - were first presented with voice rather than written down;
> - have uncomplicated and unorchestrated music and lyrics; and
> - can be performed without musical accompaniment (or if accompanied, using only acoustic instruments).

> The lyrics to "The Battle Hymn of the Republic" were written by a woman, Julia Ward Howe.

---

[5] **peril** (n) danger; a possibility of serious harm or death

Author Mercedes Hardey performs folk music for Cultural Horizons, a nonprofit organization that provides multicultural music education to schools and to the community at large.

fore it must be inferior. We now know that its different sound was not because it was inferior, but because Native American music was generally based on the pentatonic or five-toned scale, most commonly associated with Oriental music, whereas the Pilgrims' music was based on the eight-toned scale of European origin. Another difference between Anglo-Saxon and Native American music was that Native American songs and their various parts were rehearsed *meticulously*[6] and performed without mistakes of any kind. On the other hand, the songs sung by the Pilgrims were spontaneously performed, often with many mistakes, and were constantly changing in lyrics and melody.

8   During the Colonial Rebellion, Americans began to create original songs based on the events happening around them. This music was based on an emerging sense of being a new, free breed of people, apart from their British rulers.

9   Although America finally defeated the British and won its independence, our most common musical influences remain British. Most American folk songs are in the form of what is known as "broadside ballads," a combination of two distinct, British-based song styles, each with a long and distinguished history in its European homeland. The ballad was a type of solo song where the singer recounted events connected with a multitude of situations ranging from romance to heroism in battle. The lyrics were usually taken from literature and helped provide the listener with a realistic frame of reference for the event taking place. Broadsides were the opposite. They were shorter, local stories, often sensational gossip such as our "tabloids," and written on one side of the paper so as to be easily read. They were often called "singing newspapers." In addition, the dances of our British ancestors manifested themselves in American music. The jigs and reels of the Irish and Scottish people, who settled primarily in the Appalachian and Blue Ridge mountain areas of the United States, became square dances, and dance tunes like "Lord McPherson's Reel" became the uniquely American dance tune "Turkey in the Straw."

10   American folk music also had regional flexibility and adaptability. A song could start out one way in one region, and by the time it would end up in another part of the country, there would be changes in lyrics or

The Julliard School, in New York City, is the most famous college for the study of music in the United States.

---

6 *meticulously* (adv) carefully and thoroughly

melody more particular to that area. An example of this is one of the most popular American railroading songs in existence, called "John Henry." This song was originally from West Virginia, based on a true story there. As the song migrated west, however, the characters in it often changed names as well as roles to fit more local scenarios and stories.

11 As America moved into the first half of the twentieth century, the slower pace of a predominantly agricultural society was replaced by the more frenetic pace of a people in the grip of industrialization. With the advent of more sophisticated and efficient technology to perform jobs which were once done manually, the whole routine of daily life speeded up to become more productive and time-efficient. Even the music of the times, jazz, reflected the fast and furious pace of the years immediately following the Industrial Revolution. The slow, relaxed pace of the folk music sing-a-long was forgotten, at least temporarily.

12 But by the middle of the twentieth century, amidst all the *rampant*,[7] self-seeking materialism embraced by much of the American public, there appeared a small group of individuals dedicated to the preservation of the folk music tradition which had sustained this country for over 150 years. The prominent poet Carl Sandburg used his status as a Lincoln scholar to popularize American folk music once again, as well as British historian Cecil Sharp, who although being English, recognized the tremendous musical wealth of his adopted homeland. John and Alan Lomax were also folklorists and music historians who traveled throughout the United States, collecting folk songs from everywhere and from anybody who'd sing them into their little tape recorder. Their recordings *Roots of the Blues*, *Negro Spirituals*, and *The Blues Roll On* allow audiences to share this music of the black South. They put all their recordings onto albums through the United States Library of Congress, thereby preserving them for *posterity*.[8] In their travels they discovered Woody Guthrie, America's most famous folksinger. Guthrie traversed the plains and mountains of our nation, writing songs about the common working men and women of our land, who because of the recent Depression and resulting hard times, had not been able to work and provide for themselves and their families. Woody Guthrie also sang about the relentless grabbing of material wealth by the privileged. He sang about immigrant groups and their troubles, and he sang about his land's natural beauty as well as its treacherous dust storms and tornadoes.

13 Many followed in Woody Guthrie's footsteps as this folk music revival continued in the fifties and sixties. Young people fervently began to question the consuming desire of their parents' generation to acquire material wealth and comforts. With this questioning came many singers and songwriters who desired to make "music with a message," and who, like Woody

A record "goes platinum" when it sells over a million copies.

---

[7] *rampant* (adj) uncontrollable and widespread
[8] *posterity* (n) future generations of people alive after one's death

Guthrie, saw America's beauty not in her material wealth, but in the work-weary and worn hands of the diverse people who called her "home."

14   Pete Seeger, Joan Baez, Theodore Bikel, Phil Ochs, The Kingston Trio, The Weavers, Malvina Reynolds, Buffy St. Marie, and Bob Dylan (often considered Woody Guthrie's modern-day successor in terms of style and content) are only some of the great folksingers to come out of the folk music revival that started in the forties and continues to this day with artists whose songs cross over a variety of traditional and nontraditional styles and whose subject matter *encompasses*[9] all cultures and their music: Dar Williams, Ani DiFranco, Moe Tucker, Eric Clapton, Steve Earle, Willie Nelson, Iris DeMent, Mary Chapin Carpenter, David Byrne, Peter Gabriel, and Nils Lofgren, to name just a few.

15   Folk music in America will continue to evolve and develop its own unique personality. Our past history proves that no matter how advanced technologically, materially or educationally America becomes, there will always be those who will sing, in their own unique way, about the struggles of the common citizen, regardless of gender or race, and who will use the vehicle of folk music to create songs that we'll be singing along with well into the twenty-first century!

> Many large U.S. cities have special high schools for the performing arts. Students must audition to get in.

Understanding the Reading: Listing and Mapping

Using lists to develop a visual diagram or map can help you organize and remember important facts and details. Skim the reading and fill in the blanks with the missing details under each topic.

Three themes/reasons for folk songs
_____
_____
_____

Five modern-day folk singers
_____
_____
_____
_____
_____

Five kinds of folk songs
_____
_____
_____
_____
_____

American Folk Music

Three characteristics of folk songs
_____
_____
_____

Three titles of early American folk songs
_____
_____
_____

---

[9] *encompass* (v) to include

Using the Vocabulary: Vocabulary in Context

Besides using the dictionary, one of the ways to find out the meaning of a word or words is by looking for clues to its **context**, the words and phrases around it. Here are three ways to derive meaning from the context of a passage:

1. The definitions or descriptions are set off by commas, dashes, or parentheses.

2. There is a specific comparison/contrast used so that the writer is explaining what something is or what something is not. Comparison/contrast clues often use words such as: *similar to/rather than, and/but, in the same way/instead of,* and *like/unlike.*

3. The meaning is understood from general knowledge or experience.

A. *Study the sentences. Then write the type of clue* (definition, comparison, contrast, or experience) *that helps you understand the meaning of the underlined words in the blanks. Discuss your answers with your teacher and class.*

1. Folk music—music that was handed down by oral tradition—is sung in many countries.

   _____

2. Unlike classical music, folk music has its roots in rural communities.

   _____

3. As a result, what has come down to us are songs that have evolved over generations as hundreds of different people have had a turn at singing them.

   _____

4. Similar to ragtime music, Dixieland is a form of jazz.

   _____

B. *Choose the word or phrase closest in meaning to the underlined word(s) in these sentences from the reading "Folk Music in America."*

1. More than any other nation, America has had the fertile soil from which "music by and for the people" could grow.

   a. rich

   b. dry

   c. sneaky

2. Each group of settlers to America tenaciously held on to their way of life and to the culture into which they were born.

   a. silently

   b. strongly

   c. hungrily

> The Americans . . . are almost ignorant of the art of music, one of the most elevating, innocent and refining of human tastes, whose influence on the habits and morals of a people is of the most beneficial tendency.
>
> James Fenimore Cooper (1789–1851), U.S. novelist

3. Most American folk songs are in the form of what is known as "broadside ballads," a combination of two distinct, British-based song styles, each with a long and distinguished history in its European homeland.

   a. songs from a broad group of styles

   b. songs from special homelands

   c. special songs from England

4. Sometimes there were additions to the lyrics or modifications to the music. These changes could be small: a single word or a few notes of the melody.

   a. variations

   b. notes

   c. harmonies

5. The jigs and reels of the Irish and Scottish people, who settled primarily in the Appalachian and Blue Ridge mountain areas of the United States, became square dances.

   a. types of dances

   b. hilly regions

   c. film clips

6. As America moved into the first half of the twentieth century, the slower pace of a predominantly agricultural society was replaced by the more frenetic pace of a people in the grip of industrialization.

   a. relaxed

   b. fast-paced

   c. restricted

7. The ballad was a type of solo song where the singer recounted events connected with a multitude of situations ranging from romance to heroism in battle.

   a. song that tells a story and is sung by one person

   b. musical event

   c. tale that is put to music and sung in groups

8. Prior to the Revolutionary War, the major musical influence in the colonies had been from the Pilgrims, a group of Anglo-Saxon immigrants who had separated from the Church of England so that they could worship in their own way.

   a. a group who came seeking freedom of religion

   b. a group who traveled from church to church

   c. a group who became separated from the colonies

9. They brought along their collection of music called psalms, sung out of a special hymnbook called a Psalter.

a. religious song

b. gift for the poor

c. hymnal

10. However, they also believed that musical instruments <u>detracted from</u> true worship, so when they sang they did so without accompaniment of any kind.

a. added to

b. weakened

c. improved upon

C. *Now complete this paragraph with words from this list.*

ballads	frenetic	modifications
fertile	jigs and reels	tenaciously

Folk music in America grew out of the (1)_____ soil of freedom, courage, and initiative. The early settlers were influenced by their Anglo-Saxon and European ancestors, and they clung (2)_____ to their own cultures and traditions. As they worked, played, and prayed, they sang songs that expressed their emotions and experiences. Some of these songs were (3)_____ of ones they had brought from their homelands. As a result, American folk music reflects great diversity: from religious songs to broadside (4)_____ and dance tunes for (5)_____.

Thinking Together

Read the lyrics to these songs. Then write the type of song (blues, love, traveling, or protest) next to the musical note beside each set of lyrics. Then, in small groups, discuss a folk song from your native country. What type of song is it and why?

We Shall Overcome

We shall overcome,

We shall overcome some day.

Oh, deep in my heart,

I do believe,

We shall overcome some day.

_____

My Bonnie Lies over the Ocean

My Bonnie lies over the ocean,

My Bonnie lies over the sea,

My Bonnie lies over the ocean,

Oh, bring back my Bonnie to me.

_____

> Music is the world's universal form of communication. It touches every person of every culture on the globe to the tune of $38.1 billion annually, and the U.S. recording industry accounts for fully one-third of that world market.
>
> Recording Industry
> Association of America

Santy Anno

We're sailing down the river from Liverpool,

Heave away, Santy Anno,

Around Cape Horn to Frisco Bay,

All on the plains of Mexico.

Things about Comin' My Way

Ain't got no money

Can't buy no grub,

Back-bone and navel

Doing the belly rub.

This Train

This train is bound for glory, this train,

This train is bound for glory, this train,

This train is bound for glory,

Don't ride nothin' but the righteous and the holy,

This train is bound for glory, this train.

Writing about It

*Write one to two paragraphs on one of the following topics. Try to use some of the vocabulary from this reading and from **Focusing In**.*

1. Choose a song you know and judge it by the list of Hardey's criteria from the shaded box on page 107. Then write a paragraph explaining why it is or is not folk music.

2. Compare and contrast the influences on American folk music pointed out by Hardey with the influences on the folk music of your homeland.

3. Summarize some of the reasons why folk music will continue to remain popular in the United States.

Reacting to the Reading

Do you think schools should teach children the folk music of their countries in order to preserve it? Why or why not?

- To truly understand Americans and their music, one should be familiar with two types of popular music whose roots are in the South. In this article, Dan McGraw travels to Tennessee, the heartland of "real American music." He explores the roots of a music style made popular by legendary blues musician B. B. King and visits Graceland, home of "rock 'n roll" idol Elvis Presley.
- As you read, think about different types of music you have in your country. Are any cities or areas famous for the "real music" of your homeland? Read this article to find out what the musical term "true blues and country" refers to and where this type of music can be heard.

True Blues and Country

Dan McGraw

from *U.S. News and World Report*

1   Just about every city in America boasts a blues club or two, where horn sections sway and lead guitarists *contort*[1] their faces with every note they bend. But nowhere else will you find the wild abandon and emotional *exuberance*[2] of a 3 A.M. jam at Blues City Cafe in Memphis. Musicians who played with B. B. King and Elvis Presley take turns hopping on stage, while the dance floor is packed with European tourists fresh from a Graceland tour, old guys in porkpie hats, and office workers who swore they were just meeting a few friends for happy hour.

2   I had come to Tennessee to look for real American music, from Memphis blues to Nashville country, and all the rock-and-roll and gospel and rhythm and blues in between. The music of Memphis and Nashville is honored in museums and tourist attractions throughout the state. But the real history is ongoing, played by struggling musicians, not so much for a record deal and cash in the tip jar but

because no one wants the night to end.

3   Heading over the bridge into Memphis from the Arkansas side of the Mississippi, where the bottom lands are still planted in cotton, I could imagine when this place was the magnet for the best musicians in the Delta, who left their sharecropping days for the bright lights of the big city.

4   Over the years, Memphis has *billed*[3] itself as the cradle of American music, where soul and gospel and rock-and-roll all merged. Two of the city's musical institutions pay tribute to that remarkable fusion: Graceland and Beale Street.

5   As *tacky*[4] as Elvis Presley's Graceland museum can be, it is a must for fans as well as those curious to see what happens when people get what they wish for. More than a tribute to one man, Graceland pays homage to an era of excess, a slice of Americana framed in shag carpeting. . . . Sadly, Graceland is short on the significance of Presley's music—his *synthesis*[5] of gospel,

---

[1] *contort* (v) to twist the body in an unnatural manner
[2] *exuberance* (n) high spirits, enthusiasm
[3] *bill* (v) to label
[4] *tacky* (adj) cheap, not well made; lacking good taste
[5] *synthesis* (n) blend of various elements into a whole

Butch Mudbone, a Seneca Indian, sings the blues in Memphis.

country, and blues into a singular new art form. Though some would argue that he stole black music and sold it to a white audience, what Elvis did was daring and dangerous, and American music has never been quite the same. A better bet for the significance of Presley is to tour Sun Studio on Union Avenue, where recording engineer Sam Phillips took a shy kid in the early 1950s and molded him into a legend. The guided tour is informational and fun, and you can see the microphone Elvis sang into when he was transformed from Memphis truck driver to American icon.

No cotton

6   When night falls in Memphis, the *neon*[6] of Beale Street *beckons*,[7] where the music from about a dozen clubs and as many street musicians blends into a glorious din of electric guitars and screaming horns, and the musicians are as accessible as their

music. That's the beauty of Beale Street, the way local blues artists and tourists *mingle*.[8] Some long for the old days, when Beale Street featured solitary bluesmen playing three-chord songs about wayward women and picking cotton. The music now is big and brassy, geared more for tourists than for purists. The musicians of Beale Street constantly argue about the authenticity of their music. "I didn't grow up picking cotton and I don't sing about it," says blueswoman Verlinda Kertria Zeno, the Louisiana Mojo Queen. "Blues is about romance and heartache, good times and bad, about sex and love and hate. It's about real people, not race."

7   After two nights of sucking down *long-necks*[9] and dancing more than I have since college, I bolted out of Memphis and made my way to Nashville, Music City U.S.A. Rather than take the 3-hour drive up Interstate 40, I set out on U.S. 64 east and made a day of the trip. . . .

8   Heading into Nashville at nightfall, I was struck by the glittering skyline of one of the South's new power cities. But Nashville is a trap of sorts. Dreams of country-music stardom draw a swarm of aspiring musicians. Only a few will make it; the rest will hustle from one bar to the next, playing for tips and hoping a record producer will pluck them from the pack.

9   Nashville has three main areas for music: the Opryland complex, which houses the Grand Ole Opry; Music Row, the center of the country recording industry; and the downtown clubs on Second Avenue and Lower Broadway. The Grand Ole Opry is a must, if for no other reason than to say you were there. The longest continuously run-

---

6 *neon* (n) gas used to light up tubes in electric signs
7 *beckon* (v) to motion or call someone to come to you
8 *mingle* (v) to move around in a group of people
9 *longneck* (n) glass bottle of beer

ning radio show in the country, with performances on weekend nights and matinees Tuesday through Thursday, it is country's version of vaudeville, with a mix of comedy and music stars, though the fare is pretty standard.

10   After the Opry, I made my way downtown to the Wildhorse Saloon on Second Avenue—one of Nashville's hot clubs, with a dance floor about as big as a football field and mirrored balls spinning spots of light on *boot-scooters*[10] two-stepping and line dancing. The Wildhorse is where the Nashville Network tapes its country dance show (sort of like American Bandstand, but with middle-aged line dancers instead of teenagers), and the club offers free dance lessons every afternoon. But the place itself is somewhat cold, reflecting the current stale state of country music.

11   Country boomed in the '80s, and the music industry in Nashville began *churning out*[11] safe acts to keep the records selling. As a result, country music has moved toward indistinguishable ballads and novelty songs, promoted by videos of handsome guys in cowboy hats and women swirling in long dresses. Most acts copy the formula, hoping to be the next in line.

12   I thought about this current state of country music as I walked down Broadway to the *seedy*[12] clubs near the new Nashville Arena. The crowd was noticeably different from the Wildhorse's. Guys were wearing peg pants, their hair in *pompadours*.[13] Women in leather miniskirts were smoking cigars. From these bars came the sounds of bands playing tunes by Hank Williams, Johnny Cash, and Merle Haggard, along with fast-paced rockabilly.

Retro[14] bands

13   Just as punk rock revitalized rock-and-roll in the late '70s, this "retro country" music on Lower Broadway is trying to inject new life into country. The movement began a few years ago when a band called BR-549 began playing at Robert's Western World, a combination Western clothing store and nightclub. Lines would form whenever BR-549 played its rockabilly originals and covers, and it was soon signed to a record deal. . . .

14   The energy on Lower Broadway is a lot like Beale Street's, with a combination of international tourists and Nashville music hipsters mixing to form a cross-cultural scene that is breathing new life into country music. For the most part, the bands play for tips, making it tough moneywise but ensuring that the music acts and crowds get to know one another.

Big bow

15   I talked about the retro Nashville scene with singer-guitarist Autumn Haley over a few beers at Robert's. Haley favors big bows in her hair and checked gingham blouses; musically she plays a speedy guitar while covering Wanda Jackson and Janice Martin songs from the 1950s. Her cover of Jackson's "Big Iron *Skillet*[15]" ("I'm going to teach you wrong from right with my big iron skillet in my hand/I'm going to show how a little woman can whip a great big man") is fast-paced and funny, the opposite of the current country ballads.

16   "When I look at country music these days, everything runs together," she says. She and her band, the Rockin' Comets, play three nights a week at Wolfy's. "Hopefully, what's

---

[10] *boot-scooter* (n) country-western line dancer
[11] *churn out* (vp) to produce in large amounts
[12] *seedy* (adj) bad or dirty, squalid, shabby
[13] *pompadour* (n) hairdo combed high above the forehead

[14] *retro* (adj) backward, behind; here, referring to a time in the past
[15] *skillet* (n) pan used for cooking

happening down here on Broadway will get the notice of the record companies," she adds. "They need some new blood, and maybe we can give it to them by playing this older music." More than anything else, that is what this American music played in Tennessee is all about: reinventing styles based on those that have gone before.

17   On my way out of Nashville, I cruised Music Row, scouting for anyone famous coming out of the record companies' office buildings. The only stars were the *replicas*[16] in the Country Music Wax Museum (which is down the street from the Barbara Mandrell Gift Shop and Museum, the Hank Williams Jr. Museum, and the George Jones Gift Shop). I stopped for a Foot Long Houndog across from the Country Music Hall of Fame and thought of Elvis before he made bad movies and ended up playing in Las Vegas. He was the real thing before he became an imitator. In Tennessee, the real thing is still there. You just have to look for it.

Understanding the Reading: Main Ideas

Being able to find the main idea in a paragraph helps readers to understand its gist or general message. A **main idea** explains who or what the passage is about and what the writer is saying about it. It must be stated in a complete sentence. A main idea is too broad if it is vague or goes beyond what the writer is trying to say. It is too narrow if it only gives one detail that doesn't fully cover what the author says about the topic.

A. *Read this paragraph and circle the letter that best identifies the main idea. Discuss with a partner why each of the other choices is either too broad or too narrow.*

> **Famed blues guitarist B. B. King averages 250 concerts per year and says, "Now it's the highlight of my career every year when I go back to Indianola and play a free concert in the park for the kids."**

Just about every city in America boasts a blues club or two, where horn sections sway and lead guitarists contort their faces with every note they bend. But nowhere else will you find the wild abandon and emotional exuberance of a 3 a.m. jam at Blues City Cafe in Memphis. Musicians who played with B. B. King and Elvis Presley take turns hopping on stage, while the dance floor is packed with European tourists fresh from a Graceland tour, old guys in porkpie hats, and office workers who swore they were just meeting a few friends for happy hour.

a. Blues City Cafe in Memphis is one of the best blues clubs in America because of its 3 A.M. jam.

b. Horns sway and leading guitarists contort their faces.

c. Tourists and musicians have fun in Memphis because they can dance and play music together even at 3 A.M.

---

[16] *replica* (n) copy of something, often made smaller than the original

B. *Read the sentences. Circle the sentence that best expresses the main idea of the paragraph indicated from "True Blues and Country." Be ready to discuss why the other sentence is either too broad or too narrow.*

1. Paragraph 2

   a. The writer came to Tennessee to search for the heart and inspiration of American music.

   b. The writer found lots of different kinds of music in Tennessee.

2. Paragraph 5

   a. Although Graceland museum is named in honor of Elvis Presley, one must also tour Sun Studio to understand Elvis and his music.

   b. Graceland is a must.

3. Paragraph 6

   a. Beale Street offers tourists a lot to see and do.

   b. Beale Street is where blues artists and tourists mingle and play and constantly argue about the authenticity of their music.

4. Paragraph 8

   a. Nashville is one of the South's new power cities.

   b. Aspiring musicians who come to Nashville struggle to become famous.

5. Paragraph 16

   a. American country music reinvents styles that have gone on before.

   b. The Rockin' Comets play three nights a week at Wolfy's.

> Commercial to the core, Elvis was the kind of singer dear to the heart of the music business. For him to sing a song was to sell a song. His G clef was a dollar sign.
>
> Albert Goldman (1927–), U.S. author

Using the Vocabulary: Participial Adjectives

Adjectives can be formed from many verbs by adding *-ed/-en/-t* or *-ing*. The *-ed/-en/-t* adjective is passive and describes a condition (the *tired* musician) or a person or object that receives the action (the *amused* audience, the *jazzed-up* music). The *-ing* adjective is active and describes the person or object that is doing something or causing the condition (the *beating* drums, the *performing* artist). Study these examples with a partner.

1. The world was amazed by Elvis Presley's performance on stage.

2. The guide's confusing speech about Graceland puzzled the tourists.

3. His fans were shocked by his death.

> Rock 'n' roll was music from the heart and soul that gave us a feeling of freedom.
>
> Bunny Gibson, dancer on *American Bandstand*

A. *Test your knowledge of these forms by labeling the following sentences with **C** for correct and **I** for incorrect. Check your answers by referring back to the passage with a partner. Then correct any incorrect participial adjectives.*

_____ 1. . . . the real history is ongoing, played by struggling musicians . . . (par. 2)

_____ 2. . . . the best musicians in the Delta . . . left their sharecropped days for the bright lights of the big city. (par. 3)

_____ 3. . . . what Elvis did was dared and dangerous . . . (par. 5)

_____ 4. . . . I was struck by the glittering skyline of one of the South's new power cities. (par. 8)

_____ 5. Haley favors big bows in her hair and checking gingham blouses . . . (par. 15)

B. *Fill in the blanks with the correct forms for the verbs in parentheses.*

1. The story about the singer's life was _____ (interest).

2. The first songs were so long and slow that many _____ (bore) people left the nightclub early.

3. Visiting Opryland can be an _____ (entertain) experience.

4. The most fondly _____ (remember) songs of that era are preserved at the Smithsonian.

5. I liked her singing voice so much that I became _____ (fascinate) with her background.

C. *Now complete this paragraph using the correct forms of the appropriate words.*

bore	dare	guide	remember
check	fascinate	interest	struggle

Tennessee, the Volunteer State, is well known for its music. Two of its most famous cities, Memphis and Nashville, have welcomed (1)_____ musicians for years. The sights and sounds of these two cities are so (2)_____, that tourists are never (3)_____ when they visit. In fact, there are so many (4)_____ museums and attractions that it can take weeks to see all of them. One of the most popular places to see is Graceland, where visitors can take a (5)_____ tour of Presley's former home.

Reading Maps

*When reading a map, it is important to establish the directions (North, South, East, and West), to study the keys provided, and to follow roads with a pointer when necessary. Look at the map of the state of Tennessee on page 121 with a partner and then mark these statements true (**T**) or false (**F**).*

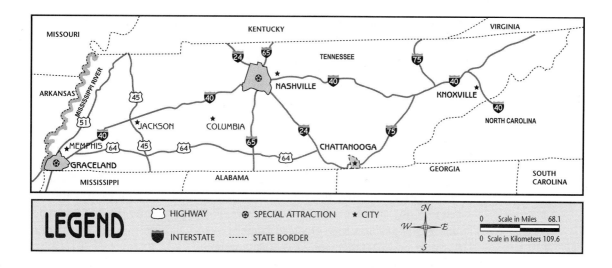

_____ 1. From downtown Memphis, take U.S. 51 south to get to Graceland.

_____ 2. The Mississippi River forms the border between Mississippi and Tennessee.

_____ 3. Knoxville is east of Nashville.

_____ 4. Chattanooga is on Interstate 75 near the Kentucky border.

_____ 5. Dan McGraw passed through the city of Jackson when he drove from Memphis to Nashville. (hint: check paragraph 7 of "True Blues and Country.")

Thinking Together

Talk about the music stars who are popular in your countries. Are there any music legends like Elvis Presley? What qualities does the person have that make him or her so unique? Check to see if these famous musicians and singers have achieved international fame by finding out if your classmates have heard of them.

Writing about It

Write one to two paragraphs on one of the following topics. Try to use some of the vocabulary from this reading and from **Focusing In**.

1. Summarize the importance of Nashville and Memphis to the music of the United States.

2. Imagine you have been visiting Tennessee. Write a letter or postcard to a friend describing some of the sights and sounds you've seen.

3. Describe Elvis Presley and his music based on what you learned by reading this article.

> In _Souls of Black Folk_, W. E. B. Du Bois defined the blues as "the music of an unhappy people, of the children of disappointment; they tell of death and suffering and unvoiced longing toward a truer world, of misty wanderings and hidden ways."
>
> W. E. B. Du Bois (1868–1963), U.S. civil rights leader and author

Reacting to the Reading

The United States has many museums and tourist attractions, such as Graceland and the Rock and Roll Hall of Fame, dedicated to its popular music icons. Do you think Americans pay too much tribute to their music idols?

- Music is part of American popular culture that spreads most easily around the world, in part because the sounds and rhythms are universal even if the language is not. In the title of this article "MTV: Tomorrow the World?" journalist Alan Bunce predicts the spread of "American rock culture through the form of the most powerful medium we've ever known."
- This article was written in 1989 when MTV was shown in only a few countries. Discuss MTV in small groups to see whether Bunce's prediction "tomorrow the world" has come true. Survey your group to see where MTV is available today. Then read the article to see why people are so receptive to this form of pop culture.

MTV: Tomorrow the World? The Music Video Channel Stakes a Worldwide Claim to the Future

ALAN BUNCE

FROM THE *CHRISTIAN SCIENCE MONITOR*

1   It's a hip language of universal images and music. It's the mindless product of a *decadent*[1] youth culture. Music video—three- or four-minute rock numbers *wedded*[2] to moving pictures—can produce both reactions. Whatever one thinks of it, the form is hugely popular with young people in America—largely through 24-hour cable television channel MTV.

2   Can this *controversial*[3] video service—with its free-flowing imagery and sometimes non-logical or even *offensive*[4] content—find happiness amid the ancient cultures of Europe, Asia, Africa, as well as Latin America?

3   Absolutely, says Tom Freston, MTV's founder and president. "We want to make MTV the world's first TV network," he states. MTV's style of entertainment is the world's pop-culture wave of the future, Mr. Freston feels, and he's staking an early claim by making costly *global*[5] deals. MTV is already in 24 countries on five continents. In Europe it has some 7 million *subscribers*[6] in more than 12 countries.

4   "Last Christmas in Greece," Freston says, "we *broadcast*[7] to about a million homes. And beginning next month in the U.K., we will be

---

[1] *decadent* (adj) in decline or moral decay
[2] *wed* (v) to bring together, marry, join, unite
[3] *controversial* (adj) causing disagreement
[4] *offensive* (adj) rude, insulting
[5] *global* (adj) relating to the world, worldwide
[6] *subscriber* (n) person who pays money to regularly receive a magazine, newspaper, or television station
[7] *broadcast* (v) to send out over the air

distributed direct to homes via the Astra *satellite.*[8] It will be our first major DBS [direct broadcast satellite] *venture*[9] outside the United States." But it will be a long haul. In Europe, for instance, Freston says, "we're in a venture that will spend tens of millions of dollars before it will *recoup*[10] one pound. We don't expect to be a big player there until the mid-1990s."

5   Why this kind of effort for such *long-deferred*[11] rewards? After all, MTV in the U.S. already has some 44.8 million subscribers, is viewed by 23 or 24 million people a week, and is adding about 15,000 new customers every day, seven days a week. Because the global audience is worth waiting for, answers Freston. He foresees an international generation of young MTV viewers eager to tune in.

6   "There's a world music today," he says, "a world pop culture and *sensibility*[12] among 12- to 34-year-olds. If you take 23-year-olds in Australia, Austria, and the United States, they have more in common with each other than they do with their parents. They have a viewpoint, attitude, consumer habits that have been shaped by the last 25 years of advances in technology, communications, and transportation. They wear the same clothes, drink Coca-Cola, watch movies made in France, the U.S., and U.K. And as for music, there is no entertainment form that crosses boundaries more readily and successfully than popular rock and roll."

7   Music video is a born world traveler, say its fans. It uses primitive *metaphors*[13] unencumbered by *literalism*[14] or even logic—a stimulating flow of pictures and ideas to dress up the music. For a global network, what could be more appropriate than a universal language like that? Plenty, say many observers who are frightened by the vision. They see an American cultural *Goliath*[15] crushing indigenous forms.

8   "This will probably be the biggest threat of cultural *imperialism*[16] ever seen," says Garth Jowett, a cultural historian and professor of radio and television at the University of Houston. "There is a *mystique*[17] about American popular culture that has been dominant in this century and particularly since the end of World War II," Mr. Jowett continues. "One only has to look at the impact of American movies. More than 60 percent of screen time throughout the world is still devoted to the showing of Hollywood product. People may resent the United States military and throw eggs at our soldiers but they love its popular forms."

9   And each time a new form comes on the scene, the problem looms again, Jowett charges. After World War II it was comic books—there was a big debate in Europe about them.

10   "Now," he says, "we're dealing with American rock culture through the form of the most powerful medium we've ever known: television. They've been trying to conquer Europe for a long time with American TV. But not all of it translated. Rock videos obviously do translate. In the words of Cole Porter, you don't have to know the language—even for English speakers."

MTV's philosophy "Think globally, act locally" has helped it expand to almost 300 million households in 82 territories around the world.

---

[8] *satellite* (n) man-made object that circles another in outer space

[9] *venture* (n) new business deal with risk

[10] *recoup* (v) to gain back something after losing it

[11] *long-deferred* (adj) put off for a long time

[12] *sensibility* (n) appreciation for and response to influences and impressions

[13] *metaphor* (n) figure of speech that suggests similarity between one thing and another

[14] *literalism* (n) exact meaning of a word or words

[15] *Goliath* (proper n) giant; (biblical) Philistine warrior whom David killed with a stone from a sling

[16] *imperialism* (n) system of one nation controlling the political or economic life of another nation

[17] *mystique* (n) mysterious and unusually attractive quality

11   In the past, local cultures have tended to absorb the *onslaught*[18] of aggressive new entertainment forms. But this time, with the combined power of rock and video, Jowett says, "There will be no stopping it." If the reaction of a viewer like Christine Bohuom of France is any indication, MTV can indeed look forward to an enthusiastic welcome from many European viewers.

12   "I love American music videos," Miss Bohuom said while on a recent U.S. visit. "I would like a chance to have more of it." Does she have any problem with an American-produced form of entertainment invading her native land?

13   "No, not at all," she states. "I think the videos are very good, and lots of my friends watch them all the time."

14   Not surprisingly, Freston also feels the imperialism issue is an *unfounded*[19] fear. He claims MTV will be working closely with people in each country: "MTV would never work if you just took music *tailored*[20] to the American audience and put it into a different country," he asserts. "It requires some significant changes. Yes, the music is always rock-and-roll based, but the selections are different country to country."

15   He cites MTV's experience in Japan, where it introduced a *prototype*[21] for other world ventures. "We programmed with a sensitivity to the Japanese audience," says Freston. "We wove the elements of a video show together: some American, some European, some Japanese. Rock, at its roots, is an Anglo-American art form; so we try to be sure we are playing the music that is most *in sync with*[22] what different countries want to hear."

16   Even Jowett acknowledges international MTV could well create a desirable cross-current of talent. "This may be an opportunity for European musicians and video people to become a part of MTV and, in turn, have a reverse kind of effect in the U.S.," he suggests. "One only has to look at the effect of British pop musicians and now, to some extent, Australian and, to a lesser extent, European in the U.S."

17   That's exactly the view held by Joe Kotarba, a sociologist and colleague of Jowett's at the University of Houston. He teaches popular culture and is writing a book about rock listeners. "It would be much too *glib*[23] to entertain terms like 'cultural imperialism,'" he asserts. "There's a market out there. Young people around the world can't get enough. MTV is simply responding to that demand, and the content is representative of local tastes."

18   Freston calls it a "*pent-up*[24] demand" resulting from decades of government control and few outlets for this kind of entertainment. Government resistance has been a major obstacle to MTV's global efforts.

19   "Many countries object to the whole notion of a pan-European anything," Freston says, "let alone a rock-and-roll network. The young people have been underserved, and, lo and behold, here comes a 24-hour network!"

20   Not so fast! says J. C. Combs, a professor of percussion and an active jazz musician at Wichita State University in Kansas. He feels MTV's global designs are less about serving youth than serving profits.

21   "It has very little to do with young people pounding on the table and saying, 'Give us MTV,'" he states. "Record producers have discovered another way of promoting their *wares*.[25] The rock scene among the kids there features all the current music on MTV over here. They don't seem deprived that they haven't seen it on MTV."

22   Even if they were *clamoring*[26] for it, Mr. Combs has a problem with the form itself—specifically the scenes accompanying the

---

[18] *onslaught* (n) violent attack, either physically or with words

[19] *unfounded* (adj) false, not based on fact

[20] *tailor* (v) to make something to specific requirements, to customize

[21] *prototype* (n) working model used to test an idea before producing the final version

[22] *to be in sync with* (idiom) to be together in timing or ideas

[23] *glib* (adj) spoken quickly and easily, without thought, usually not true

[24] *pent-up* (adj) closed in and blocked from escaping; frustrated

[25] *wares* (n pl.) items of the same general kind that are for sale

[26] *clamor* (v) to make loud, noisy demands or protests

music—and says he'd hate to see it spreading into other countries. For one thing, he thinks the music and video run on two different and often nonparallel tracks. "Music video is a wonderful tool if used properly—like Michael Jackson," he states. "There a video and an artist seem to meet, with video and music going hand in hand. But often it's as if a poem you were proud of was set to music that overpowered it to the point no one even cared about the words. The visual part runs in its own direction to hype the product as much as possible. It's two different *idioms*.[27]"

23 Jowett calls it "an assault upon the eye" and says, "It's somewhat *anarchistic*.[28] There's chaos involved. It's not linear; you just sit there, and images are flashed at you quickly. It's almost an *avant-garde*[29] form of art."

24 Combs voices another concern shared by many about music video. "Some of them are pretty *blatant*[30] and sexually explicit," he

charges. "I don't understand what that has to do with musicians who are trying to make music. If it's for shock value, I suppose, that gets the job done."

25 They must be watching another network, according to Freston, who points to the good standards he says MTV maintains. "We refuse hundreds of videos a year," he points out, "and send them back with edits and changes. We have a responsibility, and uphold it. A lot of the complaints about MTV are from people who have always held the whole of rock music in *disdain*.[31]"

26 Anyway, music video is just one of the formats MTV offers. "It's the key building block," he says, "but just putting it on MTV, you're not going to get much of an audience. We're trying to create a whole environment that has a certain style, look, and feel. It's information, news, fashion, comedy, movies— all the *spokes*[32] of the youth culture."

Understanding the Reading: Main Ideas

A. *When choosing the correct statement of the main idea, remember to avoid those sentences that capture only a part of the paragraph or that go beyond what the writer is really saying in the paragraph. Circle the best main idea for the indicated paragraph from the reading.*

I. Paragraph 1

A. MTV is considered an empty expression of problematic youth.

B. People react in both positive and negative ways to MTV.

C. There are a lot of people who don't like MTV.

II. Paragraph 6

A. The popularity of music goes beyond the boundaries of a country.

B. Rock and roll is the most popular music in the world.

C. Teenagers all over the world are more alike than they are different.

Based on Recording Industry Association of America statistics, rock is the top music genre, followed by country, R & B, rap, pop, gospel, jazz, and classical. The best-selling album as of 1998 was *Thriller* by Michael Jackson.

[27] *idiom* (n) [used in music or art] a distinct style or character
[28] *anarchistic* (adj) disregarding existing rules; disorderly
[29] *avant-garde* (adj) pathbreaking, on the forefront of art, literature, music, etc.
[30] *blatant* (adj) obvious; going against one's sense of honesty; shameless
[31] *disdain* (n) the feeling that someone or something deserves no respect; contempt
[32] *spoke* (n) a bar or rod radiating from the hub of a wheel

> The Grammy Awards are given each year to honor achievement in the recording industry.

III. Paragraph 10

    A. MTV is more successful in other countries than TV in general because the listener doesn't have to understand the words.

    B. American TV programs will never be understood by those who don't speak English.

    C. Television is the most powerful medium.

IV. Paragraph 14

    A. The MTV programs seen in other countries will be the same as those seen in the United States.

    B. Changes will be made in MTV to make it more adaptable to each country.

    C. All MTV music videos will have a basis in rock and roll.

V. Paragraph 22

    A. Coombs feels that MTV shouldn't be exported because music and video do not always go well together.

    B. Coombs feels that music videos such as those of Michael Jackson are very successful.

    C. Coombs doesn't like MTV.

B. *If the topic of the whole article is MTV and its success around the world, what is the main idea? What does the author say about this topic?*

_____

_____

Using the Vocabulary: Reviewing Compound Words and Participial Adjectives

A. *Review the formation of compound words (Chapter 3, p. 56) by skimming the reading to find at least five compound words made by combining two words to make a new word or phrase, such as* heartland, avant-garde, folk music.

    1. _____

    2. _____

    3. _____

    4. _____

    5. _____

B. *Review the formation of participial adjectives (p. 119) by skimming this reading to find at least five adjectives made by adding* **-ing** *or* **-ed/-en/-t** *to verbs (struggling musician, fast-paced rockabilly).*

1. _____

2. _____

3. _____

4. _____

5. _____

Thinking Together

Test your knowledge of American music by completing this crossword puzzle with a partner. All of the words can be found in the three readings in Chapter 5, "Keeping the Beat."

Across Clues

3. a simple song that tells a story
4. ____ and western music
6. famous rock-and-roll legend
7. the words to a song
8. a religious song

Down Clues

1. dance form
2. ____ Guthrie, famous folksinger
3. music of sadness
5. beat
9. music television video

> No change in musical style will survive unless it is accompanied by a change in clothing style. Rock is to dress up to.
>
> Frank Zappa (1940–1993), U.S. rock musician

Writing about It

*Write one to two paragraphs on one of the following topics. Try to use some of the vocabulary from this reading and from **Focusing In**.*

1. According to this writer, why is music such a universal medium?

2. What are the good and bad aspects of MTV, according to some of the critics mentioned in this article?

3. Write a letter to your local TV station expressing the idea "We want our MTV!"

Reacting to the Reading

MTV has helped spread American music and culture around the world. Do you think other countries should welcome the importation of American music via television? Why or why not?

Keeping Track of Your Reading Rate

tip **Readers are more efficient when they read with a purpose in mind. Read this article to find out why d'Amboise's National Dance Institute is so special.**

- This article, courtesy of the Kennedy Center for Performing Arts, is about Jacques d'Amboise, a famous ballet dancer and teacher.
- When your instructor gives you the signal to begin, read the story at a quick pace and mark down the time as soon as you are done. Then answer the questions without looking back at the reading.

"He makes me feel like dancing!" For more than twenty years, that is what thousands of excited children throughout the country have been saying after participating in Jacques d'Amboise's National Dance Institute. . . . As one of the finest ballet dancers of our time, d'Amboise inspired geniuses like George Balanchine and Frederick Ashton to create some of their best works for him. As one of this country's leaders in the field of arts education, he now inspires children to lead healthy, creative, and vital lives.

What he teaches to children today, he learned from experience. At seven, growing up in a rough New York neighborhood, his mother insisted he attend his sister's dance classes—not so much to participate as to keep him from joining one of the many gangs that roamed the Upper West Side. Six months later the wise teacher realized he deserved better than what she could offer, and in 1942 he joined George Balanchine's School of American Ballet.

. . . In 1976, while still a principal with New York City Ballet, d'Amboise founded the National Dance Institute. The inspiration was the hope that perhaps he could do for young children what that first dance teacher had done for him. . . . He started with thirty little boys, $3,000 out of his own pocket, and talked Balanchine into letting him use the stage of the New York State Theater between performances. Within three years, he had three hundred children in the program. National Dance Institute continues to grow in cities around the country. Asked why dance is so often the key to turning around young lives that are headed in the wrong direction, he responded, "Dance is the most immediate and accessible of the arts because it involves your own body. When you learn to move your body on a note of music, it is exciting. You have taken control of your body and, by learning to do that, you discover that you can take control of your life."

For his extraordinary contribution to the arts education of this country's young people, d'Amboise has been honored with a 1990 MacArthur Fellowship, the Capezio Award, the first Producer's Circle Award for public service in enriching the lives of New York City children, the Governor's Award for outstanding contributions to the art and culture of New York State, and the distinguished Paul Robeson Award for Excellence in the Field of the Humanities.

(400 words)   TIME _____

*Now mark these statements true (**T**) or false (**F**) without looking back at the reading.*

_____ 1. Jacques d'Amboise grew up in France.

_____ 2. D'Amboise started ballet lessons when he was seven years old.

_____ 3. Many of the students at the National Dance Institute are poor and at risk of joining gangs.

_____ 4. The National Dance Institute first started with boys and girls.

_____ 5. D'Amboise once danced with the New York City Ballet.

_____ 6. D'Amboise never became a famous dancer, but he is a famous teacher.

_____ 7. The goal of the National Dance Institute was to find and train professional dancers.

_____ 8. D'Amboise has received only one award for his contribution to the arts.

_____ 9. D'Amboise believes that dancing is an activity that can promote self-esteem.

_____10. Students must travel to New York City to have the opportunity to work with d'Amboise.

Percent correct = _____ wpm = _____

Dance Theater of Harlem, established in 1968, was the first African American dance company.

MAKING CONNECTIONS

Responding to the Readings

Prepare short oral or written responses based on your personal experience and your reactions to the readings. Try to incorporate the information and the vocabulary you have learned in this chapter.

1. What types of music do you like most, both from your own country and from other countries?

2. Describe your favorite singer and the type of music she or he plays.

3. The author of "True Blues and Country" writes, "But Nashville is a trap of sorts. Dreams of country-music stardom draw a swarm of aspiring musicians." Is there a particular city (or a place in the city) in your country where aspiring musicians gather? Describe this city or area in detail.

4. Do you think MTV goes too far in showing sex and violence on television?

5. Write a paragraph describing one of the folk songs from your homeland.

6. How important are music and learning a musical instrument in your culture?

7. Are there community music or dance programs such as the National Dance Institute in your country that try to provide an experience in the arts to disadvantaged children? If so, describe them.

8. The blues in America express sadness and despair. What kind of music do you like to listen to when you are "down and out"?

9. Discuss your reaction to one of the quotes or facts in the margins of this chapter that you find most interesting or surprising.

Editing Your Work

*A student wrote this paragraph about her favorite type of music. The paragraph has five base verbs in bold italics that require endings to turn them into adjectives. Review the rules for making -**ing** and -**ed**/-**en**/-**t** adjectives on page 119 before you add the correct ending. Make any necessary spelling changes.*

I love listening to the soundtracks of musicals such as *The Phantom of the Opera* and *Miss Saigon*. Almost always these songs are very ***touch***_____ and filled with emotions. Just like a movie, a musical can present a story,

---

We look at the dance to impart the sensation of living in an affirmation of life, to energize the spectator into keener awareness of the vigor, the mystery, the humor, the variety, and the wonder of life. This is the function of the American dance.

Martha Graham
(1894–1991), U.S. dancer and choreographer

but in a different way. With their complicated harmonies and beautifully *write*_____ lyrics, the songs carry the listeners into a *fascinate*_____ world of imagination. When I listen to Broadway music, I feel as if I am becoming a part of the story as I follow the *excite* _____ beats and flowing melodies. Thus, a musical song is like a combination of music, books, and movies, wonderfully put together that I can enjoy all at once by simply playing a CD. About a year ago, I also became a big fan of Rhythm and Blues. Whenever I hear the strongly *pronounce* _____ beat of an R and B song, I can't help singing along.

> The Nutcracker Ballet is performed all over the United States at Christmas. Thousands of aspiring young ballerinas try out each year.

Writing an Essay

Choose one of the following topics and write an essay. As a prewriting activity, read over your shortwrites and notes for inspiration. Remember to review the brainstorming techniques on pages 262–263. In your essay, use the readings, factoids, quotes, class discussions, and personal experience to support your ideas. Try to use the vocabulary you have learned in this chapter. If you choose to write a research paper, make certain to cite your sources clearly.

1. Trace the historical development of some of the music of your homeland in the same way that Mercedes Hardey analyzes American folk music. Discuss the inspiration for this music, the artists who sing it, the instruments played, and the meanings of some of the lyrics.

2. Discuss the influence of popular American music on the music and culture of your country. Has MTV arrived on television? Can people buy all types of American music in stores? Is it played on the radio or performed in concerts? Do the young people follow the dress styles and language associated with popular music? Make sure to include as many details as possible on the music and culture both in the United States and in your country.

3. Elvis Presley is a music legend in the United States. His home, Graceland, is a shrine to his version of rock and roll. Is there a music star in your country who has risen to such a degree of fame? Describe the person and his or her music. What has helped this performer achieve such fame, and what type of audience does he or she appeal to?

4. Compare and contrast the types of music that are most popular in your country with those in America. For example, country music and rock and roll dominate the American radio stations that attract young listeners, but folk music, jazz, and swing are also popular. Include enough information on the music of your country to help the readers understand the types of music that might not be familiar to them. Make reference to the articles you have read in this chapter.

5. If you play a musical instrument, write an essay about this experience. What do you play and when did you start playing? Who influenced you to choose this instrument? What kind of training did you have? Did you enjoy it? Who have you played for and with? Do you still play this instrument today?

6. Research the life and times of a famous American singer or group of any music style. Include details on background, musical influences, professional career, performances, and recording. Write about your own personal reaction to this performer. If you have ever been to a concert, make sure to describe it in detail.

Finding More Information

Magazines and Journals

American Music
The Audiophile
Billboard
Dance Magazine
Rolling Stone
Sing Out

Books

Adams, Noah, *Piano Lessons*
Guthrie, Woody, *Bound for Glory*
Jackson, John, *American Bandstand*
Lomax, Allan, *Folk Songs of North America*
Nance, S., *Music You Can See: The MTV Story*
Salzman, Mark, *The Soloist*

> **If I could tell you what it meant, there would be no point in dancing it.**
>
> Isadora Duncan
> (1878–1927), U.S. dancer

The World Wide Web

musicmatch.com—Music Match
users.aol.com/Jumpcity/horizons.html—Cultural Horizons
www.amc.net—the American Music Center
www.jazzonln.com—JazzOnline
www.riaa.com—Recording Industry Association of America
www.unfurled.com—MTV and Yahoo Guide to Web Music

Movies and Videos

Bound for Glory
Breakdancin'
Fame
La Bamba
Mr. Holland's Opus
The Music Man
Tap
Woodstock

> The real American type can never be a ballet dancer. The legs are too long, the body too supple, and the spirit too free for this school of affected grace and toe walking.
>
> Isadora Duncan
> (1878–1927), U.S. dancer

Getting the Message

Today's technology has not only changed the way we work and play, it has also changed the way we receive information and communicate with others. From the 1920s on, first radio and then television have brought the outside world into the living rooms of America. Today, from surfing the net for news to sending e-mail and faxes via modem, the computer has introduced us to a whole new realm of communication: cyberspace. Kenji Sato, a Japanese author, wrote that cyberspace "has become the ultimate embodiment of the American dream. Free from the restraints of reality, cyberspace surpasses any earthly nation in promising an unfettered right to pursue freedom and prosperity."

The "unfettered"—or uncontrolled—freedom of cyberspace bothers some Americans who think that there should be censorship—or government control—of the information highway. Although they welcome uses of the Internet by senior citizens such as those described by John Dickerson in the article "Never Too Old," they disapprove of the open accessibility of chat lines on homosexuality or online dating services such as the one described in "Online Dating: Myth vs. Reality" by Randy Hecht. While Americans are often seen as outgoing and talkative, they haven't always been this open. Although schools today encourage students to socialize and share their ideas and opinions, the influence of the Puritan background kept most Americans in the past from sharing their private lives. It wasn't until the 1960s with the advent of "consciousness raising" groups that they began to bare their souls in public. Today, this aspect of the American personality has given rise to chat lines on computers and talk shows on radio and television where the members of the audience express their opinions and emotions in public. Two readings in this chapter, "Radio Activity" by Peter Theroux and the excerpt from *Oprah!* by Robert Waldron, shed some light on why talk shows are so popular with Americans.

Do you surf the net and travel on the information highway? How many hours a day do you watch TV and listen to the radio? Discuss these questions in small groups. Then talk about the picture on page 134 and answer the question: *How has technology influenced the way we get our information?*

Are You Part of the Information Generation?
Circle the correct answers.

1. A modem is part of a
   a. computer.   b. cell phone.

2. The most popular American TV talk show host is
   a. Johnny Carson.   b. Oprah Winfrey.

3. An online dating service is
   a. a calendar program.   b. a means to meet people.

4. Radio talk shows are for
   a. speeches by government officials. b. voicing personal opinions.

5. The WWW is
   a. the World Wide Web.   b. Western World Wireless.

6. E-mail stands for
   a. electronic mail.   b. easy mail.

7. Cyberspace is
   a. outer space.   b. computer space.

8. A personal ad is
   a. an ad to sell something you own.   b. an ad to describe yourself.

Expand Your Word Power
Select the correct word from this list to complete the idioms in italics. Then use each idiom in a new sentence of your own.

air   breeze   ice   message   net

1. When trying to start up a conversation, it's often hard to *break the* _____.

2. People today turn on computers, log on, and *surf the* _____.

3. In a discussion, we try to make a point and hope the other person *gets the* _____.

4. Friends like to get together and *shoot the* _____.

5. A growing number of people tune in to radio hosts who *go on the* _____ to discuss current events.

■ Americans have a proverb, "You can't teach an old dog new tricks." This article, "Never Too Old," is about senior citizens (people over age sixty-five) and technology. Based on the title, what do you think John Dickerson's attitude about senior citizens and technology will be? What word tells you this?

■ Do you think senior citizens are too old to learn new things? As you read, think about how technology is used to enhance the lifestyles of senior citizens in your country.

Never Too Old

John F. Dickerson

from *Time*

1 Instructor George Breathitt asked an audience of 300 computer enthusiasts in Louisville, Kentucky, how many seniors in the group would like to teach other seniors about computers. A younger member of the audience *quipped*[1] *disdainfully*,[2] "Wouldn't that be the blind leading the blind?" He was promptly *booed*[3]: almost half the audience was over 50. In fact, Breathitt, 61, has attracted so many seniors willing to teach—and learn—about computers that he founded a successful firm to employ them. So far, his Silver Fox Computer Club has taught about 7,500 students and expanded into four states.

2 So who says computers are only for youngsters? The American Association of Retired Persons (AARP), the nation's largest organization of senior citizens, counts 2 million computer users among its 33 million members. And with more leisure time and *discretionary income*[4] than many youths, thousands of seniors—including many who have never before used a computer—are entering the cyberculture, burying the *hoary*[5] old-dog-new-tricks *axiom*.[6] "Once they get used to handling the mouse," says Breathitt, "they learn faster than teenagers."

3 Seniors are using their new computing power to do everything from monitoring investments to tracking genealogy to producing their *memoirs*.[7] Some have started postretirement businesses making greeting cards or performing legal research on the Internet. But the majority say they were drawn to computers because, like Jack Fowler, 75, of Sun City West, Arizona, they simply didn't want to be left behind by progress. "I couldn't keep up with my four-year-old grandson," says the retired pharmacist.

4 Ilene Weinberg, 68, a former social worker from Newton, Massachusetts, didn't want to get a computer; her typewriter worked just fine. But two years ago, her son gave her

---

[1] *quip* (v) to make a short, funny remark
[2] *disdainfully* (adv) showing no respect; scornfully
[3] *boo* (v) to make a sound of disapproval
[4] *discretionary income* (np) part of one's salary that can be used for extra things

[5] *hoary* (adj) old and gray
[6] *axiom* (n) obvious truth or saying
[7] *memoir* (n) written account of one's life

one anyway, hoping it might help make up for the *debilitating*[8] effects of her Parkinson's disease. Now she spends so much time online that she has installed another phone line. "I feel like I'm with it," says Weinberg. "I'm connecting with the present and the future."

5   One of Weinberg's chief destinations is the 15,000-strong SeniorNet, where she spends several hours a day chatting with others her age in the organization's station on America Online. Many seniors find the network a rich source of new friends and support in time of trouble as well as a handy supplier of information on such subjects as how to light a water heater or handle depression. "For many older people, computers allow them to feel as if their world is still expanding," says Mary Furlong, who founded the San Francisco–based SeniorNet in 1986. "They allow you to form new friendships and become more intellectually *mobile*.[9]"

6   For Rick and Rita Hanson, SeniorNet has led to much more than intellectual mobility. In September 1993, the former truck mechanic and his wife traded in their Bellingham, Massachusetts, house for a 28-ft.-long mobile home and embarked on a nationwide tour. "We wouldn't have considered this trip if it weren't for SeniorNet," says 59-year-old Rick. "If one of us got ill, what would the other do? But now, no matter where we are in the U.S., we're within 100 miles of friends." The *peripatetic duo*[10] has gone from Thanksgiving in Las Vegas with 60 online friends to a wedding of two SeniorNetters in Michigan. "Lord willing, we'll see all 350 people in our computer family."

7   In addition to communicating with one

An elementary school student in Irvine, California, shares her computer skills with her grandfather.

another and sharing memories about everything from the Great War to the once *ubiquitous*[11] Burma Shave highway ads, seniors are connecting with the generations below them. Children of aging parents log on for advice about health care and retirement communities or just to chat. On SeniorNet, several programs link schoolchildren and seniors. The Generation to Generation forum enables students to tap personal histories of World War I and the Depression, as well as lessons on aging. Says John Horn, professor of *gerontology*[12] at the University of Southern California: "It's the equivalent of the old folks sitting around the village square."

8   Though seniors are far from being the dominant group among computer users, their numbers are growing and are bound to *mushroom*[13] as the baby boomers age. When that happens, they will feel right at home alongside the mass of younger users in the digital future.

---

[8] *debilitating* (adj) weakening
[9] *mobile* (adj) movable
[10] *peripatetic duo* (np) two (duo) people who travel a lot

[11] *ubiquitous* (adj) found everywhere
[12] *gerontology* (n) study of the elderly
[13] *mushroom* (v) to grow rapidly in great numbers

> Man is still the most extraordinary computer of all.
>
> John F. Kennedy
> (1917–1963),
> U.S. president

Understanding the Reading: Reviewing Main Ideas and Annotation

A. *Write the main idea for each of the topics in the following paragraphs. Remember that a main idea must be stated in a complete sentence and must capture the whole idea of the paragraph rather than just one detail. Try to answer the question,* What is the writer saying about this topic?

1. Paragraph 2: computers and senior citizens

   _____

   _____

2. Paragraph 3: uses for the computer

   _____

   _____

3. Paragraph 5: seniors, computers, and communication

   _____

   _____

4. Paragraph 7: computers and connecting the generations

   _____

   _____

5. Paragraph 8: seniors and the digital age

   _____

   _____

B. *Remember that to annotate a text is to mark it in a way that is useful to you for a later purpose, such as studying for an exam or finding facts for an essay. Go back to the reading and annotate the text as indicated.*

1. In paragraph 1, circle the name of the computer club and underline the number of students.
2. In paragraph 2, circle the acronym AARP and the number of members and underline the number of members who use computers.
3. In paragraph 3, circle the five specific uses that seniors find for computers and in the margin write the note "uses for computers."
4. In paragraph 5, underline or highlight the two quotes.
5. In the last paragraph, underline or highlight the main idea.

Using the Vocabulary: Technical Computer Terms

A. *The computer age has added many new words to the English vocabulary. First, use the definitions in the list on page 139 to unscramble the vocabulary words. Then find them in the word search puzzle.*

*cyberspace*_____ 1. ycbscaerpe—the world of communications, information, and entertainment created via computers

_____ 2. dabataes—information on a general topic stored in a computer system

_____ 3. lmiae—electronic mail sent via computer

_____ 4. tenretln—the global computer network of electronic mail and information

_____ 5. swpasrod—access code for a computerized account

_____ 6. sesbewit—Internet pages that give information

_____ 7. dmome—an electronic device for sending/receiving computer data over telephone lines

_____ 8. kwernto—a system of communication lines connected via computer

_____ 9. lonnie—connected to a computer network

_____ 10. nutese—worldwide bulletin board system made up of thousands of newsgroups

O	N	F	U	A	P	C	N	O	S	T	R	X
N	L	F	U	Z	L	Y	F	Z	Y	D	Q	P
L	I	L	S	I	V	B	L	I	U	W	I	A
I	T	K	I	U	S	E	N	E	T	B	W	S
N	L	P	W	P	U	R	I	R	H	P	P	S
E	M	A	I	L	I	S	J	Y	M	T	G	W
P	E	S	N	K	C	P	O	N	J	M	B	O
C	D	A	T	A	B	A	S	E	M	L	P	R
O	P	Z	E	C	U	C	V	R	U	O	G	D
R	Q	B	R	R	G	E	Q	W	V	G	J	P
U	B	T	N	J	W	E	B	S	I	T	E	S
M	O	D	E	M	Z	J	F	R	K	N	O	A
H	N	E	T	W	O	R	K	K	A	B	R	W

B. *Now choose the correct words from the list in Exercise A to complete these sentences.*

When we enter the computer lab, our first job is to log on with a special

(1)_____. Once we are all online, our instructor usually asks us to

search for some information on the (2)_____. We have found a lot of

(3)_____ that have exercises for ESL students. Our instructor sends us

In 1996, 79 percent of fourth graders and 96 percent of eleventh graders reported using a computer at home or at school.

The Condition of Education 1998

(4)_____ at least once a week, and we have to answer her mail and also write to a classmate to practice our writing skills. Some students still don't like using computers, but most of us find the world of (5)_____ exciting and fun.

> **In 1997, more than 1,000 classes were offered "online" over computer networks.**
>
> *Los Angeles Times*

Thinking Together

In a small group, talk about the ways computers have influenced people in the United States and in your countries. Think about where computers are seen most and who uses them. What effects have they had on the lives of students, businesspeople, and seniors? Fill in the diagram to summarize the results of your discussion.

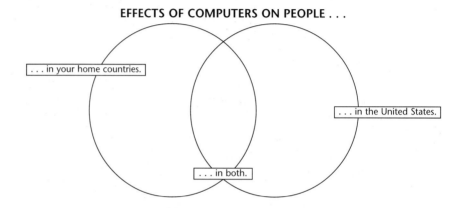

EFFECTS OF COMPUTERS ON PEOPLE . . .

. . . in your home countries.

. . . in the United States.

. . . in both.

Writing about It

*Write one to two paragraphs on one of the following topics. Try to use some of the vocabulary from this reading and from **Focusing In**.*

1. Using the information you annotated in Exercise B (p. 138) from "Never Too Old," summarize some of the benefits that seniors get from using computers and accessing the Internet.

2. Write a short speech in which George Breathitt, founder of the Silver Fox Computer Club, might try to prove that seniors are competent computer users.

3. Explain the Hansons' trip and why computers helped make it possible.

Reacting to the Reading

More and more people are feeling the pressure to buy computers that they may or may not need. Do you think the benefits of owning a computer outweigh the expense?

- The information highway has also opened up new avenues for single people to get to know others and to establish relationships. Although criticized by some, online dating has become a popular means of meeting new people, as Randy Hecht points out. Do people in your country use the Internet for this purpose?
- Match.Com is one of the leaders in online matchmaking with 750,000 registered users. Does using the Internet seem like a good way to find romance? Read this article to find out what kinds of people sign up for this service.

Online Dating: Myth vs. Reality

RANDY B. HECHT

from *Match.Com News*

1   Industry expert and Match.Com columnist Trish McDermott has seen it all. "The *stigma*[1] that was initially attached to print personals," she remembers, "was that you must be a 'loser' to 'resort' to using newspapers to advertise for a date, and that there was so much uncertainty involved: How would you know anything about the person you were going to meet? It was scary, and it was kind of a mark against your ability to get a good date in the real world. Of course, what happened was that the personals became extremely popular. It worked; many people fell in love and got married . . . and because of that the stigma has gone away." With the advent of online dating, the old fears have been revived—this time with the added twist of a kind of high-tech performance anxiety. "Now online dating is new and unknown, and for people who are not technologically *savvy*[2] there's even a further element of uncertainty about it, because they're not even certain how the technology works," McDermott says. But despite the opportunities for *anonymity*[3] in this medium, she believes online dating is a *viable*[4] and valuable option for singles. "Lots of *demographic*[5] information tells us that people who are using the Internet are college-educated, intelligent, highly functioning in terms of their ability to *navigate*[6] both in terms of communication and technology. These are certainly not what we'd call losers in life. These are people with jobs, people who can afford

[1] *stigma* (n) disgrace; a negative point on a record
[2] *savvy* (adj) smart, knowledgeable
[3] *anonymity* (n) not being named; remaining unknown
[4] *viable* (adj) workable, capable of succeeding
[5] *demographic* (adj) relating to information about groups, used especially in politics and marketing
[6] *navigate* (v) to figure out the course

The percentage of American households in which someone owned a computer rose from 7 percent in 1983 to 37 percent in 1994.

World Almanac, 1995

computers, people who are in a profession where they're using computers," she explains.

2 This brings us to another widespread myth about online dating: that most of its participants are techno-nerds who can't function in real-world social situations. Not so, says Laura Banks, author of *Love Online*, a guide to online dating services and practices. "You're meeting more people than you would in any other way. You're aggressively pursuing meeting people. And so you're going to occasionally meet someone who's a little left of center or a computer *geek*,[7]" she explains. "Everyone I met was nice and normal," she says of her own online dating experiences. "I had a couple of close encounters with men that didn't work out, but they were reasonable guys. One was a respected author, and another was a lighting designer—very attractive and literate. Not a geek."

3 Banks also talks about one online connection that changed her life in a very unexpected way: "Through someone I met online, I got turned on to traditional church, which is kind of funny for such a progressive medium."

Let's Get Serious

4 Match.Com's own statistics tell us a lot about who is searching cyberspace for a relationship. Fran Maier, the company's vice president, reports that, like Internet users overall, "Match.Com users are well employed and well educated. Over 56 percent have college degrees, 55 percent hold managerial/professional jobs, and an additional 17 percent are in technical fields."

5 Of course, education and employment status aren't absolute indicators of someone's behavior in social or romantic situations, but they are among the first indicators of *compatibility*[8] most people seek in any forum for connecting with prospective dates or other new social contacts. "On Match.Com," Maier says, "primarily because we are more upscale than chat environments and because we require a subscription fee, our members are a bit older. This makes sense because it is not until people approach their 30s that they become more serious about finding a date. Most of our users have been on the Internet for well over a year."

6 What else do we know about online daters? The median age of Match.Com members is in the mid 30s; trial members and those who log on as guests are younger. The male-to-female ratio is more balanced than you might think, too; though active, regular users of the World Wide Web remain predominantly male, women account for nearly 50 percent of Match.Com's visitors and more than one-third of its members.

---

[7] **geek** (n) nerd; one who doesn't fit in with current styles
[8] **compatibility** (n) ability to get along well together

The proportion of gay Match.Com users, 10 percent, mirrors the proportion of gay people in society at large, and there are a growing number of online dating services created specifically for this audience.

Looking for Love in All the Right Places?

7 What draws these people to a medium that still makes so many people so nervous? The same thing that leads to their investing a small fortune each year in other singles services: they want to fall in love. "There are at least 85 million singles in the U.S. alone," Maier says, "and that number is expected to break 100 million within a few years. Trends in the workplace (issues with sexual harassment, smaller companies, etc.) make it difficult to date or find someone at work. Older singles are tired of the bar scene and are looking for something new." And when they look to the Internet, they find it offers them 24-hour access from home or work, the ability to be anonymous and secure in ongoing interactive conversations, a level of immediacy newspapers cannot offer, and an opportunity to screen prospective dates.

An outdoor setting provides a safe way to screen prospective dates.

8 If she's read this far, even Mom will have to admit that online dating isn't as scary as she thought it was. "People look down on it because they don't understand it, or because they don't have the courage to do it themselves. There's this whole western civilization theory that you just accidentally slam into somebody and fall in love," author Banks says. But finding the right relationship is hard work, and this technology is just another tool for helping us to get the job done. And more and more people are finding success in their online romantic searches. Of course, just as not all marriages end as successful relationships, not all successful relationships end in marriage. But those of you who are seriously marriage-minded will delight in knowing that Match.Com just announced the wedding of the 150th couple who met through the service.

9 Yes, online dating is a gamble, Banks concedes. But meeting new people—whether online or in reality, always involves a risk, she points out.

In October, 1998, the one millionth member joined Match.Com.

"It's either that, or go back in your house, close the door, order Chinese food in, and never meet anyone."

10   Thanks to Match.Com and other online dating services, more and more of us can look forward to ordering that takeout meal for two.

Understanding the Reading: Fact versus Opinion

Distinguishing between **facts** and **opinions** requires understanding the difference between (1) something that is true and can be proved, and (2) someone's personal view. Opinions often use words like *too*, *should*, and *best*. Discuss these examples.

Examples:

a. _O_ Most online dating services are better than newspaper ads.

b. _O_ Everyone should be married by the age of twenty-five.

c. _F_ You can find a diverse selection of personal ads on the Internet.

Using the information in the article, write **F** *for fact and* **O** *for opinion in the blanks.*

_____ 1. People who use online dating tend to be well educated.

_____ 2. Online dating is the best way to meet others.

_____ 3. Meeting people online is exciting and fun.

_____ 4. Online dating services for the gay audience are growing in number.

_____ 5. People who go online in search of romance are not usually losers or geeks.

_____ 6. Computer dating services often make successful matches.

_____ 7. The best matches are made online, not through newspapers and magazines.

_____ 8. Too many people use the personals online to look for love.

_____ 9. Online dating is still new and unfamiliar to many people.

_____ 10. Single people should use online dating services.

Understanding the Vocabulary: Abbreviations and Acronyms

In 1997, one-quarter of Americans owned pagers and one-third used cell phones.

Consumer Electronics Industry Association

A. *Abbreviations and acronyms are formed by omitting letters in a word or using only the first letters of words. Match the abbreviations on the right with the correct meanings on the left. If you are uncertain, work with a partner and look them up in the dictionary.*

_____ 1. INS   a. Federal Bureau of Investigation

_____ 2. CEO   b. Independent Nature Society

_____ 3. CPA   c. As Soon as Possible

_____ 4. CPR   d. Ku Klux Klan

_____ 5. ETA   e. Chief of Engineering Operations

_____ 6. KKK   f. Auto-Immune Deficiency Syndrome

_____ 7. AIDS   g. Répondez s'il vous plaît

_____ 8. NAACP   h. Cardio-Pulmonary Resuscitation

_____ 9. RSVP   i. Immigration and Naturalization Service

_____10. YMCA   j. Chief Executive Officer

_____11. ASAP   k. Cardiovascular Problems and Results

_____12. FBI   l. Environmental Trust Agency

                     m. National Association for the Advancement of Colored People

                     n. College of Physicians and Attorneys

                     o. Faithful Believers in Ideology

                     p. Keys to Knowledge and Karma

                     q. Certified Public Accountant

                     r. Estimated Time of Arrival

                     s. Young Men's Christian Association

> **The advanced computerized telecommunication networks make information more readily accessible and make it more difficult to restrict information flow. What we need to balance, to some degree, is the right of the individual to obtain free access to information with the right of individuals to control and limit access to their personal information.**
>
> Lorne Bruce, U.S. librarian

B. *Work with your class to make a list on the board of other abbreviations you are familiar with. Then categorize these abbreviations and the ones in Exercise A by placing them in the correct column in the chart that follows.*

Professions	Medical Terms	Quantities/ Measurements	Organizations	Geographic Areas	Others
M.D.	EKG	lb.	A.M.A.	L.A.	CD

Reading Ads

Work with a partner. Read the ads below. Use the Key to Abbreviations to help you.
Then circle the answer that best completes each sentence.

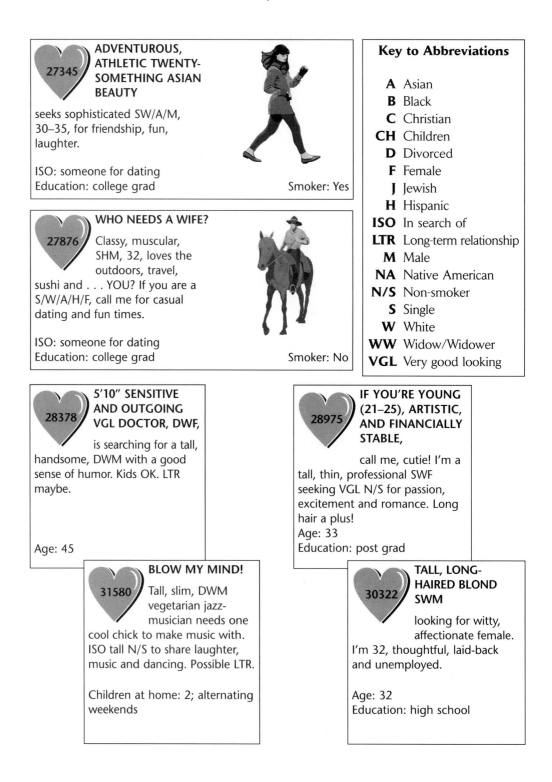

ADVENTUROUS, ATHLETIC TWENTY-SOMETHING ASIAN BEAUTY

27345

seeks sophisticated SW/A/M, 30–35, for friendship, fun, laughter.

ISO: someone for dating
Education: college grad

Smoker: Yes

Key to Abbreviations

A	Asian
B	Black
C	Christian
CH	Children
D	Divorced
F	Female
J	Jewish
H	Hispanic
ISO	In search of
LTR	Long-term relationship
M	Male
NA	Native American
N/S	Non-smoker
S	Single
W	White
WW	Widow/Widower
VGL	Very good looking

WHO NEEDS A WIFE?

27876 Classy, muscular, SHM, 32, loves the outdoors, travel, sushi and . . . YOU? If you are a S/W/A/H/F, call me for casual dating and fun times.

ISO: someone for dating
Education: college grad

Smoker: No

5'10" SENSITIVE AND OUTGOING VGL DOCTOR, DWF,

28378

is searching for a tall, handsome, DWM with a good sense of humor. Kids OK. LTR maybe.

Age: 45

IF YOU'RE YOUNG (21–25), ARTISTIC, AND FINANCIALLY STABLE,

28975

call me, cutie! I'm a tall, thin, professional SWF seeking VGL N/S for passion, excitement and romance. Long hair a plus!
Age: 33
Education: post grad

BLOW MY MIND!

31580 Tall, slim, DWM vegetarian jazz-musician needs one cool chick to make music with. ISO tall N/S to share laughter, music and dancing. Possible LTR.

Children at home: 2; alternating weekends

TALL, LONG-HAIRED BLOND SWM

30322

looking for witty, affectionate female. I'm 32, thoughtful, laid-back and unemployed.

Age: 32
Education: high school

ARE YOU SWEET, SMART, AND SPIRITUAL?
27988

Well-educated SBF seeks a S/B/A/M, 35–45, to share sunsets, sailing, and spirituality.

ISO: someone for dating
Age: 39
Smoker: No

VGL ATHLETIC SWM
28534

seeking an LTR with healthy, sensitive SBF 26–32 to share excitement, exploration, and deep thoughts.

Age: 41
Education: college grad

 ARE YOU MY GAL?
19845

Wealthy, professional DWM (tall, dark and handsome) seeks DWF C or J who looks like a model. Let's enjoy a sensitive and special LTR.

Age: 50
Education: post grad
Children at home: No

1. 27345 would make a good match for 27876 because

   a. they are both Asian.

   b. they are both looking for a casual relationship.

   c. they are both smokers.

2. 28378 and 31580 would make a good match because

   a. she's short.

   b. he's a vegetarian.

   c. they share a sense of humor.

3. 28975 would probably <u>not</u> enjoy meeting 30322 because

   a. he has long blond hair.

   b. he's too young.

   c. he's not financially stable.

4. 27988 and 28534 would <u>not</u> make a good match because

   a. she is black.

   b. she's too old.

   c. he's too old.

5. 19845 would rather meet

   a. 28975 because he is 50 and wants a long-term relationship.

   b. 28378 because she fits his description and is open to a long-term relationship.

> We are always talking about being together, and yet whatever we invent destroys the family, and makes us wild, touchless beasts feeding on technicolor prairies and rivers.
>
> Edward Dahlberg (1900–1977), U.S. author, critic

Thinking Together

The instructor will divide the class into two groups and distribute one set of numbered colored cards to each group. Work in pairs to write a personal ad seeking a partner, such as the one that follows, based on a fictitious person. Remember to use the key to abbreviations on page 146. The completed personal ads will be passed around the class. Each pair of students will choose the partners that best match the description in their ad, write down the card numbers, and pass the cards on. Share your matches and be ready to defend your choices.

Spark Up Your Life

Cheerful, charming, cultured NASWM in Mandeville, N/S, 5'9" 160, black hair, brown eyes, employed and ambitious ISO educated, intelligent 45–50 SNAF. Enjoys candlelight dinners, fireplace chats, cozy companionship. CH welcome. LTR possible.

Writing about It

*Write one to two paragraphs on one of the following topics. Try to use some of the vocabulary from this reading and from **Focusing In**.*

1. Discuss some of the myths about online dating that this article tries to disprove.

2. Pick two people from the ads that you think would make a good couple and explain why.

3. According to the article, there are several reasons why people might not want to use personal ads to meet strangers. Write a paragraph describing some of these reasons.

Reacting to the Reading

Has this article convinced you that online dating is a better way to meet people than traditional ways? Why or why not?

- The desire to "reach out and touch someone" has added a personal touch to technology. Computers offer access to chat lines, and television and radio have talk shows that encourage people in the audience to actively participate. Peter Theroux writes about Southern Californians' strong desire to stay in touch with their world while they commute to work.

- Read this article to see why talk shows are so popular in the United States. Do these reasons apply to people in other parts of the world?

Radio Activity

Peter Theroux

from *Avenues*

The Trend toward Talk

1   Whenever Southern Californians hit the road, it's the technology of the *Fireside Chat*[1] we seek. Drivers listen to the radio more than they listen to anything else, and Wall Street Journal research has shown that the better-educated among them listen to talk radio.

2   The morning and evening commutes are the motorist's equivalent of prime time. Some drivers talk back to the radio on their cell phones, expressing their opinions on various issues or perhaps dutifully reporting traffic conditions. This is the drive-time version of the fine art of conversation, since—in greater L.A., anyway—more than 80 percent of commuters travel alone.

3   And the trend is toward more talk, according to Tom Looney, one of Southern California's radio authorities. A self-proclaimed radio addict, Looney publishes an industry "fax-azine" five times a week called Talk Radio Replay. He also writes a monthly column, "The Looney Point of View," for Los Angeles Radio Guide. (The

Looney sermon always begins the same way: "Got the top down and my radio turned up loud.") "You even hear more talk on FM these days," Looney points out. "The big boast used to be 'More music. Less talk.' But now the stations are talking more. KROQ 106.7 has *Loveline*. There's more talk on KYSR 98.7, and KLSX 97.1 went all talk."

4   Southern California includes America's second-largest radio market (after New York), and its airwaves *encompass*[2] too diverse a population for its radio programming to stay traditional. The region's *cornucopia*[3] of talk radio offerings overflows day and night with news, celebrity interviews, psychoanalytic advice, and movie reviews, plus information about gardening, pets, travel, and sports.

5   For example, Michael Jackson's soft English voice has been purring over California's airwaves on KABC AM 790 for more than 30 years, mostly interviewing the top rank of celebrities: Placido Domingo, Cher, Charlton Heston, Gore Vidal, B. B. King, former U.N. Ambassador Abba Eban,

---

[1] *Fireside Chat* (proper n) informal radio talk made popular by President Franklin D. Roosevelt

[2] *encompass* (v) to include
[3] *cornucopia* (n) large supply, abundance

Hillary Rodham Clinton, and, you can safely say, just about everyone else.

6   Known for his courtliness and nonconfrontational manner with celebs, Jackson has had a simple motto for years: "enlighten, inform, entertain." But this doesn't mean he *shies away from*[4] straight, direct talk. He once asked mobster Mickey Cohen, "Did you ever kill anyone?" Cohen asked him to rephrase the question, whereupon Jackson replied, "Is there anyone no longer around as a result of some course of action you've taken?"

7   Lots of morning chatter is less serious than that on Jackson's show, of course—sometimes much less so. Whether they are inching over the Sepulveda Pass or through the Orange Crush, odds are that many of the commuters listening to local radio are tuned in to Mark and Brian—Mark Thompson and Brian Phelps, the quick-witted team on KLOS 95.5 FM from 5 A.M. to 10 A.M. "They're about the nicest morning radio guys," says Jo Beth McDaniel, a Long Beacher who commuted for several years to Westwood. "They have great guests, and they're fun. . . ."

8   For Spanish-speaking commuters, the equivalent to Mark and Brian's cheery morning chatter and pranksterism is *Humberto en la Manana*, the Humberto Luna show on all-talk Spanish radio KTNQ AM 1020, one of the most popular talk radio stations in the L.A. market. Luna, who has been on the air for more than 20 years, uses his *charisma*[5] and lighthearted sense of humor to attract callers of all ages. Luna's show, which airs from 5 A.M. to 10 A.M. Monday through Friday, recently converted to all talk. He used to play four or five records an hour,

but now he uses his flair for comedy to discuss local current events. "People like to call in and share experiences with me and with other listeners," Luna says. "Kids call in to tell me jokes. I let them as long as they promise not to be late for school. This is very much a family show."

9   And in case you hadn't noticed, talk radio isn't "just a guy thing anymore"—at least, not since the recent emergence of Tracey Miller and Robin Abcarian, "two chicks on the radio" who host a talk show from 5 A.M. to 9 A.M. on KMPC AM 710. The program is an easy mix of commentary by the two women on topics ranging from current political issues to lifestyle concerns, guest interviews, live cutaways to "woman in the street" interviewer Shelly Herman, and listener call-ins.

10   "We consider it our job to be informative and *provocative*,[6] to have opinions," says Abcarian, who considers herself a "bona fide feminist" and who also writes a column for the *Los Angeles Times*.

11   Miller, a veteran radio personality, thinks of herself as more politically moderate than Abcarian and regards the show as "an excellent alternative" to everything that's on at the same time. "We're not comedy-based and we're not *bombastic*,"[7] Miller says. "We're passionate about issues, and we want to get you thinking, but we don't want to hit you over the head."

12   The *Tracey and Robin Show* intentionally takes a woman's perspective, but the tone is congenial rather than confrontational or abrasive. Miller and Abcarian regularly chat on the air with "news guy" Joe West, the show's "*testosterone*[8] counterbalance," and

---

[4] *shy away from* (vp) to move away from something with fear or disgust
[5] *charisma* (n) charm and appeal

[6] *provocative* (adj) stimulating
[7] *bombastic* (adj) sounding overly important or grand
[8] *testosterone* (n) male hormone

on Fridays a regular feature is a tongue-in-cheek "Defend Your Gender" listener call-in segment. "Women's voices have been slighted for years in radio," Abcarian says. "We're happy that the station feels confident we can carry a show. Listener response has been very positive."

Moving into Midday

13   Much of the *bounty*[9] of Southern California's radio variety surfaces during midday. For instance, KFI offers an hour of medical advice from 2 to 3 in the afternoon with Dr. Dean Edell, about the time *Bookworm* with Michael Silverblatt of the highly rated *Marketplace* can be heard on KCRW. The eclectic tastes of Southern California radio listeners support more experimental *fare*[10] as well.

14   Southern California listeners launched KFI's Dr. Laura Schlessinger, whose advice to callers is now heard on about a dozen California stations. She "preaches, teaches, and *nags*"[11] on stations in New York, Boston, Chicago, and many other cities as well. Of KFI's talk show hosts, only Schlessinger and Michael Jackson make *USA Today*'s 1995 list of radio's top talkers nationwide. "She's second in popularity only to Rush Limbaugh [the ultra-conservative talk show host]," Looney says. "Her popularity grew very fast, and now she's in more than a hundred cities. She listens to her callers, and she's very direct. When there are family troubles, she asks, 'How are the kids?' She's very pro-kid. Her program on KFI is from noon until 2, because she has to pick her son up from school at 2:30. That's what she *espouses*.[12] Her son comes first."

The (Long and Winding) Road Home

15   After putting in a full day at work, Gil Bamford gets back in his car for the long drive home. His afternoon commute, like his morning one, is nearly ritualized. "I save my CDs for the weekend," Bamford says. From 5 to 6, he checks in on John and Ken on KFI—he enjoys the *irreverence*[13] and the chemistry of the expatriate *New Jerseyites*.[14]

16   Commuters such as Bamford often drive home tired, and many depend on their radios to keep them alert. The best way to do that, in the opinion of some, is to listen to something you hate—or something you love, which may account for the popularity of sports talk shows. If there's not a game to listen to, chances are you'll find sports fans tuning in—and maybe calling in—to one of the many afternoon sports programs.

The *Tracey and Robin Show* provides an avenue for women to voice their views on KMPC.

---

[9] *bounty* (n) plenty, a generous amount
[10] *fare* (n) choices
[11] *nag* (v) to remind someone repeatedly; to pester
[12] *espouse* (v) to believe in and support

[13] *irreverence* (n) lack of respect; poking fun at
[14] *New Jerseyites* (proper n) people from or living in New Jersey

17   "Prime Sports: the home of the HITS," bellows the promo spot on KWNK AM 670, followed by the loud crunch of bodies slamming against bodies. It's a fitting intro to Bob Golic's show: This relative newcomer to sports talk was a pro football player for 14 years. . . .

18   Golic uses contacts he's made in his college and pro years, often putting players and coaches on the air to comment on the previous night's game or the latest news. When Joe Delamielleure was nominated to the Hall of Fame, he called Golic—a former teammate—to discuss his career and the nomination. With Golic's show beaming out to more than 50 affiliates across the country, it's not just the local sports enthusiasts who are tuning in.

19   Radio programming that makes you think can also keep you attentive on the drive home. "Radio has a lot to offer, a lot of *spontaneous*[15] points of view," Gil Bamford says. "And you really listen— you're not distracted by appearances." His view is shared by an in-studio fan of radio whom Bamford frequently listens to.

20   "Radio is powerful and intimate," says Larry Elder, the self-styled Sage from South Central, who is poised to rule the afternoon drive-time airwaves. "You can do other things while you listen. And there's something of a bond, because it's interactive."

21   This African American, L.A.-born lawyer would seem an unlikely success story for California radio. The common wisdom is that in talk radio, anger is entertainment, but Elder is *urbane*[16] and rational. Ten months after moving into the drive-time slot at KABC, Elder pulled virtually even with KFI's mighty afternoon duo, John and Ken.

22   "Buuueeennnoosss tarrrrdes, Los An-he-les!" Elder calls into his mike (although he is heard as far away as San Diego and Canyon Country). The sharp, recorded *whack*[17] of a *gavel*[18] sounds. "Court is back in session!" Elder says, and then delivers a brief monologue, generally his take on some hot issue or the striking *hypocrisy*[19] of some public person or policy. He then informs his audience, "Ladies and gentlemen, you have just heard THE WORD. . . ."

23   Rick Lalor tunes to XTRA AM 690, all-sports radio. Albert Peyton is catching *Marketplace* on KUSC. Gil Bamford alternates between Larry Elder and John and Ken. Like nearly every motorist between San Ysidro and Death Valley, they carefully check the traffic updates, which now come thicker and faster. Everywhere, drivers who nine hours ago were making their way to work are navigating their way to the *hearthside*.[20] And, like a miniature North Star, the dimly illuminated dial on their dash is helping to keep them awake, entertained, informed, and safe.

---

[15] *spontaneous* (adj) not planned
[16] *urbane* (adj) well mannered and worldly
[17] *whack* (n) sharp blow or knock
[18] *gavel* (n) small wooden hammer used by officials to get attention or to bring order to a gathering

[19] *hypocrisy* (n) act of saying one thing while believing or doing another
[20] *hearthside* (n) kitchen fireplace, symbol of home and family

Understanding the Reading: Fact versus Opinion

A. *Using the information in the article, label the following statements fact (**F**) or opinion (**O**).*

_____ 1. Commuters who are well educated tend to listen to talk radio.

_____ 2. It is amazing that more than 80 percent of commuters travel alone.

_____ 3. Talk shows can provide information and advice on gardening and pets.

_____ 4. Talk shows help keep drivers alert.

_____ 5. Mark and Brian invite really interesting guests to speak on their show.

_____ 6. Southern California has diverse, nontraditional radio programming.

_____ 7. Talk shows appeal to both male and female listeners.

_____ 8. Listening to talk radio broadens the mind.

_____ 9. Spanish-speaking commuters enjoy *Humberto en la Manana*.

_____10. More and more celebrities should host talk radio shows.

B. *Work with a partner to fill in this chart with the missing information (station, frequency, program topics, hosts).*

Talk Radio Programs

KTNQ

790
Interview celebrities

710
Women's issues

KLOS
morning commute
Mark and Brian

> The new electronic independence re-creates the world in the image of a global village.
>
> Marshall McLuhan (1911–1980), Canadian author

Using the Vocabulary: Phrasal Verbs

A **phrasal verb** is an idiomatic expression made up of a **verb + adverb** (*down, up, on*) or **verb + preposition** (*in, for, to*): *depend on, walk down,* for example. The addition of the adverbs/prepositions can change the meaning of the verb: *get on / get off, look up to / look down on.*

A. *Circle the correct preposition or adverb to complete the phrasal verbs in this exercise. Make sure to pay attention to the context. When you are finished, highlight the phrasal verbs in the reading with a colored pen or marker.*

1. My best friend *listens* _____ several talk radio shows.
   (for, to, in)

2. Today's talk radio audience *accounts* _____ a large percentage of commuters.
   (for, to)

3. While driving, they regularly *switch* _____ the radio to get the weather report.
   (on, off, to)

4. Then they *tune* _____ to their favorite radio stations.
   (in, on, out)

5. On their way to work, many commuters *put* _____ time listening to traffic updates.
   (in, on, off)

6. If they become unhappy with one topic, they can easily *convert* _____ another.
   (from, to, into)

7. For instance, Bill Handel never *shies* _____ or avoids controversy.
   (away from, at)

8. He *talks* _____ his listeners and sometimes insults them.
   (at, back to, over)

9. Many people enjoy listening to Dr. Laura Schlessinger, so they *call* _____ to ask for advice.
   (off, in, out)

10. Rita Juarez, for example, recently *heard* _____ cancer treatments on a local radio station.
    (about, on, out)

> I find television very educational. Every time someone switches it on I go into another room and read a good book.
>
> Groucho Marx
> (1895–1977),
> U.S. comic actor

B. *Now complete this paragraph with the correct phrasal verbs from Exercise A.*

Talk radio is enormously popular across the nation. While inching through traffic, many commuters like to (1)_____ their radios and (2)_____ to their favorite station. They can (3)_____ and voice their opinions on various issues to the hosts and guests. On some of these talk shows, the audience can (4)_____ discussions of very controversial topics. The hosts argue about issues, (5)_____ their listeners, and openly challenge them to respond. Their audience can depend on them to surprise and shock listeners because they never (6)_____ from confrontation.

Thinking Together

In groups of four, talk about radio and television talk shows in the United States and in other countries. Choose one member to act as the talk show host. Choose a controversial topic to discuss. Then write a dialogue that you might imagine would take place on a talk radio show. Be prepared to put on a short performance for your class.

Writing about It

*Write one to two paragraphs on one of the following topics. Try to use some of the vocabulary from this reading and from **Focusing In**.*

1. In his article, Peter Theroux states that "morning and evening commutes are the motorist's equivalent of prime time. . . . This is the drive-time version of the fine art of conversation." Write a paragraph explaining why radio talk shows are so popular in the United States. Use the information in the article to help you.

2. Write a letter to the newspaper describing the advantages or disadvantages of radio talk shows.

3. Imagine yourself as a talk show host or hostess. Describe the type of program you would like to have and what celebrities or guests you would invite on the air.

Reacting to the Reading

Is listening to radio talk shows or watching talk shows on television a waste of time? Why or why not?

Keeping Track of Your Reading Rate

- The following passage is from *Oprah!*, a book by Robert Waldron on the popular talk show host Oprah Winfrey.
- When your instructor gives you the signal to begin, read the story at a rapid speed and mark down the time as soon as you are done. Then answer the questions without looking back at the reading.

> **tip** Reading word by word slows you down. Reading in meaningful phrases helps speed up the reading process.

When asked by *USA Today* if the upcoming premiere of "The Oprah Winfrey Show" made her edgy, Oprah answered, "If I'm tense, I'll be open about it. I'll tell the audience, 'Hey, this is a pretty big deal!'". . .

"A lot of people didn't know what to expect, but all the response we have gotten so far has been very positive," Jack Mazzie, vice president and general manager of WEEK-TV told Robert Feder of *The Chicago Sun-Times*. He added that viewers thought Oprah was "bouncy, full of life, very vital, and extremely intelligent." . . . Bill Mann of *The Oakland Tribune* wrote "Oprah isn't so full of herself that she'll avoid asking the question most viewers would like to ask."

The talk shows are stuffed full of sufferers who have regained their health.

Calvin Trillin (1935–), U.S. journalist

. . . When Oprah appeared on "Nightlife" with David Brenner, he kidded her about some of the guests that have appeared on her show. "I saw transsexual parents, gay bashers," said David Brenner.

"People make fun of talk shows because we do transsexuals and their parents," Oprah responded. "But I feel if something is going on in the world and it is happening to somebody, maybe somebody else is interested in it. I really think you can do anything with good taste."

"Let me just say this," Oprah added later, "because talk shows get a bad rap, all the time, about doing these sensational things. But we also do some incredible shows that make a difference in people's lives. We did a show with children of divorced parents, with children crying, because it was the first chance they had had to express their feelings about it. We did a show with people who were terminally ill and won't be around six weeks from now. We did a show with women who had been dumped by their husbands. . . . With all the poking fun of it and everything, which I know critics like to do, but to the people that these things happen to, it is very serious."

. . . Despite her success, Oprah told "Entertainment Tonight," "People don't treat me like a star or a celebrity. They treat me like I'm one of them. . . ." Of course, with the phenomenal success of "The Oprah Winfrey Show," Oprah differed from her audience in a very significant way. In December 1986, *Variety* reported that Oprah could become the highest-paid performer in show business, earning even more than Johnny Carson or Bill Cosby. It was estimated her salary could reach as high as $31 million.

(400 words)   TIME _____

Now mark these statements true (T) or false (F) without looking back at the reading.

_____ 1. Oprah was not even afraid to be open and honest with the audience at her premiere.

_____ 2. Oprah Winfrey is quiet and shy.

_____ 3. The public response to the premiere of "The Oprah Winfrey Show" was negative.

_____ 4. Oprah asks her guests questions that she thinks viewers would like to ask.

_____ 5. According to Oprah, talk shows do not have bad reputations.

_____ 6. Talk shows often get criticized for focusing on sensational topics.

_____ 7. Oprah feels that talk shows can help people.

_____ 8. One of Oprah's shows featured terminally ill people.

_____ 9. "The Oprah Winfrey Show" has been only slightly successful.

_____10. Oprah may be the highest-paid entertainer in her profession.

Percent correct = _____   wpm = _____

MAKING CONNECTIONS

Responding to the Readings

Prepare short oral or written responses based on your personal experience and your reactions to the readings. Try to incorporate the information and the vocabulary you have learned in this chapter.

1. Do you and other people in your country enjoy listening to talk shows on the radio? What type of shows do most people listen to?

2. Explain who decides what American movies and TV shows can be seen in your country.

3. Write to one of the people in the ads in "Online Dating" on pages 146–147 explaining why you think she or he could meet a friend of yours. Make your letter serious or humorous.

4. Explain some of the possible dangers of online dating.

5. Do you think people can become addicted to the Internet? How can spending too much time online affect your life?

6. Have you ever had any experience with censorship of movies, television, radio, newspaper, or computer information?

7. Discuss your reaction to one of the quotes or facts in the margins of this chapter that you find most interesting or surprising.

Editing Your Work

*A student wrote this paragraph on computers without editing carefully for articles. Remember that an **article** (a/an/the) precedes singular count nouns. **The** precedes all superlatives (the best, the longest). Articles are also part of some expressions of quantity such as* a few, a lot of, one of the men, *and* a great deal of. *Edit this paragraph by inserting the five missing articles.*

Without the computer, we would still be in the Dark Ages. Computer has helped people to have better lives and better living conditions. It can do things faster than people can. The computer has also helped advance our communication and transportation systems. As we become more advanced, we need more computer engineers to create a better world for future. There will be lot of jobs for computer engineers. This is excellent career for someone who enjoys cyberspace. Computer Engineering is one of best majors for me.

> Thank God we're living in a country where the sky's the limit, the stores are open late and you can shop in bed thanks to television.
>
> Joan Rivers (1935–), U.S. comedian

Writing an Essay

Choose one of the following topics and write an essay. As a prewriting activity, read over your shortwrites and notes for inspiration. Remember to review the brainstorming techniques on pages 262–263. In your essay, use the readings, factoids, quotes, class discussions, and personal experience to support your ideas. Try to use the vocabulary you have learned in this chapter. If you choose to write a research paper, make certain to cite your sources clearly.

1. Write an essay on the types of television or radio programs that are popular in your country. Discuss television or radio in general and then choose a few specific programs to discuss in detail. Classify the programs and what type of audience they are particularly popular with. Discuss the programs that are produced nationally and those that are imported from other countries. Talk about your own favorite program as well.

2. Write an essay discussing the types of information accessible to people today and the debate over the need for limits. Is it dangerous for people to be able to access anything they want on the Internet? Should people be allowed to read banned literature, meet strangers, and learn to build bombs simply by surfing the net? Should the governments around the world establish guidelines and pass laws to limit such access? How would such an idea be accepted in the United States? in your country?

3. Compare and contrast the ways technology is used in everyday life in the United States and in other countries. What types of technology are most common? For example, does every home have a dishwasher, a television, a telephone, and a computer? Do people have cell phones and laptop computers? What forms of technology are becoming more widely used? Compare this to some of the points raised in the readings.

4. Write an essay discussing the ways technology has influenced society in your country. Include all aspects of society including school, business, and home life. How has technology influenced the way you live, study, and work? Discuss how you think it will change people's lives.

5. Research one technological advancement such as telephones, radios, computers, or satellites. Find information about its discovery and development. What people were involved in its conception and growth? What areas of society does this product affect or influence? Would you say this technology has improved or hurt society in general?

Cox Communications Cable TV in Southern California offers over 100 television stations to its subscribers.

Finding More Information

Magazines and Journals

Information Week
Wired
Talkers Magazine
Mixmatch
PC Magazine

Books

Banks, Laura, *Love Online*
Gates, Bill, *The Road Ahead*
Kidder, T., *The Soul of a New Machine*
Toffler, Alvin, *Future Shock*
Waldron, Robert, *Oprah!*

The World Wide Web

www.cdt.org—Center for Democracy and Technology
www.hotwired.com—Hotwired Defining the Web
www.match.com—Match.Com Online Matchmaking
www.sscl.uwo.ca/explore/#computers—Computer and Technology links
www.tvtalkshows.com—TV Talk Show links

Movies and Videos

Hackers
The Net
Sleepless in Seattle
The Truth about Cats and Dogs
You've Got Mail

> The medium is the message. This is merely to say that the personal and social consequences of any medium—that is, of any extension of ourselves—result from the new scale that is introduced into our affairs by each extension of ourselves, or by any new technology.
>
> Marshall McLuhan (1911–1980), Canadian author

Making History

> The ordinary man is involved in action, the hero acts. An immense difference.
>
> Henry Miller (1891–1980), U.S. author, *The Books in My Life*

Out of the struggles and hard work of immigrants and pioneers, the American hero emerged. Sam Wilson, the man on whom "Uncle Sam" is based, symbolizes one definition of the American hero—the common man who succeeds through his own efforts and hard work. This quintessential American personifies all that the ideal American is supposed to be—self-made, good-natured, imaginative, charitable, and religious. Another American hero is the "lone ranger" who comes into town, saves someone in distress, and rides off into the sunset. Yet another is the person who helps ensure that everyone has a chance to achieve the American Dream of prosperity and security. Because America is very protective of its freedoms, heroes are also defined as those who defy rules and regulations or who speak out for or act on their beliefs.

More recently, the unsung hero has become more appreciated. As pointed out by Peggy Noonan, presidential speechwriter and author, "Most people aren't appreciated enough, and the bravest things we do in our lives are usually known only to ourselves. No one throws ticker tape on the man who chose to be faithful to his wife, on the lawyer who didn't take the drug money, or the daughter who held her tongue again and again. All this is anonymous heroism."

This chapter presents a number of American heroes, some who are well known and some who are not. The American Red Cross, described here in its own publication, epitomizes the volunteer spirit. *Jackie Robinson*, by Avonie Brown, highlights one outstanding American who broke racial barriers in one of the country's favorite sports. In the *New York Times* article, "Lawbreakers We Have Known and Loved," readers will catch a glimpse of some acts they may or may not consider heroic. The last passage reminds readers of a more traditional hero—Amelia Earhart.

Do you know what it takes to be an American hero? Discuss this question in small groups. Then talk about the picture on page 160 and answer the question: *Do you know who this man is and what he represents?*

How Heroic Are You?

Check all the statements you think are true about yourself. Calculate your score. Then, with a partner try to match the name of an American with each description.

☐ ____ 1. I would risk my life making speeches in front of people who disagreed with my ideas.

☐ ____ 2. I would jump a motorcycle over a row of cars.

☐ ____ 3. I would play on a sports team even if half of the players didn't want me to.

☐ ____ 4. I can leap tall buildings in a single bound.

☐ ____ 5. I would stand up for the rights of women.

☐ ____ 6. I would try to fly a plane around the world alone.

☐ ____ 7. I would risk a civil war to free people from injustice.

☐ ____ 8. I would be brave enough to walk on the moon.

☐ ____ 9. I would never tell a lie.

☐ ____10. I would dedicate my life to helping those in need.

a. George Washington

b. Neil Armstrong

c. Evel Knievel

d. Susan B. Anthony

e. Dr. Martin Luther King, Jr.

f. Superman

g. Abraham Lincoln

h. Jackie Robinson

i. Amelia Earhart

j. Clara Barton

Score: 1–3: Not too heroic   7–9: A true hero
         4–6: On the road to heroism   10! Can we have your autograph?

Test Your Word Power

Take this vocabulary quiz. Then compare your answers with a partner so you will be better prepared to understand the readings.

____ 1. heroic (adj.)

____ 2. feat (n)

____ 3. assassination (n)

____ 4. idealize (v)

____ 5. fascinate (v)

____ 6. idol (n)

____ 7. daredevil (n)

____ 8. self-made (adj)

a. one who is greatly admired

b. successful due to one's own efforts, not due to money or help from others

c. murder of someone (usually a political figure)

d. act of bravery or great deed

e. showing courage or unusual ability

f. one who takes risks to perform difficult acts

g. to think of something as better than it really is

h. to interest greatly, to command attention

- In 1835, the famous French historian Alexis de Tocqueville wrote that Americans have "an inclination to organize nonpolitical groups to achieve common purposes." Americans respect those unsung heroes who, in spite of being driven by the belief that "time is money," find time to volunteer, working without pay to help better the lives of others.
- This article outlines the history of one of America's oldest and most revered charities. As you read this article, try to remember any circumstances you have heard of when the American Red Cross helped people in need. Are you aware of any work that the Red Cross has done in your country?

The History of the American Red Cross

from the American Red Cross Organization

The Early Years of the American Red Cross, Pre-1900

1   In October 1863, The International Red Cross and Red Crescent Movement was created in Geneva, Switzerland, to provide *nonpartisan*[1] care to the wounded and sick in times of war. The Red Cross *emblem*[2] was adopted at this first International Conference as a symbol of *neutrality*[3] and was to be used by national relief societies. . . .

2   The founding of the American Red Cross in 1881 was due to the devotion and dedication of Clara Barton. Because the American Association of the Red Cross depended solely on volunteer help and public contributions to conduct its work, it was important to *rally*[4] public support of the organization, especially during disasters. Directly supervising the operations, Clara Barton sometimes brought Red Cross *relief*[5] workers to the scenes of disasters and rallied local volunteers to *alleviate*[6] the pain and suffering of victims. In 1884, as flood waters raged along the Ohio and Mississippi Rivers, six children initiated the first known Red Cross youth activity in Waterford, Pennsylvania. The children produced a play in their town and raised $50.00, which Clara Barton reportedly used to help a large family that suffered greatly from the flood. In the letter accompanying their contribution, the children wrote: "Sometime again when you want money to help you in your good work, call on the Little Six."

The American Red Cross Enters the Twentieth Century, 1900–1919

3   In the early 1900s, the Red Cross developed safety awareness and health care practices that would help Americans help themselves, including services

Let your heart feel for the affliction and distress of everyone; let your hand give in proportion to your purse, remembering always the estimation of the widow's plight.

George Washington
(1732–1797),
first U.S. president

---

[1] *nonpartisan* (adj) not representing just one side or viewpoint
[2] *emblem* (n) symbol
[3] *neutrality* (n) condition of being neutral, not siding with anyone
[4] *rally* (v) to gather together in support of something
[5] *relief* (n) aid
[6] *alleviate* (v) to soften; to reduce; to ease

in nursing, first aid, and water safety. Christmas Seals were created to fund the battle against *tuberculosis*.[7] To highlight the importance of safe usage of railroads and streetcars, the Red Cross printed over 60,000 posters that were hung in railroad stations and on trolley cars urging people to take precautions against accidents. Red Cross President Mabel Boardman's philosophy guided the organization—an ounce of prevention is worth a pound of cure.

4   The First World War helped transform the American Red Cross into a powerful social force. At the onset of the war, the American Red Cross had 562 *chapters*[8] and about 500,000 members. Millions of volunteers joined the Red Cross, and by the end of the war, there were 3,724 chapters, 17,000 branches, and over 31 million members (including children and adults). Within weeks of the outbreak of the war in Europe in 1914, the Red Cross sent a mercy ship on a short mission to provide assistance to soldiers of all nationalities, marking the beginning of wartime service that continued until 1916. After the United States went to war in 1917, the American Red Cross focused its attention on American soldiers. Red Cross staff and volunteers tended to the needs of the wounded and sick, and the able-bodied and disabled veterans. Institutes for the blind and the crippled were opened, and valuable contributions were made in veterans hospitals. When the *armistice*[9] was signed in France in 1918, Red Cross personnel were scattered from the British Isles to Siberia's far reaches.

> **Society is looking for new heroes.**
>
> Edward James Olmos, U.S. actor, Hispanic leader

The American Red Cross: Still the Greatest Mother in the World, 1920–1939

5   Following the First World War, the American Red Cross faced new challenges. Public support and the number of volunteers for the organization decreased, but the great demand for services continued. . . . Reorganization was necessary if the Red Cross was to survive. Starting in 1921, under its new chairman Judge John Barton Payne, the Red Cross showed that it could survive and be strong without war, and without reliance on emergency work to justify its existence. Payne believed that if the Red Cross was to endure and prosper, it must satisfy social demands not met by other agencies. Staff and volunteers worked together to achieve Payne's vision, and the Red Cross regained its former popularity.

American Red Cross volunteers provide disaster relief to home owners following hurricanes, floods, and tornadoes.

---

[7] *tuberculosis* (n) disease of the lungs
[8] *chapter* (n) group that belongs to the same organization
[9] *armistice* (n) treaty of peace; truce

> A nation reveals itself not only by the men it produces but also by the men it honors, the men it remembers.
>
> John F. Kennedy
> (1917–1963),
> U.S. president

Between 1923 and 1939, the Red Cross responded to calls for help from victims of floods, drought, and the Great Depression, as it commenced preparation to provide assistance to the victims of another world war.

The American Red Cross: Through Fire and Storm, 1940–1959

6   As the Second World War began, the doors of Red Cross chapters were thrown open to thousands of new volunteers who wanted an outlet for their frustration over Japan's surprise attack on Pearl Harbor. The Red Cross quickly expanded its services to the *armed forces*,[10] *recruiting*[11] nurses on behalf of the military, as well as more social workers and recreation specialists to ease the discomfort of civilians being drafted.

7   In January 1941, the Red Cross blood donor project was organized at the request of the Surgeon General of the Army and Navy. During the four-year period beginning in February 1941, when the Blood Donor Service was established in New York City, six million Americans donated blood. During the Second World War, millions of Americans joined the Red Cross effort as volunteers in the Nurse's Aide Corps, the Gray Lady Service, the Junior Red Cross, the Hospital and Recreation Corps, and in other services benefiting the armed services and the war effort.

8   The 1950s were marked with labor *disputes*[12] and chronic unemployment, as well as natural and man-made disasters. Throughout the time period, the Red Cross *persevered*[13] and volunteers continued to give their time and money to help provide relief to citizens of the United States and the world at large.

A New Frontier: Volunteers, Vietnam, and the Age of Technology, 1960–1979

9   The period between 1960 and 1979 was marked by rapid social and technological change. The Civil Rights Movement, labor disputes, chronic unemployment, and the Vietnam War marked some of the divisions within American society. As new technologies emerged, the Red Cross relied increasingly on radio communications, computers, and satellites. The new technology also forced the Red Cross to solve problems caused by man-made *calamities*,[14] such as chemical plant accidents, oil spills, and the first nuclear accident at Three Mile Island. Red Cross chapters provided assistance to veterans returning from Vietnam, as well as tens of thousands of Vietnamese refugees, the elderly, the mentally ill, and other forgotten segments of society. In spite of Red Cross continued involvement in numerous activities, two Harris polls in 1973 and 1976 revealed that few Americans understood the vital role that the organization played in their daily lives.

---

[10] *armed forces* (n) military (Navy, Coast Guard, Marines, Army)
[11] *recruit* (v) to search out in order to hire or sign up
[12] *dispute* (n) fight; disagreement
[13] *persevere* (v) to persist; to carry on
[14] *calamity* (n) disaster

10   In 1964, Chairman E. Roland Harriman proposed a plan at the National Convention to end distinctions among Red Cross volunteers, a dream that would not be realized completely for ten years. He stated that the organization needed volunteers who could serve the whole Red Cross rather than just a segment of the organization. To cease differentiation among chapters and Red Cross volunteers, a standard light blue uniform with a Red Cross *insignia*[15] became the official uniform. Young people, retirees, minorities, and the underprivileged were all encouraged to join its volunteers corps as the Red Cross expanded its activities into federal programs such as Headstart and VISTA. By 1974, Harriman's dream of just "one Red Cross" was realized.

The American Red Cross: Into a New Century, 1980 to the Present

11   Entering its second century, the American Red Cross continued its tradition of providing relief to victims of natural and man-made disasters. One hundred years had passed since Barton had carried in her purse the funds to conduct the tiny Red Cross operations. The organization had greatly expanded from the small association founded by Clara Barton in 1881. Yet, the millions of relief workers of the 1980s and 1990s were motivated by the same concern for human life and well-being as the relief workers who had provided aid during the first American Red Cross relief efforts. An early 1990s national survey by Yankelovich Partners showed that the American Red Cross was the most highly regarded of major U.S. charities, and *Money* magazine named the Red Cross one of the ten best-managed charities in the country. Proud as the Red Cross is of its achievements, the organization *endeavored*[16] continuously to prepare itself and to make its service efforts more efficient and more effective.

Understanding the Reading: Outlining

*To **outline** is to provide a summary sketch of a reading. Imagine you will have a test on the American Red Cross. Prepare an outline to help you study the information. Use the bold titles in the reading to help you organize the information.*

I. The Early Years of the American Red Cross, Pre-1900

    A. International Red Cross and Red Crescent Movement

        1. Year: _____

        2. Purpose: to provide nonpartisan care to the wounded and sick during war

    B. American Red Cross

        1. Year: 1881

        2. Founder: _____

• **H I N T** •

Creating an outline is a useful study guide. Use the bold headings and italicized words in your textbooks to help you create an outline.

---

[15] *insignia* (n) symbol; emblem
[16] *endeavor* (v) to try or attempt

> I think of a hero as someone who understands the degree of responsibility that comes with his freedom.
>
> Bob Dylan (1941–),
> U.S. singer, songwriter

II. The American Red Cross Enters the Twentieth Century, 1900–1919

   A. Early 1900s safety awareness and health care practices

      1. Nursing

      2. _____

      3. _____

   B. Red Cross president Mabel Boardman's philosophy: _____

      _____

   C. First World War activities

      1. _____

      2. _____

III. _____

   A. New challenges following First World War

      1. Decrease in _____

      2. Meeting the demand for services

   B. Chairman Payne, 1921, and his vision to satisfy social demands and justify the existence of the Red Cross

   C. Work between 1923 and 1939; responding to calls for help from victims of:

      1. _____

      2. _____

      3. _____

IV. The American Red Cross: Through Fire and Storm, 1940–1959

   A. Second World War activities

      1. Recruiting nurses

      2. _____

   B. Volunteer Groups

      1. Nurse's Aide Corps

      2. _____

      3. _____

      4. _____

   C. Problems during the 1950s

      1. Labor disputes

      2. Chronic unemployment

V. _____

   A. Red Cross solves problems caused by man-made disasters

      1. _____

      2. Oil spills

      3. _____

B. Red Cross chapters provide assistance to:

1. _____

2. Mentally ill

3. _____

C. Chairman Harriman's changes

1. Emphasis on unity

2. _____

VI. The American Red Cross: Into a New Century, 1980 to the Present

A. Tradition: _____

B. Public opinion: _____

C. Continuous endeavors to stay prepared, efficient, and effective

Using the Vocabulary: Suffixes

In Chapter 3 (page 62), you learned three common noun endings: *-ment*, *-er*, and *-ion*. Other noun endings include *-ity* and *-ance/-ence*. Some verbs can be changed to nouns with *-ence/-ance* (*disturb–disturbance*). Some adjectives can be changed to nouns by adding *-ity* (*national–nationality*).

A. *Fill in the charts with the noun form of the following adjectives and verbs. Make any necessary spelling changes.*

Adjective	Noun
able	
active	
charitable	
flexible	
neutral	
popular	

Verb	Noun
assist	
exist	
rely	

American awards include the Carnegie Hero Medal, the J. C. Penney National Volunteer Award, and the Presidential Medal of Freedom.

> The final test of a leader is that he leaves behind him in other men the conviction and the will to carry on.
>
> Walter Lippman, U.S. essayist, in a tribute to President Franklin D. Roosevelt

B. *Complete this paragraph using the nouns from the charts in Exercise A. Make them plural when necessary.*

In 1881, due to the devotion and dedication of Clara Barton, the American Red Cross came into (1)_____. Over the years, citizens of the United States have come to rely on the generosity and bravery of American Red Cross volunteers. These volunteers have come to the (2)_____ of countless Americans during natural disasters, civil disturbances, and wars. Some Red Cross (3)_____ include first aid and CPR training, blood donor drives, and HIV/AIDS education. Because of its (4)_____, the Red Cross is also able to enter any country at war to lend a hand and ease human suffering. In spite of difficult times over the past 100 years, the (5)_____ of this humanitarian organization has helped it grow into one of the most highly regarded charities in the world.

Thinking Together

In a small group, make a list of volunteer and relief organizations around the world with which you are familiar. Compare and contrast these organizations with the Red Cross. What needs do these groups help meet? What is the biggest organization? Does your group think that people do enough to help others, or is there more work that needs to be done? Discuss your findings with the class.

Writing about It

Write one to two paragraphs on one of the following topics. Try to use some of the vocabulary from this reading and from **Focusing In***.*

1. Using your outline from **Understanding the Reading** (pp. 165–167), summarize the changes in the Red Cross that have taken place during the last century.

2. Describe some of the problems the American Red Cross had to contend with during the early twentieth century. According to the article, why was it important that the organization solve these difficulties?

3. Write a letter from an American Red Cross volunteer trying to recruit young people to join the work to help others around the world.

Reacting to the Reading

Do you think schools should require all students to work for the benefit of those in need, by participating in programs such as tutoring, running clothing drives, and feeding the homeless? Why or why not?

- American heroes can be presidents, scientists, volunteers, or athletes. Baseball player Jackie Robinson died in 1972, but in 1997 people across America celebrated the fiftieth anniversary of his first game with the Brooklyn Dodgers. Avonie Brown describes Robinson's legacy here.
- Do you know why Jackie Robinson is considered an American hero? Read this article to find out what contribution he made to baseball and to American history.

Jackie Robinson

A V O N I E   B R O W N

from afroam.org

1   Jackie Robinson is a legendary figure and his name is now synonymous with the *desegregation*[1] and redefinition of professional sports. Yet, our collective knowledge of the historical process that created this American icon has been reduced to an occasional *"color commentary."*[2]

2   Jackie Robinson and Branch Rickey, owner of the Brooklyn Dodgers, are forever linked in American history. Rickey understood the *psyche*[3] of white America. While Rickey's motives are still unclear, history has proven that his "great experiment" to *integrate*[4] baseball ultimately had less to do with baseball and more to do with challenging deep-seated attitudes about race.

3   The process had to be systematic, and Jackie Robinson not only had to have all the required physical and emotional *assets*,[5] he had to be willing to make the necessary sacrifices. Sam Lacy, the *AFRO-American's* sports editor from 1944 through the present, confirms that while Jackie Robinson was not the most talented black player in the Negro Leagues, he was the best choice for integrating the Major Leagues. Like Rickey, Mr. Lacy believed that Jackie's early experiences playing and working with whites at UCLA [University of California, Los Angeles] and in the Army gave him an understanding many other black players did not have, as most had only lived and played in segregated arenas.

4   The racial divide was rigidly practiced and reinforced by white America in the most elemental human experiences: where you drank water, ate, sat, used the bathroom and even where and with whom you interacted. Consequently, because of this racial divide, black athletes were forced to establish their own professional teams and leagues as early as 1920.

> A life is not important except in the impact it has on other lives.
>
> Jackie Robinson (1919–1972), U.S. baseball player

---

[1] *desegregation* (n) end of a system in which members of different races are kept separate
[2] *color commentary* (np) statement about race relations
[3] *psyche* (n) human mind or spirit
[4] *integrate* (v) to put different types of people together
[5] *asset* (n) quality

> Heroes are people who struggle and do more than what is asked of them and their particular set of skills. That is to say, Babe Ruth is not a hero but Jackie Robinson is. You are really looking for that which will make a deposit in the sum of human progress and Jackie Robinson certainly does.
>
> Ken Burns,
> U.S. baseball historian

5   The Negro Leagues provided a showcase of the very best black players throughout the country and a popular social occasion for the community. Players had to be competitive and versatile. They played multiple positions as rosters were small; wages fluctuated, and road trips were long and potentially dangerous, especially in rigidly segregated southern towns.

6   White owners profited also from the Negro Leagues because in some cities, black teams had to rent these stadiums, at inflated rates, to play their games. In addition, competition against a Negro League team and a Major League team attracted a large and curious crowd to the ballpark.

7   After leaving the Army, Jackie joined the Kansas City Monarchs, a Negro League team, in April 1945. He was paid $400 a month to play *shortstop*.[6] In 41 games with the Monarchs, Robinson batted .345 with ten *doubles, four triples, and five home runs*,[7] and was chosen to play in the annual All-Star Game. Jackie got to play against some of the leagues' greatest players like Satchel Paige, Josh Gibson and Cool Papa Bell. Unlike most players in the Negro Leagues, whose athletic *finesse*[8] *languished*[9] in relative *obscurity*,[10] Jackie was noticed by *scouts*[11] for Branch Rickey of the Brooklyn Dodgers. In October 1945 he met with Branch Rickey for the first time.

8   When Jackie turned up in Cuba for the 1947 spring training, several Dodger players signed a petition refusing to play. Their protest was short-lived because Rickey threatened to fire all the protesters. Games on the road were especially difficult: Jackie couldn't room with the white players in some towns, and fans and rival players took every opportunity to target Jackie. His first series with Philadelphia was one such brutal occasion. Led by manager Ben Chapman, the Phillies verbally *assaulted*[12] Robinson with *racial slurs*[13] every time he would go on the field. But, from his first game with the Montreal Royals in April 1946, until the 1949 season, Jackie was forced to passively respond to racist taunts and threats. In fact, the required silence was his most difficult sacrifice, as it went against how he had chosen to live his life.

9   Runners intentionally went after him, when he played at second base, and occasionally *spiked*[14] him. In St. Louis, the Cardinals tried to organize a *strike*[15] against Jackie and the Dodgers in 1947, hoping other teams would follow suit. But the story was leaked and National League president Ford

---

[6] *shortstop* (n) position in baseball between second and third base.
[7] *double* (n) hit that advances runner to second base; *triple* (n) hit to third base; *home run* (n) hit that advances runner around all three bases and scores a run
[8] *finesse* (n) fine skill and smoothness
[9] *languish* (v) to be without energy or spirit
[10] *obscurity* (n) condition of not being seen or well known
[11] *scout* (n) person looking for talented people
[12] *assault* (v) to attack
[13] *racial slur* (n) unkind statement against someone from another racial group
[14] *spike* (v) to hit someone with the bottom of a shoe that has sharp points
[15] *strike* (n) work stoppage

Frick defended Jackie and threatened to *suspend*[16] any player that went on strike. Fellow teammates like Pee Wee Reese also publicly defended Jackie's right to play.

10   But, through it all Jackie remained silent even though he wanted to respond verbally and physically. Jackie was forced to honor the two-year agreement he had with Rickey. Rickey insisted that Jackie could not respond to any of the inevitable racial taunts or attacks; he had to live a life on the field and off that was *circumspect*[17] and without fault, so as not to further *infuriate*[18] whites and *derail*[19] the integration experiment.

11   Jackie and the black community had to bear the burden for the morality of the white community. Rickey even met with black community leaders and erected signs in the black section of the ballpark, encouraging black spectators to control their own behavior and not respond to any expressed racism. He believed that the actions of black spectators could affect Jackie's acceptance by the white community.

"Once Jackie broke the color barrier, I guess the thinking was that if you could break it in baseball, anything else was possible."—Sharpe Jones, mayor of Newark, N.J.

12   Threats on his life were the most severe of racist attacks. In 1951, Jackie received one particularly threatening letter warning against playing at Crosley field in Cincinnati. The FBI investigated the threats and undercover agents were assigned to patrol the stadium. Fortunately, the game proceeded without incident.

13   Jackie did not let racist ignorance stop him from performing or, eventually, from speaking out against injustice. The key to his success was his ability to challenge injustice without compromising his personal *integrity*[20] and beliefs. When he was free to speak out, it became clear that he had his own athletic and political agenda to *pursue*.[21] Throughout the whole experience, especially in his final years in baseball, he used his athletic stature and popularity to turn society's focus towards humanity and equality for blacks and whites.

14   Today with the *dominance*[22] of black players in professional sports, it seems *unfathomable*[23] that just under 50 years ago not only were black athletes absent in all mainstream sporting arenas, it was simply not an option and even illegal in some states. Robinson is heroic, in part, because of the excellence of his athletic achievement; and equally important, for his political commitment to racial equality. He reaffirms for blacks in America that ours is a history of struggle, survival and accomplishment.

---

[16] *suspend* (v) to take away someone's membership; to stop
[17] *circumspect* (adj) cautious; guarded
[18] *infuriate* (v) to make very angry
[19] *derail* (v) to send off course
[20] *integrity* (n) strong morals; honesty
[21] *pursue* (v) to chase or go after
[22] *dominance* (n) great power and influence
[23] *unfathomable* (adj) unimaginable

> If a man does not
> keep pace with his
> companions, perhaps
> it is because he
> hears a different
> drummer.
>
> Henry David Thoreau
> (1817–1862),
> U.S. philosopher, writer

Understanding the Reading: Drawing Conclusions

Readers think about what they are reading and **draw conclusions**, or make judgments, based on the author's words. These must be logical decisions based on the information provided and critical thinking on the part of the reader. The reader should not let personal opinions and biases influence his or her thinking.

Put a check next to the statements that are conclusions that can be drawn based on the information in this reading. Do not check statements that do not have enough evidence in the reading or that say something contrary to what the author has said.

_____ 1. Jackie Robinson is an American hero because he was a good baseball player.

_____ 2. Even in the 1940s there was a great deal of racism in the United States.

_____ 3. The laws governing people's behavior are different from state to state in America.

_____ 4. Not all players discriminated against Robinson when he started playing in the Major Leagues.

_____ 5. The Negro League players were better athletes than the Major League athletes.

_____ 6. Branch Rickey wanted Robinson on his team because he wanted the best shortstop money could buy.

_____ 7. Jackie Robinson helped break the race barrier in sports.

_____ 8. In the 1940s some hotels and ballparks were still racially segregated.

_____ 9. Black athletes are able to compete with much less difficulty today.

_____10. Racism is no longer a problem in the United States.

_____11. Jackie Robinson graduated from UCLA.

_____12. Rickey had to fire some Dodgers in 1947 because they refused to play with Robinson.

_____13. Eventually Robinson spoke out against the racism he experienced.

_____14. Rickey didn't want Robinson or others to protest because he wanted to win the battle against racism in a quiet way.

_____15. Robinson became an American hero because of his athletic skill and his commitment to equality.

Using the Vocabulary: Prefixes

A. *Analyzing parts of words, such as **prefixes** and **suffixes**, helps readers decode meaning. First study these prefixes and the sample words from the text. Then choose the best meaning for the words in the sentences that follow.*

Prefix	Meaning	Examples
circum-	around	circumspect
de-	from, away, out	desegregation, derail
il-	not	illegal
in-	not	injustice, inevitable
inte(r)-	between, together	interact, integrating
re-	again	redefinition, reaffirm
un-	not	unlike, unclear

1. The baseball player's <u>uncertainty</u> caused her to _____

   a. hesitate and miss the ball.

   b. respond quickly and catch the ball.

2. If I draw a line for the <u>circumference</u> of the area, I will be drawing a line
   _____ it.

   a. next to

   b. through

   c. around

3. An <u>integrated</u> sports team is one that is _____

   a. multiracial.

   b. segregated.

4. When our instructor asked me to <u>reevaluate</u> the reasons for my conclusion
   before handing in my paper, he wanted me to _____

   a. change my decision.

   b. copy my reasons onto the paper.

   c. think over my reasons.

5. When an immigrant is <u>deported</u> by the Immigration and Naturalization Service,
   she or he is _____

   a. sent back to her or his country.

   b. given citizenship in the United States.

   c. allowed to enter the United States under special circumstances.

B. *Now use the correct words from the chart in Exercise A, column three, to complete
the sentences on page 174.*

California has twenty-seven cities with schools, plazas, libraries, parks, or streets named after Cesar E. Chavez, founder of the United Farm Workers.

Perhaps it was (1)_____ that discrimination against blacks in America would eventually decrease, but it happened much more smoothly due to the patience and sacrifices of American heroes such as Dr. Martin Luther King, Jr. and Jackie Robinson. These black men were committed to (2)_____ all areas of American life. (3)_____ slavery, which was ruled as unconstitutional in 1865 by the 13th Amendment, it was still permissible for states to make sure that blacks and whites did not (4)_____, even in the 1940s and 1950s. Today, although racism still exists in America, it is (5)_____ to discriminate against blacks in the workplace, in schools, and in housing.

Reading Timelines

Timelines, outlines of events in chronological order, are common visual aids in history books. Work with a partner to study this timeline about the civil rights movement in the United States, and then answer the questions about it.

CIVIL RIGHTS TIMELINE
1946 ➤ Jackie Robinson becomes the first black player in major league baseball
1954 ➤ U.S. Supreme Court bans segregation in public schools
1955 ➤ Bus boycott in Montgomery, Alabama, is started by Rosa Parks when she refuses to give up her seat to a white person
1956 ➤ Montgomery buses are desegregated
1957 ➤ First black students enter a Little Rock, Arkansas, high school
1960 ➤ Sit-ins begin as a protest against all-white lunch counters in Woolworth's stores all across America
1961 ➤ Freedom Riders (black and white civil rights activists) ride around the South challenging segregation
1962 ➤ James Meredith is the first black student at the University of Mississippi
1963 ➤ Civil rights leader Medgar Evers is murdered
➤ March on Washington of 250,000 people supports civil rights legislation; Dr. Martin Luther King, Jr.'s "I Have a Dream" speech
1964 ➤ President Johnson signs the Civil Rights Act of 1964
1965 ➤ Black leader Malcolm X is murdered
1966 ➤ Bill Russell becomes the first black coach in a professional sport (Boston Celtics basketball)
1968 ➤ Dr. Martin Luther King, Jr. is assassinated
1979 ➤ Dr. Jerome Holland becomes the first African American chairman of the American Red Cross
1989 ➤ Douglas Wilder is elected as the nation's first African American governor (in Virginia)

U.S. citizens have won the most Nobel Prizes in every area except literature.

1. What three black leaders were killed between 1963 and 1968?

2. What did Rosa Parks do in 1955 that began a protest movement?

3. When did Dr. Martin Luther King, Jr. make his famous "I Have a Dream" speech?

4. Which U.S. president signed an important Civil Rights Act in 1964?

5. In what year did the first black student enter the University of Mississippi?

> There are American Halls of Fame for rock and roll (Cleveland, OH) and baseball (Cooperstown, NY).

Thinking Together

Jackie Robinson was chosen by Branch Rickey to be the first black to break into the all-white baseball system for a number of reasons. Work with a partner to write down those reasons. Talk about other historical figures you know of who have tried to make a difference in society, such as Abraham Lincoln, Susan B. Anthony, Eleanor Roosevelt, Ghandi, Dr. Martin Luther King, Jr., and Mother Teresa. What type of person do you think helps bring about change most easily—an outspoken activist or one who believes in passive resistance? Does it depend on the situation?

Writing about It

Write one to two paragraphs on one of the following topics. Try to use some of the vocabulary from this reading and from Focusing In.

1. Write a character description of Jackie Robinson.

2. Write a letter from a baseball fan to the commissioner of baseball arguing for the integration of major league baseball.

3. Write a short newspaper piece commemorating Jackie Robinson after his death in 1972.

Reacting to the Reading

Some national holidays or other celebrations have been named after important people such as Jackie Robinson and Dr. Martin Luther King, Jr. Should governments do this to make sure that people like these are remembered more for the heroism of their acts than for the controversy they caused at the time?

■ Every country has its own special heroes. In this article from the *New York Times*, reporter Robert McG. Thomas Jr. writes about some heroic feats that might surprise you.

■ Before you start reading, use the title to predict what type of hero Thomas will be describing. Why do you think this article was chosen for a chapter on American heroes and "making history"?

While reading, readers process information and draw conclusions. These conclusions may be confirmed as the reader continues reading, or new conclusions may need to be drawn. As you read each paragraph in this article, look at the statements in boxes and put a check if you feel each stated conclusion is valid up to that point, based on what the author has said.

Lawbreakers We Have Known and Loved

ROBERT MCG. THOMAS JR.

FROM *THE NEW YORK TIMES*

1   They walk where they're not supposed to walk. They climb where climbing is not allowed. They jump where they shouldn't jump, and yes, they drive trains they have no business driving. They are the daring and *endearing*[1] fools who rush in where angels fear to tread, and when they do, it is generally the angels who lead the applause.

> _____ *People admire those who do dangerous things.*

2   For their feats, as illegal as they are daring, almost invariably capture the collective imagination of a generally law-abiding population, which cheers their *defiance of the laws of gravity*[2] and established authority even as the authorities are clearing their throats and filing criminal charges. The details aren't important. It hardly matters whether they're leading

the New York police on a 10-mile chase in a hot air balloon, *parachuting*[3] into Shea Stadium—or taking the A train out for a spin.

> _____ *People who do dangerous things are crazy.*

3   That was more or less the case last week when word got around that one Keron Thomas, a 16-year-old Trinidad-born train buff from Brooklyn, had walked into a Transit Authority terminal in upper Manhattan the previous Saturday, nodded to *dispatchers*[4] and *blithely*[5] driven off with a New York City subway train. By the time the police arrested him several days later, Mr. Thomas seemed well on his way to becoming as much a local hero as George Willig and Philippe Petit were before him, and Adie Walford was before them.

> _____ *Since Mr. Thomas was caught and arrested, he will surely be punished for stealing the train.*

4   It was Mr. Walford who took a *stroll*[6] across the Williamsburgh Bridge on June 1, 1901,

---

[1] *endearing* (adj) likable
[2] *defiance of the laws of gravity* (np) refusal to accept the natural force that pulls objects to the ground
[3] *parachute* (v) to jump from a plane protected by an umbrella-like device

[4] *dispatcher* (n) person who keeps track of transportation or shipments
[5] *blithely* (adv) casually
[6] *stroll* (n) slow, casual walk

when the bridge was no more than a few thin cables stretched across the East River.

> _____ *Only Americans perform dangerous acts.*

He had been long forgotten by the time Philippe Petit, a French high-wire artist, stretched a tightrope between the towers of the World Trade Center on Aug. 7, 1974, and walked from one to the other, turning the Trade Center into an icon of *derring-do.*[7]

5   On July 22, 1975, Owen J. Quinn, an unemployed construction worker, parachuted off the North Tower, and on May 26, 1977, George Willig, a mountain climber, scaled the South Tower, assisted in his preparations by Ronald DeGiovanni, who had delighted New Yorkers six months earlier by riding a hot air balloon from Staten Island to Queens by way of Lower Manhattan.

> _____ *Defying gravity is enough to make a feat heroic.*

6   Why are the Walfords and Willigs of the world so *lionized*?[8] Dr. Joyce Brothers, the psychologist whose public practice gives her special insights into public emotions, didn't have to consult her files. "We are tickled to death," she said. "They are fulfilling our own *Walter Mitty*[9] dreams. Everybody has fantasies. They actually go out and do them."

> _____ *We admire these people because we secretly want to be like them.*

7   A key appeal of such feats, Dr. Brothers said, is that they are *illicit*[10] as well as daring. Skydivers, for example, have been employed for years to help promote sporting events, and nobody paid much attention when parachutists were engaged to help celebrate the

"The thirst for adventure is a fundamental aspect of the American character. . . . High-risk sports add spice to the humdrum of American lives." — Brendan Koerner, sports writer, *U.S. News and World Report*

1986 Little League World Series in Williamsport, PA.

> _____ *To be truly admired, acts must be dangerous and illegal.*

But two months later, when Michael Sergio made a distinctly unscheduled parachute landing in the Shea Stadium infield during the first inning of Game 6 of the World Series, it was an immediate sensation. Dr. Brothers sees a little *vicarious*[11] fantasy *larceny*[12] in us all. "We *root*[13] for them," she said, "because our lives are filled with rules, and *petty bureaucrats*[14] are always finding ways to make things more difficult for us."

---

[7] *derring-do* (n) reckless courage
[8] *lionize* (v) to honor
[9] *Walter Mitty* (proper n) character in a James Thurber story—an ordinary man who fantasizes about greatness
[10] *illicit* (adj) illegal

[11] *vicarious* (adj) felt through the experiences of another person
[12] *larceny* (n) theft
[13] *root* (v) to cheer
[14] *petty bureaucrat* (np) unimportant government worker

8   After an initial *bluster*,[15] the bureaucrats generally back down. When Mr. Willig completed his climb, he was arrested and *sued*[16] for $250,000 to cover the city's cost and trouble.

> _____ *Daredevils can expect to receive harsh punishment from New York City authorities.*

Two days later he was given a hero's welcome at City Hall by Mayor Abraham D. Beame, who made clear that he had not authorized the suit, which was settled for $1.10, a penny for each of the tower's 110 stories.

9   Whether Mr. Thomas is treated so gently remains to be seen. If convicted of all charges that have been lodged against him, including reckless endangerment, he could spend more than seven years in prison.

> _____ *The author is sure Mr. Thomas will be punished.*

10   While such a sentence seems unlikely, not everyone sees him as a hero, even though his adventure seems certain to be memorialized in a television movie. Parachuting off a skyscraper to a deserted street is one thing. Risking the lives of thousands of subway passengers is something else again, even though the evidence would suggest that the passengers on Mr. Thomas's A train were in capable hands.

> *Mr. Thomas seemed to be a competent motorman while driving the A train.*
> _____

Until he took a curve faster than the 20-mile speed limit and tripped the automatic brakes, Mr. Thomas, who was just two stops from the end of the line, had driven 45 miles without incident and made 85 smooth stops, picking up and dropping off 2,000 passengers during the three-and-a-half hour run. Indeed, there were those who expressed admiration for him precisely because he was so dedicated in his *obsession*[17] with subway trains that he had pored over the official operator's manual and assembled his own set of operating tools.

11   And while there are those who believe he belongs in jail, a common reaction to his adventure was that he should be hired by the Transit Authority and given full motorman's training.

> *Dr. Brothers believes Mr. Thomas is a hero.* _____

Given that, Dr. Brothers said that she would not hesitate to ride a train driven by the young man, who, she suggested, has given evidence of another rare and admired quality shared by popular heroes. "He cares," she said.

Understanding the Reading: Drawing Conclusions

Now that you have completed the article, check to see which of your conclusions were confirmed as you finished reading. Put a check in the third column in this chart if they were. Discuss with your class why some of the conclusions were incorrect.

Paragraph No.	Conclusion	Confirmed ✔
1	People admire those who do dangerous things.	
2	People who do dangerous things are crazy.	
3	Since Mr. Thomas was caught and arrested, he will surely be punished for stealing the train.	

> That's one small step for [a] man, one giant leap for mankind.
>
> Neil Armstrong, U.S. astronaut, stepping onto the moon on July 20, 1969

---

[15] *bluster* (n) loud or threatening speech
[16] *sue* (v) to file a legal claim against someone
[17] *obsession* (n) mind-controlling interest

Paragraph No.	Conclusion	Confirmed ✔
4	Only Americans perform dangerous acts.	
5	Defying gravity is enough to make a feat heroic.	
6	We admire these people because we secretly want to be like them.	
7	To be truly admired, acts must be dangerous *and* illegal.	
8	Daredevils can expect to receive harsh punishments from New York City authorities.	
9	The author is sure Mr. Thomas will be punished.	
10	Mr. Thomas seemed to be a competent motorman while driving the A train.	
11	Dr. Brothers believes Mr. Thomas is a hero.	

Using the Vocabulary: Analogies

Analogies are like word puzzles which show the relationship between two pairs of words. The relationship could be that the words are synonyms, antonyms, a category and an example, and so on.

Analogies are read, "A is to (:) B as (::) C is to (:) D."

Example:

big : small :: hot : cold. *Big* is to *small* as *hot* is to *cold.* The relationship here is one of antonyms. *Big* is the opposite of *small,* as *hot* is the opposite of *cold.*

A. *First figure out the relationship between the words in the first pair. Then fill in the blanks to complete each analogy. The italicized words are footnoted vocabulary from the reading. The first one has been done for you.*

1. icon : cross :: vehicle : *car*_____

2. high : low :: *stroll* : _____

3. *hero* : Superman :: _____ : Amazon

4. *endearing* : hateful :: good : _____

5. punish : _____ :: *lionize* : hero

6. teacher : school :: *bureaucrat* : _____

7. build : carpenter :: *sue* : _____

8. *obsession* : desire :: beautiful : _____

9. assassinate : _____ :: endanger : threaten

10. *larceny* : _____ :: honesty : truth

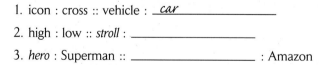

> Heroes are created by popular demand, sometimes out of the scantiest materials.
>
> Gerald W. Johnson (1890–1980), U.S. author

> When Charles Lindbergh became the first person to fly across the Atlantic Ocean (in 33 hours in 1927), Dean Robbins, a New York minister, said, "No greater deed of personal prowess and adventure appears on the pages of man's conquest of nature."

B. *Now choose the correct words from Exercise A to complete this paragraph. Make any necessary changes in form.*

assassinate	lionize	punish	teacher
hero	obsess	risk	vehicle

There are all kinds of (1)_____ in society. Some do brave deeds when they (2)_____ their lives to protect people. Others are admired for dedicating their lives to helping society. Doctors, (3)_____, and ministers fall into this group. Many times heroic deeds go unnoticed or unrewarded. When a leader has been (4)_____, like Dr. Martin Luther King, Jr. or John F. Kennedy, he or she becomes more famous and gains a special place in history. Some "lawbreakers" become famous because they do dangerous and daring things that are often illegal. We admire these people, however, and even (5)_____ them because they give us a vicarious sense of danger.

Thinking Together

Many Americans consider heroes to be cowboys and adventure seekers depicted by actors such as John Wayne and Harrison Ford. Work in a small group to figure out why this is true. How would your group describe the typical American popular hero? How is this similar to or different from the typical heroes from your countries? Compare your answers with other groups.

Writing about It

*Write one to two paragraphs on one of the following topics. Try to use some of the vocabulary from this reading and from **Focusing In**.*

1. Write a short newspaper article on Mr. Thomas's actions.
2. Summarize Dr. Brothers's views on the type of American hero described in this reading.
3. Write a letter to the mayor from one of the passengers on Mr. Thomas's stolen train; support punishment or forgiveness for Mr. Thomas.

Reacting to the Reading

Do you think that people like Mr. Thomas who do dangerous and sometimes illegal stunts should be considered heroes or fools?

Keeping Track of Your Reading Rate

- This article is about a famous American hero. It was written by Susan Ware and published in a book entitled *The Reader's Companion to American History.*
- When your instructor gives you the signal to begin, read the passage as rapidly as you can and mark down the time as soon as you are done. Then answer the questions without looking back at the reading.

tip Pointing your finger or moving your lips slows down the reading process. Avoiding these behaviors will help you read more quickly.

Amelia Earhart symbolizes the fascination that aviation held for Americans in the 1920s and 1930s. Like Charles Lindbergh, she became a national celebrity because of her exploits in the air. Her modest demeanor and short, tousled hair made her a perfect heroine for a media-conscious age. She used her fame to promote two causes dear to her: the advancement of commercial aviation and the advancement of women.

Earhart's entire life had a restless quality. By 1928, when New York publisher George Palmer Putnam asked if she wanted to be the first woman to fly the Atlantic, she readily agreed. The June 1928 flight from Newfoundland to Burry Port, Wales, made her an instant celebrity. When she crossed the Atlantic Ocean alone in 1932, another first for women, she proved that 1928 had not been a fluke.

After the 1928 flight, Earhart turned her hobby of flying into a paying career. As a lecturer, author, and airline industry vice president, she preached her message that flying would soon be an accepted part of everyday life. Many of her well-publicized flights—the 1932 transatlantic crossing, her 1935 solo from Hawaii to California, the 1937 round-the-world attempt—hastened the introduction of commercial air routes. Her career was managed by Putnam, whom she married in 1931. Earhart kept her own name professionally and made no plans to have children. She continued to identify herself publicly with feminism and served as the first president of the Ninety-Nines, an organization of women pilots.

Amelia Earhart had a poet's appreciation of flight, and she flew because she wanted to, which to her individualistic mind-set was the best reason of all. She was delighted when Purdue University presented her with a Lockheed Electra so advanced she dubbed it "the flying laboratory." Now she could fulfill her ambition to fly around the world. On July 2, 1937, during the hardest leg, a 2,556-mile segment from New Guinea to Howland Island, Earhart and her navigator, Fred Noonan, disappeared.

The circumstances of Earhart's "popping off" (her matter-of-fact phrase) have been a source of speculation ever since. Was she on a spy mission for Franklin Roosevelt? Did she land on a desert island and become a Japanese prisoner? The weight of evidence suggests that her plane ran out of fuel somewhere near Howland Island and then sank quickly. But given the aviator's hold on the popular imagination, the search for Amelia Earhart continues.

(400 words)   TIME _____

When John Glenn made his historic trip into space in 1998, thirty-six years after being the first man to orbit earth, NASA administrator Dan Goldin told him, "You're a true American hero. You got back in that shuttle because you believed you'd improve life here on earth."

*Now mark these statements true (**T**) or false (**F**) without looking back at the reading.*

_____ 1. Amelia Earhart became a celebrity during the 1920s and 1930s.

_____ 2. She grew famous for her exploits in the sky.

_____ 3. One adjective that might describe Earhart is "timid."

_____ 4. Earhart supported three causes: aviation, civil rights, and children.

_____ 5. She was married to her career manager, George Putnam.

_____ 6. Most of her flights were not well publicized.

_____ 7. She had probably never really thought about becoming a famous pilot before she got married.

_____ 8. She and her husband planned on having a large family.

_____ 9. Earhart and her navigator disappeared during their flight around the world.

_____10. People are still fascinated with the mystery surrounding her disappearance.

Percent correct = _____   wpm = _____

MAKING CONNECTIONS

Responding to the Readings

Prepare short oral or written responses based on your personal experience and your reactions to the readings. Try to incorporate the information and the vocabulary you have learned in this chapter.

1. Write your own definition of a hero.

2. Describe an ordinary person who has done something extraordinary, and explain what he or she has done to be classified as a hero.

3. Describe one of your country's national heroes.

4. How can a person who volunteers contribute enough to society to make him or her a hero? Give an example.

5. Describe a nontraditional hero you know of. It might be a cartoon character, a daredevil, or an animal.

6. Do you think it is harder for men or for women to achieve heroic status? Why?

7. Discuss your reaction to one of the quotes or facts in the margins of this chapter that you find most interesting or surprising.

Editing Your Work

*This passage was written by a student who forgot to use the passive when necessary. Remember to use the **passive voice** (**be** + **verb ending in** -**ed**/-**en**/-**t**) when the action of the sentence is not being done by the subject. Find and change the five verbs that require the passive voice.*

When my life was on the edge, my mom risked her life to save me. I can still recall the moment when we were on a boat sailing to America. Our boat ran out of fuel and the engine shut down. My mom gave me all her food that left over. After a few days passed, we rescued by a boat, but only a certain number of people could saved. With such a generous heart my mom told them to take me and she would stay behind. Luckily the decision made to take everyone. Though some moms out there are the same as mine, I still think my mom is the best. Amelia Earhart and Rambo not considered my idols. They do represent what heroes are, but my idol is someone that has done so much for me.

American comic superheroes include Superman, Batman, and the Power Rangers.

Writing an Essay

Choose one of the following topics and write an essay. As a prewriting activity, read over your shortwrites and notes for inspiration. Remember to review the brainstorming techniques on pages 262–263. In your essay, use the readings, factoids, quotes, class discussions, and personal experience to support your ideas. Try to use the vocabulary you have learned in this chapter. If you choose to write one of the two research papers, make certain to cite your sources clearly.

1. Jackie Robinson said, "A life is not important except in the impact it has on other lives." Describe a person who has had an impact on your life or on the life of someone you know. You might first give your own definition of a hero and then go on to describe this special person. Make sure to include details so that your reader can clearly see why she or he is heroic.

2. Compare and contrast the types of figures who become heroes in the United States with those in your country. First define the national images of a hero. Choose at least one example from each country. Make sure to include enough background information to clarify the similarities and differences.

3. The media influence our perceptions of who is a hero, and they often create heroes. Write about an American hero that the media have popularized. It might be a human being or a fictional or cartoon hero, but it must be one that you are familiar with. Write in detail about the qualities that this hero has. Show why the public admires his or her feats or accepts him or her as a hero.

4. The traditional hero is one who always does the right thing. However, some people are admired for being daredevils, for taking ridiculous risks, or for breaking the law. Write an essay that defends or argues against extending the definition of heroism to include this type of person. Do you think someone like Evel Knievel (who jumped amazing distances) or Keron Thomas (who drove off with a New York City subway train) should be given hero's status? Is someone like Robin Hood really a hero?

5. Write a research paper on a volunteer organization you know about or that you would like to find out more about. Do a detailed analysis of the organization similar to the article on the American Red Cross. Find out the organization's background and origins, its purpose and goals, and its activities. What kind of person volunteers? Who does the organization serve? Try to interview someone who is involved to add a personal dimension to your essay.

6. Research an American hero. You might want to find out more about someone from this chapter or another person you admire. Find out about his or her life and times, education, and family background. What circumstances influenced this person's course of action? Be sure to describe the contributions that made this person heroic. Did he or she fight against some type of injustice, inspire others to succeed, or forge new frontiers?

Finding More Information

Magazines and Journals

AmeriCorps Vista Voice
Awards Program/Take Pride in America
Habitat World
Life
People

Books

Blair, W., *Tall Tale America: A Legendary History of Our Humorous Heroes*
Crane, Stephen, *The Red Badge of Courage*
Fishwick, M., *American Heroes: Myth and Reality*
Grier, R., *Rosey Grier's All-American Heroes: Multicultural Success Stories*
Millhauser, Steven, *Martin Dressler: The Tale of an American Dreamer*
Ware, Susan, *Letter to the World: Seven Women Who Shaped the American Century*

The World Wide Web

amarillonet.com/black_history/heroes.html—African American Heroes
lcweb2.loc.gov/ammem—The Library of Congress, American Memory
www.geocities.com/Pentagon/Quarters/7737—Hall of Heroes, Pueblo, Colorado
www.lifeheroes.com—*Life* Celebrating Our Heroes
www.redcross.org—American Red Cross

Movies and Videos

All the Unsung Heroes
Superman
Hero
Indiana Jones
Malcolm X
Tombstone

> Superstars strive for approbation; heroes walk alone. Superstars crave consensus; heroes define themselves by judgment of a future they see it as their task to bring about. Superstars seek success in a technique for eliciting support; heroes pursue success as the outgrowth of inner values.
>
> Henry A. Kissinger (b. 1923), U.S. secretary of state, 1973–1977

CHAPTER 8

Hitting
the Books

> A teacher affects eternity; he can never tell where his influence stops.
>
> Henry B. Adams (1838–1918), U.S. historian, in *The Education of Henry Adams*

America's goal for universal education is best stated by Richard Riley, the U.S. Secretary of Education: "The story of America in this century is the story of giving each new generation the opportunity to advance themselves through education." Parents in seventeenth- and eighteenth-century America taught their children at home or sent them to one-room schoolhouses. As the population grew, the one-room schoolhouse grew, too, becoming a complex system of elementary schools, middle schools, and high schools governed by local school boards and funded by the federal government and local taxes. Today public education in America is free through high school, and all students are required to attend school from the age of five until they have reached age sixteen. Government funded community colleges offer all high school graduates the chance to pursue a higher education, and state colleges and universities are open to all who demonstrate the ability to succeed academically.

Each year the U.S. Secretary of Education summarizes the state of American education in a public address. In 1995, Richard Riley spoke on "Turning the Corner: From a Nation at Risk to a Nation with a Future." In spite of his positive outlook on the public school system, many parents still choose home schooling for their children, as Peggy Goetz describes in "Standard Classrooms Aren't Necessary for Learning in Home School Program." Equal access to education helps even older Americans improve their lives, as the four adults in "Fresh Start" by Dennis Hevesi demonstrate. Education is seen as the key to unlocking the door to opportunity in the United States. Therefore, Americans believe that the right to public education is fundamental to all citizens. Albert Shanker, educator and former president of the American Federation of Teachers (AFT), spent much of his life defending this right, as an article from the AFT publication *On Campus* points out.

Are American schools doing a good job of educating students? Discuss this question in small groups. Then talk about the picture on page 186 and answer the question: *How is this classroom picture similar to or different from a classroom scene in other countries?*

What Do You Think?

How true do the members of your group think the following stereotypes about Americans are? Be prepared to share your opinions, reasons, and experiences with the class.

1. American parents are dissatisfied with public education.
2. Parents are not involved in their children's education.
3. American children lag behind those in other countries in math and science.
4. Children do not spend enough time in school.
5. American children spend too much time in after-school activities.

Test Your Word Power

Take this vocabulary quiz. Then compare your answers with a partner so you will be better prepared to understand the readings.

_____ 1. curriculum (n)

_____ 2. academic (adj)

_____ 3. G.E.D. (n)

_____ 4. principal (n)

_____ 5. scholarship (n)

_____ 6. extracurricular activity (np)

_____ 7. distance learning (n)

_____ 8. high school dropout (np)

_____ 9. alumni (n pl.)

_____ 10. AP class (n)

a. money awarded for a course of study

b. head of a school

c. someone who leaves high school without graduating

d. graduates of a school

e. education by means of television or computers

f. program beyond regular coursework, such as sports or music

g. diploma certifying work completed in place of a regular high school program

h. course of study

i. concerning education

j. college-level course taken in high school

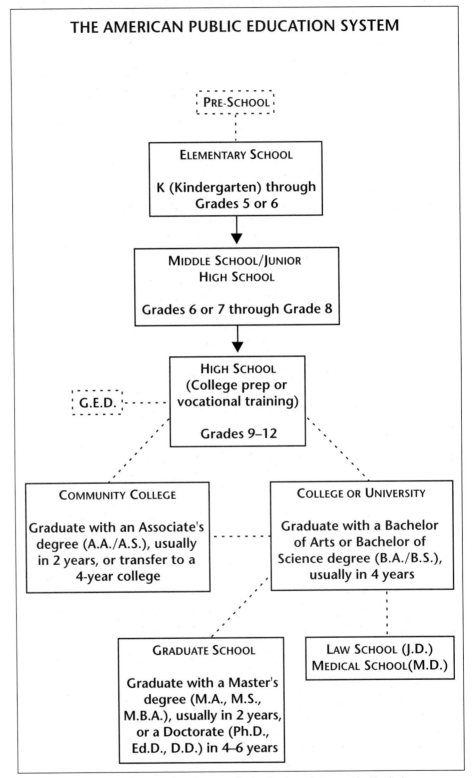

THE AMERICAN PUBLIC EDUCATION SYSTEM

PRE-SCHOOL

ELEMENTARY SCHOOL

K (Kindergarten) through Grades 5 or 6

MIDDLE SCHOOL/JUNIOR HIGH SCHOOL

Grades 6 or 7 through Grade 8

HIGH SCHOOL
(College prep or vocational training)

Grades 9–12

G.E.D.

COMMUNITY COLLEGE

Graduate with an Associate's degree (A.A./A.S.), usually in 2 years, or transfer to a 4-year college

COLLEGE OR UNIVERSITY

Graduate with a Bachelor of Arts or Bachelor of Science degree (B.A./B.S.), usually in 4 years

GRADUATE SCHOOL

Graduate with a Master's degree (M.A., M.S., M.B.A.), usually in 2 years, or a Doctorate (Ph.D., Ed.D., D.D.) in 4–6 years

LAW SCHOOL (J.D.)
MEDICAL SCHOOL(M.D.)

Note: Dotted lines represent educational paths that are optional and go beyond those required by the law.

- Each year the U.S. Secretary of Education reports to the American people on the problems and successes in the public schools. Americans feel they have the right to know what is going on and they are not reluctant to demand change when they think it is necessary.
- Before reading this article, think about whether you believe that the state of education in the United States is improving or declining. Then, while you read this speech, see if you can list some of the problems in American schools that the government is trying to address.

Turning the Corner: From a Nation at Risk to a Nation with a Future

2nd Annual State of American Education Address

RICHARD W. RILEY

Introduction

1   . . . we are no longer a nation at risk, but a nation on the move . . . a nation turning the corner, raising its standards and reaching for excellence for the twenty-first century. It is so appropriate that we should come together at a school named in honor of Thomas Jefferson—the president who wrote to John Adams that he could "not live without books," and the founder of a great American institution of higher learning, the University of Virginia. Were he alive today, I have no doubt that Jefferson, ever the scientist and inventor, would be, at this very moment, in the computer lab uplinking to the Internet's World Wide Web.

2   But Jefferson would have to be quick because the classrooms and computers here at Thomas Jefferson are always in use. This school is a community bursting with energy and learning, day and night. Thomas Jefferson is a school that reflects many of the new dynamics shaping the future of American education.

3   We are, for example, in the midst of another baby boom. In the next ten years, an additional 7.1 million children are going to get up in the morning and go to school. Another 7.1 million children. And at the same time that we are helping these brand new students become part of America's strength, we must raise standards and teach Americans of all ages some very new and demanding skills. Now, every child still must learn the basics. I am a great believer in the fundamentals. You simply can't get ahead if you cannot read, write and figure out how much change the checkout clerk should give you. But in this day and age, using computers and recognizing the discipline of the arts and the power of science all have to be seen as new fundamentals for all our children.

4   This is a critical time for American education . . . a turning point.

> There were 14,470 school districts in the United States, governing over 80,000 elementary, middle, and high schools.
>
> *Peterson's Guides,* 1995

Many American high school students enjoy the relaxed atmosphere of an open campus.

Turning the Corner: A Nation on the Move

5   So what, then, is the state of American education today given these and other new dynamics? I believe that we are, at long last, turning the corner . . . moving from being a nation at risk to a nation with a hopeful future. We are starting to win the battle for excellence and good citizenship in American education. Why am I becoming optimistic? Student performance in reading, science and math is on the rise, and we have made up much of the ground we lost in the 1970s. The number of high school students taking the core academic courses is increasing, up 27 percentage points since 1983, and still rising. Many more students, particularly minority students, are participating in the advanced placement [AP] process. The dropout rate has declined in the last decade, and young people are getting the message that graduation from high school is only the stepping-stone to more learning. There is a new seriousness and appreciation for the value of education. The percentage of students attending college is higher than [that of] any other developed country. Community colleges are filling up as never before. And our great institutions of higher learning still produce world-class graduates. . . .

The Uniqueness of Goals 2000

6   So I am pleased to report to you today that just eight months after the President signed Goals 2000 into law, 44 states are now moving forward in designing—from the bottom up—an education system for the twenty-first century. Goals 2000 is the driving force behind the ongoing effort across this country to raise standards, to get technology into the classroom, and to make sure that we set high expectations for every young person, every teacher and every parent. . . .

7   The American people believe in education, and they believe it should be made a national priority. They know that education is an act of building—the building of people, the building of our nation, and the building of our future. Every poll that I have read drives home this essential point: the American people want to invest in education that works. The results of the November election do not tell me that the American people want to go backwards. There is nothing that tells me that they want cuts in student aid for college, nor that they want Congress to cut education that helps the American people become more *self-reliant*.[1]

---

[1] *self-reliant* (adj) able to take care of oneself without outside help

8   I pledge my full cooperation to the new Congress. We will make an honest review of what federal education programs are working and which ones have seen their time come and now must go. But the need to reduce the federal budget deficit must be balanced against our need to invest in America's future. The reduction of the deficit and investing in education are two of the most important and essential ways we can secure this nation's prosperity. In this new Information Age, education must be seen as a national priority. . . .

A Social Contract for Public Education

9   This is why I continue to place great importance on supporting the American family. Last year on this occasion, I announced a new effort to encourage parent involvement in the education of our children. As I said at that time, "thirty years of research tells us that parent expectations and parental involvement" are the starting point for improving American education. . . .

10   Listen to these words from a pledge that young people take every day at school in Independence, Missouri: "I am the one and only person who has the power to decide what I will be and do. I will accept the consequences for my decisions. I am in charge of my learning and behavior. I will respect the rights of others and will be a credit to myself, my family, my school, and my community." I believe this is what the American people want for their children. And I agree with them. . . .

Turning the Corner: Looking Toward the Future

11   As we look to the future, let us also recognize that we live in a time of great learning and technological achievement. New discoveries by the Hubble telescope are leading astronomers to rethink the very age of the Universe, even as we *marvel*[2] at the recent *unearthing*[3] of 20,000-year-old prehistoric paintings in caves in Southern France. Scholars are *deciphering*[4] the Dead Sea Scrolls and the technology of *virtual reality*[5] is helping to teach disabled children how to drive wheelchairs. Machines the size of molecules are being created by dedicated scientists to heal the sick, and scientists are announcing that they have isolated the DNA of dinosaurs. It is all rather extraordinary.

12   Dr. Pat Graham, the former Education Dean at Harvard, wrote in her book, "In this nation, we have never had a 'golden age of learning.' We have had a golden age for some," she said, "but not one for the nation." If ever there was a time for this great nation of ours to have a "golden age of

---

[2] *marvel* (v) to regard with wonder and admiration
[3] *unearthing* (n) discovery from underground
[4] *decipher* (v) to figure out the meaning of
[5] *virtual reality* (n) technology used to make life-like games or to practice skills such as driving or flying

The number of American high school students taking Advanced Placement exams for college credit increased from 50 per 1,000 in 1984 to 131 per 1,000 in 1996.

Educational Testing Service

> In 1920, schools spent an average of $54 per year per student. In 1995, the figure was $7,163.
>
> National Center for Education Statistics

learning" for all of our people, now is the time to have it—to create a new *ethic*[6] of learning—a new standard of excellence.

13 Now all this is going to take some decision making, and here, I want to end by telling you a story about a funeral I attended when I was governor of South Carolina. The *deceased*[7] was an elderly lady named Katie Beasley. Katie Beasley was a *sharecropper*,[8] the mother of six or seven children, who spent her entire life just getting by. At her funeral, an old friend stood up and said that he had spent a good long while trying to think through what made Katie Beasley so special—how it was that she had so little and yet all of her children got an education, got good jobs and were community leaders themselves. And he had decided, after a great deal of thought, that what made her special was that she was a decision-maker. This is what he said: "Katie decided that an education for her children was important, and she was determined to see that they were all educated. She never looked back."

14 We are at a time for decision making in this country. If we believe, as Katie Beasley believed, that education is a serious matter, and that all of our children must be educated, we too can be successful. It is a matter of having the human spirit to believe in ourselves as a people—and to make the decision to move forward. Everything is in place to educate America—and I think we will with your help. Thank you.

Understanding the Reading: Evaluating Evidence and Language

A. *Secretary Riley makes many claims in his speech on American education. Does he provide **evidence** (support or proof) for all of them? Read the following quotes from his speech and put a check next to those statements you feel are supported with sufficient evidence. The quotes are listed in order of their appearance in the reading. Check those you are sure of first, and then go back and read over the passages in the speech.*

_____ 1. We are, for example, in the midst of another baby boom.

_____ 2. . . . we have made up much of the ground we lost in the 1970s.

_____ 3. The number of high school students taking the core academic courses is increasing . . .

_____ 4. Many more students, particularly minority students, are participating in the advanced placement process.

_____ 5. Community colleges are filling up as never before.

---

[6] *ethic* (n) code of moral or correct behavior
[7] *deceased* (n) dead person
[8] *sharecropper* (n) person who does farm work in exchange for part of the crops or money earned

_____ 6. . . . states are now moving forward in designing—from the bottom up—an education system for the twenty-first century.

_____ 7. . . . the American people want to invest in education that works.

_____ 8. We will make an honest review of what federal education programs are working and which ones have seen their time come and now must go.

_____ 9. . . . we live in a time of great learning and technological achievement.

_____10. . . . Katie Beasley believed, that education is a serious matter . . .

B. *When politicians want to glorify the facts that they are giving, they often use language full of slogans, inspirational phrases, and images such as "a nation on the move" (par. 1) and "a community bursting with energy" (par. 2). Look at paragraph 5 and underline as many of these phrases as you can find. Compare your findings with a partner. What kind of emotional reaction is Riley trying to get from his audience with these phrases?*

Using the Vocabulary: Word Forms

A. *Fill in the blanks with the correct form (adjective, adverb, noun, verb) of each word.*

1. *education*

   a. The teacher insisted on working after school to _____ her students.

   b. The professor wanted to make certain that his students had a strong _____ background.

   c. His desire to get a good _____ drove him to work hard.

2. *information*

   a. The purpose of his speech was to provide more _____ to the faculty and staff.

   b. It's vitally important to _____ students of their many options.

   c. Her _____ essay helped him to make a choice.

3. *expectation*

   a. Goals 2000 is one model of how we can raise standards and set high _____ for our country.

   b. Teachers _____ students to participate freely in the classroom.

4. *cooperation*

   a. So far, legislators have _____ in passing bills to improve education.

   b. Richard Riley has promised his complete _____ to the new Congress.

> By the end of the twentieth century, over 20 percent of Americans over the age of 25 had a college degree.
>
> U.S. Census Bureau

c. Students need to work _____ with others on classroom projects.

5. *election*

a. The voters decided to _____ the governor to another term in office.

b. Why didn't he win the voters' approval in the recent November _____?

B. *Now complete the paragraph with the correct words from Exercise A. Be sure to change the word form whenever necessary.*

Government officials, such as Richard Riley, try to address the concerns raised by Americans during (1)_____ by enacting laws and setting standards while they are in office. In his 1995 address, Riley spoke about designing a(n) (2)_____ system for the future. He stressed the significance of technology in the classroom as well as the importance of setting high (3)_____ for students. Riley's optimistic message about the state of American education was inspirational and (4)_____. He pledged his full (5)_____ to secure the future of this nation's education.

Thinking Together

In a small group, discuss the objectives of Goals 2000 in the United States. Talk about how these goals could be met in the United States and how they have been or could be met in other countries represented by members of your group. Fill in the first column with the three objectives proposed by Secretary Riley in paragraph 6 of the reading. Then fill in the other columns with ideas from your group. Be prepared to share your information with the class.

The number of American school children whose parents are immigrants and whose home language is not English will increase from 5.1 million in 1990 to 7.4 million in 2000.

National Center for Educational Statistics

Goals 2000 in the United States

Objectives	Ways to achieve objectives in the United States	Ways to achieve objectives in other countries

Writing about It

*Write one to two paragraphs on one of the following topics. Try to use some of the vocabulary from this reading and from **Focusing In**.*

1. Given the evidence or lack of evidence you saw in **Understanding the Reading**, write a reaction to Secretary Riley's positive view of American education.

2. Write a response to Secretary Riley's speech with some comments and questions.

3. Use the chart in **Thinking Together** to write a short paragraph comparing and contrasting the objectives of education in your home country and those in the United States.

Reacting to the Reading

Do you think the state of American education is as good as Richard Riley would like Americans to believe? Why or why not?

> What we want to do is to weave multicultural perspectives into the entire fabric of the American story.
>
> Thomas Sobol, New York State commissioner of education, 1990

- Today home schooling in the United States is becoming more and more popular. It has been growing at a rate of 15 percent per year since 1990. By the end of the twentieth century, more than one million children were being taught by their parents at home instead of in public and private schools.
- How much do you know about home schooling? Do you think you'd enjoy learning at home instead of in school? See whether your opinion changes as you read.

Standard Classrooms Aren't Necessary for Learning in Home School Program

PEGGY GOETZ

FROM THE *IRVINE WORLD NEWS*

1 Would it really be education without school bells and *recess*[1] and 20 to 30 kids in a classroom? Does teaching your child at home sound impossible?

2 With the help of the school district's Irvine Home School, it can be the best of home and the best of school, according to the program's lead teacher, Peggy Frick.

3 This year, the program has served 90 children in kindergarten through eighth grade and their parents. It is a part of the regular school district and uses the same curriculum as the elementary and middle schools in the district.

Taught by Parents

4 The big difference is the students are taught by their parents, mostly mothers, on a daily basis and the classrooms are at home—and out in the world.

5 "Most parents choose to do this because they think they can meet their kids' needs

---

[1] *recess* (n) short break during the school day

Students in a home school program meet to collect water samples in the wilderness area of a park in California.

better than a classroom can, and that mostly has to do with size (of classes)," said Frick, who has headed up the program since it was established eight years ago.

6   Other parents *opt for*[2] home schooling for health reasons and others because of professional, mostly performance, commitments on the parts of children.

7   Frick said that one *myth*[3] is that the majority of parents choose home schooling for religious reasons.

8   "I can't think of even one family in our program who's doing this for religious reasons," she said.

9   The Irvine Home School program provides curriculum materials like books, teachers' guides and other instructional material without cost. The school district receives the same state monies for home-schooled students as it does for children in regular programs.

Weekly Workshops

10   Frick and the two other teachers in the program also provide student workshops every week, two monthly field trips and an organized monthly outdoor activity called Park Day. The Park Days are planned by parents around themes.

11   Workshops include those on science topics, writing, public speaking and using comput-

ers. Students participate in the district music programs. A speech contest is coming up.

12   The teachers meet weekly with students and parents and provide tutoring as needed.

13   Frick, who oversees the middle school students, works individually with students on writing and other topics. She said she can do much more working one-to-one than a teacher can do in a classroom with even 20 students, let alone 32.

14   "I love this because you see so much happen. I am like the coach and help guide the overall picture, and the parents are like the trainers and take it home and to work every day," she said.

Open Nature

15   Frick and Barbara Tanner talked excitedly about the more open nature of home schooling. Tanner oversees the fourth through sixth grade students and teaches fourth through eighth grade science.

16   Taking away the necessary but arbitrary year-to-year structure of larger scale education gives students and teachers, who are primarily the parents, greater freedom for creative learning, according to Frick.

17   "When you have parents who really love to learn, who enjoy learning right along with the kids, you see *awesome*[4] things happen," she said.

18   Tanner said her fourth grade students don't know they aren't supposed to be using eighth grade science and sixth grade vocabulary. They just do it because it's fun. Although attendance is not *mandatory*[5] at all activities, attendance is excellent, said Frick.

19   "I sometimes ask (classroom) teachers what their classes would be like if children could choose not to come," she said.

20   And do the kids like home schooling? Don't they miss all the social things from school?

21   "No, we have great friends here," said Michelle and Jessica Barnes with no hesitation. The two are twin seventh graders who live in Woodbridge.

School Hours Required

22   Their mother, Mary Lou Barnes, teaches them all the curriculum subjects. Parents are

---

[2] *opt for* (vp) to choose, decide on
[3] *myth* (n) popular belief

[4] *awesome* (adj) amazing, wonderful
[5] *mandatory* (adj) required, dictated by law

required to provide daily instruction during normal school hours.

23   "This mom has done a great job with writing. The girls have produced some amazing work," said Frick.

24   The girls' mother also teaches them algebra, and they said the process of learning it along with her has taught them a lot about how to learn.

25   Their father, Gary Barnes, also helps teach them math and helps with some writing and computer research. He also takes them on field trips.

26   "I liked school, too," said Michelle, "but I love the classes here (at the Home School office), especially the art and the acting classes. One thing we really enjoy is—like for research projects we have to go on the Internet and now we spend a lot of time on the Internet."

27   Jessica *rattled off*[6] information she had found about a volcanic eruption that took place on May 5 that ties into a project she's working on.

A Big Commitment

28   Frick said that home teaching is a big commitment for parents, but many parents like the kind of partnership it provides.

29   "It's a learning community, that's what it is. The kids and the parents are always bringing in things for us. We learn things all the time," she said.

30   Even for parents who do not choose home schooling, the idea of a true partnership in the education of their children is something everyone can benefit from, said Frick, whose own two daughters have gone through the regular classroom program in Irvine schools.

31   "With this job I have realized how critical parents are in the education of their children. I am their (my kids') teacher and the classroom teacher is there to assist me. Once you have that mentality, it's really different," she said.

Understanding the Reading: Myth versus Reality

*Distinguishing between myth and reality is similar to understanding the difference between opinion and fact (see page 144). A **myth**, however, is usually an opinion or belief shared by a number of people. According to this article, which of the following statements reflects a myth (**M**) or reality (**R**)?*

_____ 1. Children attend home schools primarily because of religious reasons.

_____ 2. Most home-schooled children resent not being able to see their friends.

_____ 3. Parents who teach their children at home become involved in their children's learning process.

_____ 4. Flexible scheduling provides more opportunities for creative learning in home schooling.

_____ 5. Home-schooled students are not exposed to the diversity that regular schools have.

_____ 6. The school district provides the same state funding for home schooling as it does for regular schooling.

_____ 7. Students in home schooling miss the types of activities that are available in regular schools.

_____ 8. One of the reasons for home schooling is that the children have professional commitments, such as acting, or athletic training.

> I'm sure there were points when I was just miserable and said, 'How could my parents do this to me?' but I don't think there was ever a time that I wanted to be in school.
>
> Tad Hauer, Brown University student, when asked about home schooling

---

[6] *rattle off* (vp) to say quickly, without thinking

> What does education often do? It makes a straight-cut ditch of a free, meandering brook.
>
> Henry David Thoreau (1817–1862), U.S. philosopher

Using the Vocabulary: Crossword Puzzle

A. *Test your knowledge of words related to education in this article by completing the crossword puzzle.*

Across Clues

4. level at school
6. teach
9. place where students meet to learn

Down Clues

1. guide or trainer, in school or sports
2. short break during the school day
3. course of study
5. in-depth investigation or study
7. private teacher
8. gain knowledge

B. *Different forms of the following words can be used to complete the sentences in this paragraph. Read the passage and choose the word that best fits the meaning of each sentence. Then fill in the blanks with its correct form.*

attendance	creative	curricular	instruct	tutoring

Public education in the United States today has many critics. Although most people admit that educators try to deal with these criticisms (1)_____, many parents, such as the ones described in this article, choose alternative forms of education. Some of the complaints parents have relate to the problems school systems face in trying to address the individual needs of students. Research supports the belief that students who do not speak English, for example, should receive (2)_____ in their first languages for a certain period. Some schools provide (3)_____ in the classroom who help these students keep up with the class. However, critics claim that this policy takes money

away from other areas. Other parents object to the modern school
(4)_____ that has units on sex education or interpretations of
history that concentrate on minority views. For these reasons, some parents choose
to abandon the public school system. Although it is compulsory to
(5)_____ school in the United States until the age of sixteen,
most states recognize home schooling as one legal alternative.

Thinking Together

Peggy Goetz, the author of this article, talked about the advantages and disadvantages of home schooling. Discuss your views and the views of the author with a partner. Then summarize them by writing down the advantages and disadvantages to see which way the scale tips.

Writing about It

Write one to two paragraphs on one of the following topics. Try to use some of the vocabulary from this reading and from **Focusing In.**

1. Write a letter to your local school board explaining why you have decided to teach your children at home.
2. Summarize some of the activities that can be done by students at home but not in a typical classroom.
3. Write a dialogue between a child who is taught at home and one who is taught in public school.

Reacting to the Reading

Based on what you have read, do you think home schooling can provide an education that is as complete as that of traditional schooling? Why or why not?

> Our time-bound mentality has fooled us all into believing that schools can educate all of the people all of the time in a school year of 180 six-hour days.
>
> National Education Commission, 1994

■ Americans believe that it is never too late to learn something new and change their lives. American colleges are full of adults who are doing just that. Dennis Hevesi describes four of them here.

■ While you read about the adults who "return to school and life," think about the opportunities for adult education in other countries. Do the same possibilities exist there?

Fresh Start—Adults Who Return to School and Life

Dennis Hevesi

from *Education Life*, a supplement to *The New York Times*

1   If opportunity is a thread woven through the American dream, then continuing education is a *spool*[1] that *unravels*[2] new lines of possibility for people whose lives seem to have *frayed*.[3]

2   A young woman who, after a long *hippie*[4] journey, finds she has got nowhere; a "classic underachiever," fresh out of *the service*,[5] who doesn't want to *heft*[6] sticky soda cases; a newly divorced mother with three children, uprooted and in a new town; a drug-addicted multiple *felon*[7] with too much *time to do*.[8]

3   They are among the millions—5.7 million last year alone, according to the National University Continuing Education Association, and constituting about 40 percent of all college enrollees— who have seized that second chance.

4   The hippie heads for law school. The underachiever is a college professor. The divorced mother is now commissioner of a major state agency. The convict graduates *cum laude*.[9] They cannot be seen as the only shining stars of continuing education, but they are lights among the *firmament*.[10]

Roy Eddington

5   Roy Eddington was a "B and E man"—as in breaking and entering. "No sense hiding it," he said. "I've been convicted of burglary, larceny, possession of drugs and one charge of unarmed robbery." . . . Mr. Eddington has graduated from all that. In 1989, after having spent 13 of his 37 years in prison, he earned a bachelor's degree from the University of Massachusetts at Amherst. Now *out on parole*,[11] he is working on a master's degree. Three months ago he received the Outstanding Non-Traditional Student Award from the National University Continuing Education Association.

6   The transformation of Mr. Eddington, who is from Springfield, Mass., began in

---

[1] *spool* (n) cylinder of thread
[2] *unravel* (v) to unwind or separate
[3] *fray* (v) to become thin or worn
[4] *hippie* (n) nonconformist, particularly of the 1960s
[5] *the service* (n) the Armed Forces of the United States such as the Army, Navy, or Marines
[6] *heft* (v) to lift

[7] *felon* (n) criminal
[8] *time to do* (idiom) time to spend in prison
[9] *cum laude* (adv) with honors
[10] *firmament* (n) heavens; sky
[11] *out on parole* (idiom) out of prison early due to good behavior

1971 when, while serving time "for a variety of crimes," he signed up to study for a high school graduate-equivalency diploma "because it was there."

7   "Either you play basketball or tell your war stories or lay up in your bunk and read," he said. Mr. Eddington read a lot. "I had nothing going for me and figured a G.E.D. would help me down the line with employment." It didn't. In 1983, after more turns of the revolving jailhouse door, Mr. Eddington found himself at North Central Correctional Institution in Garner, Mass., where Mount Wachusetts Community College offered courses toward an associate degree. "It started as something to kill time," Mr. Eddington said. "But I stuck with it."

8   "In 1987, having kicked his drug habit, and with his associate degree in hand, Mr. Eddington signed up for the Prison Education Project offered by UMass [the University of Massachusetts]. When he graduated two years later, he was the bearer of a bachelor's degree in general studies. "My grade point average was 3.46," he said. "That is cum laude." He is working toward his master's degree at UMass's School of Education.

9   "My hope is to do substance-abuse counseling," Mr. Eddington said. "Right now I am involved with a group called Prisoners Against Drugs. They made videos with inmates[12] saying, 'This is what drugs got me.' I show these videos to kids."

10   Could Mr. Eddington return to drugs and crime?

11   "Me end up back in the joint?" he responds. "I would have to say, yes. Right now, though, I have a lot more reasons and

Over 40 percent of American college students are age 25 or older.

resources at my disposal to help me stay away from drugs. Plus I've got people around me who care."

Lee Gutkind

12   It was the *stickiness*[13] that got to Lee Gutkind. He enjoyed driving a beer truck. "I liked the *camaraderie*,[14]" the 47-year-old University of Pittsburgh professor said. "I made some good friends." He didn't mind the heavy lifting, hard as it was, . . . but driving a beer truck really meant driving a beer-and-soda truck, and a large part of the job was picking up the empties—hundreds of not-quite-empty, really sticky empties. "You got it on your hands, on your pants. The pants stuck to your skin. By the end of the day, yeech!"

13   Lee Gutkind also liked selling ladies' shoes. Compared with hauling bottles, it was light work, and clean, he said. The problem was, "You know you're not going anywhere." Prospects had never seemed bright for Mr. Gutkind. In high school, "I was a strong D

---

[12] *inmate* (n) prisoner
[13] *stickiness* (n) quality of sticking or adhering to things
[14] *camaraderie* (n) friendship

student and had behavioral problems—fighting, smoking, drinking." From Pittsburgh, where he lived, he applied to "the three worst colleges in the area. When even they rejected me, I joined the Coast Guard."

14 Soon after his discharge, back in Pittsburgh and feeling at a dead end with only the beer-truck and shoe-selling jobs to show for his life, Mr. Gutkind took a walk. "I walked through the city, wondering what I wanted to do with my life," he said. "It was one of the most important walks in my life. I ended up at the Cathedral of Learning," 36 stories high and then the main building of the University of Pittsburgh.

15 He had walked into what is now called the Continuing Education Office but was then the School of General Studies. He was told he could *enroll in*[15] night school, *on probation*.[16] Over the next two years, he earned straight As. It was in freshman English that the idea of becoming a writer struck. The instructor read one of his essays aloud and said, "You ought to consider being a writer."

16 By the time Mr. Gutkind completed his degree, he had been published in several magazines, had started a novel, and, soon after, had his first contract for a book. That book, *Bike Fever*, about Mr. Gutkind's motorcycle travels around the nation, sold 15,000 hardback copies. In September, his seventh book, "One Children's Place," a behind-the-scenes look at a pediatric hospital, will be published. Last year, "Many Sleepless Nights," a look at the world of organ transplantation, received the American Heart Association's Blakeslee Award for Outstanding Scientific Journalism.

17 It is with a certain mischievous pride that Mr. Gutkind, former beer trucker and shoe salesman, points out that he is now a full professor of English at the University of Pittsburgh. "As far as I know, I'm the only *tenured faculty member*[17] and full professor at the university not having an advanced degree," he said. "I never got past my bachelor's degree."

Barbara Patton

18 Barbara Patton took a traditional route—high school, marriage, two children, all in five years—with no hint of the changes and challenges to come.

19 "I graduated from All Saints Commercial High School in Brooklyn in 1961," said Ms. Patton, now 46, who lives in Freeport, L.I. [Long Island, NY]. "Three years later I was married and as immediately as possible after that I had two children. I was a housewife, *den mother*,[18] parish council member, and *P.T.A.*[19] mom."

20 The only hint of a future in politics and public service was the envelope-licking and *petition-gathering*[20] she sometimes did for local candidates in Canarsie, the Brooklyn neighborhood where she and her husband, a meat cutter, bought a co-op apartment. Then in 1974, to get a job that required a degree, Ms. Patton enrolled as a business major at Kingsborough Community College. "My first semester," she said, "I took a course in business law. It turned my world around. I knew I was going to be a lawyer.

21 In 1976, divorce threw Barbara Patton's life into upheaval. "I completely changed my life. I left the apartment. I left

---

[15] *enroll in* (vp) to register for; to sign up for

[16] *on probation* (phrase) period of testing a person's character or ability

[17] *tenured faculty member* (np) permanent teaching staff member at a university

[18] *den mother* (n) leader of a Boy Scout troop

[19] *P.T.A.* (n) Parent Teacher Association, a group that volunteers in schools

[20] *petition-gathering* (n) acquisition of signatures in support of an issue

Brooklyn." Moving to Freeport with her children and an associate degree, Ms. Patton qualified for a scholarship at Hofstra University in Hempstead. She went to school at night and worked during the day as a clerk in the law office of Alan Dorfman, the president of the Freeport Democratic Club.

22   After graduating with a 3.8 grade point average in 1979, she enrolled at Hofstra's law school. Two and a half years later she was a lawyer. Then in 1982, Mr. Dorfman asked his law clerk if she would like to run for the New York State Assembly. "It was a newly created district," said Ms. Patton, who is black, "the first time one had been drawn to make sure a minority person would be elected from a *suburban*[21] district."

23   Ms. Patton hit the streets, shaking hands and making her face known in every election district. And so, in November 1982, she said, "I woke up one morning and I was a legislator," having won 58 percent of the votes. "I went to the library and took out every civics book I could find."

24   Assemblywoman Patton learned quickly. As chairwoman of the subcommittee on Persons in Need of Supervision, she created programs under which young people who got into trouble with the law were given counseling before being brought before a judge—as long as their parents participated. She was elected twice more, in 1984 with 67 percent of the vote and in 1986 with 70 percent. . . .

Karen James

25   Life was a "hippie trip" for Karen James—some *dabbling in*[22] drugs, a *sojourn*[23] in Paris to learn *mime*,[24] an escape from a *cult*.[25] She finally found herself through an ad in the Yellow Pages. Now 37, Ms. James, who lives in Culver City, Calif., is the daughter of the former owner of a nationwide chain of dress stores.

26   "I went to *prep school*[26] and I was getting into drugs," Ms. James said. "So my parents sent me to a Christian Science boarding school to get me away from drugs. But they were plentiful there, too." After high school, Ms. James went to Pitzer College in Claremont, Calif. But she got bored and in 1971, dropped out.

27   "I was drifting," Ms. James said, "just didn't know what I wanted in life." She soon *developed "a crush" on* [27] a man who was going to France to study mime. She left for Paris. That man already had a girlfriend, and Ms. James discovered her talent for mime was minimal. She returned to California, sold clothing, was a hostess at a hamburger restaurant, sold cosmetics in a department store, worked as a sound-effects assistant in film.

28   "I went to school to become a nursery-school teacher, got a certificate in early-childhood education" from the Center for Early Education, a private school in Los Angeles, she said, "and found out I didn't enjoy working with kids all day."

29   Then, in December 1982, she got married. "It lasted a year," she said. "We had a baby," Kayla, who is now 6. The marriage disintegrated in part because Ms. James and her husband had moved to Mesa, Ariz., to join what turned out to be a cult. "People would gradually give up all their money in large counseling fees to 'The

---

[21] *suburban* (adj) outside of a town or city
[22] *dabble in* (vp) to try, or experiment with, but not very seriously
[23] *sojourn* (n) stay, visit
[24] *mime* (n) the art of using action without language to show meaning

[25] *cult* (n) group believing in a particular religion, usually non-traditional
[26] *prep school* (n) private school that focuses on college preparation
[27] *develop a crush on* (idiom) to fall in love, but not seriously

Community,'" she said. "You would constantly be 'processed,' analyzed, verbally assaulted."

30   Ms. James moved to Los Angeles, where she worked first as a messenger and then as a proofreader for a mortgage-document service for about three years. "I realized I could not make more money to support myself and Kayla," she said. "I looked in the Yellow Pages and started calling technical schools." One ad was for the University of California at Los Angeles Extension Program, which offered a four-month training course for paralegals. "I quit my job and got a loan through UCLA," Ms. James said. "I moved in with my parents."

31   Her first day in class, Ms. James said, "I felt I was in the right place. I was fascinated by what I learned. I had a knack for it—how a lawyer thinks."

32   Shortly after graduating, with honors, Ms. James was hired by the Los Angeles law firm of Kumetz & Glick. "Mr. Stephen Glick took me as a temporary," she said. "The first day I started writing a motion. The second day I went down to court to trace the ownership of some property. He was so happy with my work that he offered me a full-time position. Now I supervise a paralegal and a law clerk. I draft important motions. When I draft one and it's argued in court, and the judge reads it and we win, I feel such a sense of success."

33   Ms. James is saving money so that, in a year or two, she can enroll in law school. "When I tell people where I came from," she said, "they can't believe it, because I'm so normal now."

Understanding the Reading: Charting Information

This article tells the story of four "adults who return to school and life." First, test your memory by filling in this chart with information about each of the adults. Then with a partner, skim the reading to fill in the information that you did not remember.

STUDY·NOTE

A chart like this is a good way to write down information for later use. Use it as a study tool.

Name	Previous job	Special problem	College attended	Degree attained	Field of study	New job
Roy Eddington						
Lee Gutkind						
Barbara Patton						
Karen James						

Using the Vocabulary: Figurative Language

Writers often use **figurative language**, describing one thing in terms normally associated with another. This creates images in the readers' minds. Two forms of figurative language are similes and metaphors. In both cases, the writer compares one thing to another. In a **simile**, the words *like* or *as* are used to make the comparison clear (*her feet were as cold as ice*). In a **metaphor**, the writer directly substitutes an image for the original word and leaves the connection up to the readers (*her eyes were a river of tears*). In this reading, "Fresh Start," the writer uses a number of images. The most notable is the one in the first paragraph:

> If opportunity is a thread woven through the American dream, then continuing education is a spool that unravels new lines of possibility for people whose lives seem to have frayed.

A. *Complete these sentences about the metaphors in the reading.*

1. In this metaphor, opportunity is compared to a "thread woven through the American dream," and continuing education is compared to

   _____.

2. By saying that people's lives "seem to have frayed," the writer is describing lives as _____.

3. In paragraph 4, the word "stars" refers to _____.

4. In paragraph 20, "turned my world around" means to _____.

5. The phrase "turns of the revolving jailhouse door" in paragraph 7 is used to show that Mr. Eddington _____.

6. In paragraph 23 when Ms. Patton "hit the streets," she was really

   _____.

B. *Work with a partner and convert some of the metaphors in Exercise A to similes.*

C. *Hevesi also uses special phrases and idioms to talk about the four different people whose stories he is telling. Identify each person that fits these expressions from the reading.*

1. _____

   was out on parole

   ended up in the joint

   served time

2. _____

   dabbled in drugs

   developed a crush on

   had a knack for it

3. _____

   picked up empties

   had prospects that never seemed bright

   felt at a dead end

4. _____

   threw life into an upheaval

   turned her world around

   took the traditional route

Reading Schedules

Schedules are written in columns, like tables, but without lines between them. The titles are usually only at the top of each column. To read a schedule accurately, it is often helpful to use your finger or a ruler to scan down and across the columns looking for information. Work with a partner to answer these questions about choosing classes from this community college schedule.

```
  code  days  times              instructor     room    credits

ENGLISH AS A SECOND LANGUAGE

ESL 5 READING DEVELOPMENT IN ESL

   1100  MWF   9:30-10:30AM       WONG            LA41    3.5

ESL 6 BASIC GRAMMAR AND WRITING 1

   0442  TTh   12:00-1:30PM       ADAMS           LA34    3.5
               +1.5 Wkly hrs by arr

   2207  M     6:30-9:30PM        JACOBS  R       LA32    3.5
               +1.5 Wkly hrs by arr

ESL 10 BASIC LISTENING AND SPEAKING 1

   0443  TTh   9:00-10:30AM       STAFF           LA41    3.5
               +1.5 Wkly hrs by arr

   2208  Th    6:30-9:30PM        GARCIA          LA34    3.5
               +1.5 Wkly hrs by arr

ESL 20 BASIC READING AND VOCABULARY 1
Credit/No Credit Option.
   0444  MWF   8:30-9:30AM        SIMON           LA34    3.5
               +1.5 Wkly hrs by arrangement

GEOLOGY

GEOL 1 PHYSICAL GEOLOGY
Nature, properties, and distribution of earth material, vol-
canoes, and earthquakes.

   0509  MWF   9:30-10:30AM       HERMAN T        SM34    4.0
         &T    8:30-11:30AM                       SM47

   0510  MWF   9:30-10:30AM       HERMAN T        SM34    4.0
         &T    11:30-2:30PM                       SM47

   2235  Th    6:00-10:00PM       SHADI           SM47    4.0

GEOL 15 GEOLOGY OF CALIFORNIA
Geologic development of California in space and time.
   2236  W     6:30-9:30PM        HERMAN T        SM47    3.0
```

In 1995, 40 percent of adults reported participating in some form of adult education activity.

National Center for Education Statistics

1. Can a student enroll in both ESL 5 and ESL 6?

2. What will a student learn in ESL 20?

3. Can a student enroll in ESL 10 and GEOL 1 during the day?

4. What four classes could a night student enroll in?

5. How many credits will a student earn in ESL 20?

6. In what room does GEOL 15 meet?

7. How many classes does Professor Jacobs teach?

8. How many extra hours beyond class time do the students in ESL 6 have to meet?

9. Does Professor Herman teach in the day or evening?

10. What is the course code for GEOL 15?

Thinking Together

*In groups of four, compare your charts from **Understanding the Reading**. Share your thoughts and reactions to each of the four adult students. Then work together using your notes to write a short summary of the article in your own words. Try not to look back at the article; this will help you avoid plagiarizing. Start out with the general idea that the writer is trying to show or prove. Then pass the paper around and give each group member a chance to write as you collaborate on your summary.*

Writing about It

*Write one to two paragraphs on one of the following topics. Try to use some of the vocabulary from this reading and from **Focusing In**.*

1. Mr. Eddington is a counselor in the Prisoner Against Drugs program. Write a short speech that he might give to young adults about how to change their lives.

2. Write a report for a school newsletter on the success of one of the four adults in this article.

3. Write a short piece explaining which of the four adults overcame the greatest difficulties to obtain an education.

Reacting to the Reading

Should taxpayers' money be spent on educating adults who need new chances or new skills, such as the ones Dennis Hevesi writes about in his article? Why or why not?

In 1995–1996, 19 percent of full-time undergraduate students reported working full-time while attending college. On average, 80 percent of full-time students at private colleges and 50 percent at public colleges receive financial aid.

National Center for Education Statistics

Keeping Track of Your Reading Rate

tip Pausing too often during reading slows down the reading process. Try to pause only two or three times per line.

■ Albert Shanker was the president of the American Federation of Teachers (AFT), the professional teachers' union, from 1974 until he died in 1997. His life is described in this AFT article.

■ When your instructor gives you the signal to begin, read this short biography of Shanker as rapidly as you can and mark down the time as soon as you are done. Then answer the questions without looking back at the reading.

On February 28, 1997, family, friends, and colleagues gathered at New York City's Stuyvesant High School to honor an old alumnus, someone who had dedicated his life to advancing the work and workers of Stuyvesant and public schools nationwide.

It was a memorial to Albert Shanker, the late AFT president, who over the last two decades was public education's defender as well as one of its harshest critics. . . . From the humblest of backgrounds, Shanker rose to become a major force in American unionism and education, thanks in no small measure to the rigorous public education he received as a child. For him, quality public schools meant opportunity. He wanted no less for any other kid.

Born on Manhattan's Lower East Side on Sept. 14, 1928, Albert Shanker was the son of Russian immigrants and grew up as the only Jew in an Irish and Italian neighborhood. His father delivered newspapers from a pushcart. His mother was a sewing machine operator. . . . She instilled in her son a deep appreciation of trade unionism and a love of spirited debate. Shanker, who didn't speak a word of English when he entered first grade, was often reduced to hiding in his apartment to escape beatings from the neighborhood toughs. . . . He was picked on for his appearance (6 foot 3 inches by age 12), his language (Yiddish only when he began first grade), and his ethnicity (at age eight, bullies put a rope around his neck, shouted anti-Semitic insults at him, and left him hanging, briefly, from a tree).

At Stuyvesant, Shanker discovered a major escape route from isolation. "It was not the gang atmosphere. [Stuyvesant] was a bunch of bright kids from all over the city. It was an intensely competitive school." He flourished in math and chemistry, headed the school's debating team, and graduated in the top fifth of his class.

Shanker enrolled at the University of Illinois at Urbana-Champaign in 1946, majoring in philosophy. . . . After graduating with honors from the University, Shanker pursued a doctorate in philosophy at Columbia University, completing all but his dissertation before money ran out. In 1952, he took a teaching job at PS 179 in East Harlem. . . . In 1959 Shanker quit as a Manhattan junior high school math teacher to become a full-time organizer for the Teachers Guild, which in March 1960 would merge with break-away elements of a rival high school teacher organization to form the United Federation of Teachers.

(400 words)   TIME _____

The liberally educated person is one who is able to resist the easy and preferred answers, not because he is obstinate but because he knows others worthy of consideration.

Allan Bloom (1930–1992), U.S. educator, author

*Now mark these statements true (**T**) or false (**F**) without looking back at the reading.*

_____ 1. Shanker's parents were born outside of the United States.

_____ 2. Most of the people in Shanker's neighborhood were of the same ethnic background as his family.

_____ 3. Shanker did not speak English well when he started elementary school.

_____ 4. Shanker was a very tall child.

_____ 5. Shanker attended private schools in New York.

_____ 6. Shanker taught briefly before he started to work as a union organizer.

_____ 7. Shanker received his Ph.D. from Columbia University.

_____ 8. Shanker's parents were probably fairly wealthy.

_____ 9. Shanker was an excellent student.

_____10. People never appreciated the work Shanker did for the public school system in the United States.

Percent correct = _____   wpm = _____

> **New York City has more than ninety universities and colleges.**

MAKING CONNECTIONS

Responding to the Readings

Prepare short oral or written responses based on your personal experience and your reactions to the readings. Try to incorporate the information and the vocabulary you have learned in this chapter.

1. Would you like to be schooled at home or in a traditional classroom?

2. American schools try to educate the "whole child" to make him or her more well-rounded. Is this the same goal in your country?

3. Do you know of any other countries where adults are encouraged to go back to school throughout their lives?

4. American schools are often criticized for being too open and liberal, while in other cultures teachers are strict and follow specific guidelines. Which system would you like better?

5. Describe a teacher who helped change your life.

6. Explain one clear difference between the U.S. education system (based on the chart on page 188) and one you are familiar with.

7. Albert Shanker was the son of immigrant parents and spoke only Yiddish when he started school. What are some of the educational challenges immigrants must face?

Although Harvard University cost almost $31,000 in 1997, 75 percent of undergraduates attended public colleges or universities that cost less than $8,000 per year.

The College Board Review

8. Discuss your reaction to one of the quotes or facts in the margins of this chapter that you find most interesting or surprising.

Editing Your Work

*This passage on test anxiety was written by a student who forgot to edit carefully for word form errors. Remember that the ending of a word often indicates its part of speech. For example, some common noun endings are -**ance**, -**ity**, and -**ion**; adverbs usually end in -**ly**; common adjective endings are -**ous**, -**able**, and -**ful**. When in doubt, check a dictionary. Find and correct the five word form errors in this paragraph.*

When taking a test, many people form what's called "test anxiety." Test anxiety is fearful of ruining the test. Test anxiety is a problem for students who have to take many tests. As a student myself I take many exams, and every time I take the tests I get test anxiety. I think "what if I do poor on the test?" Once I had to take the SAT test. It was a big test. Of course I had to do well because it would put me into a college. The pressure on me was enormously. Once I started the test, I wasn't ability to remember anything. It was in my head, but I was so nerves the things I had studied were flooding my head, so obviously I did badly on the SAT test.

Writing an Essay

Choose one of the following topics and write an essay. As a prewriting activity, read over your shortwrites and notes for inspiration. Remember to review the brainstorming techniques on pages 262–263. In your essay, use the readings, factoids, quotes, class discussions, and personal experience to support your ideas. Try to use the vocabulary you have learned in this chapter. If you choose to write a research paper, make certain to cite your sources clearly.

1. Write an essay about someone you know who has changed his or her life through education. Like the author of the article "Fresh Start," make sure to give background on the life of the person so that the changes before and after the educational experience are clear. Tell about the type of school the person attended and mention any particular teachers or programs that were especially helpful.

2. Compare and contrast the educational system in the United States with that of your country. First explain the general structure of the educational system. Is it open to everyone? Then go on to give details about special programs and the testing required to get into them. Refer to the articles in this chapter for information on U.S. schools. Do programs in adult education and alternatives such as home schooling exist in your country? Analyze what you see as the strengths and weaknesses of both, but do not judge one as better than the other.

3. Describe a memorable experience from your education that affected the way you learned. This might be a year with a special teacher, a move to another country, having to learn in a new language, or a test or presentation you

feared. Make sure to include enough details to help your readers understand the importance of this experience.

4. What are the components of a good educational system? Consider some of these questions when formulating your proposal: Should the program include reading, writing, math, foreign language study, and sports, as well as social skills? Should all students be able to attend school through college level if they want to, or should tests be used to advance only the very best students? Should students receive a liberal arts education, or should they only specialize in their own specific professional fields? Write an essay in which you present a program for the ideal school system.

5. Research the educational systems in different countries and find out which countries have been judged as most successful according to studies and test results. This is a difficult topic but one which has received a lot of attention in worldwide newspapers. See if you can find a relationship between factors that determine what countries are most successful in educating their youth.

Finding More Information

Magazines and Journals

American Education
Cyberschool Magazine
Education News
Homeschooling Today
Parents' Journal of School Related Issues

Books

Barzun, Jacques, *Teacher in America*
Biddle, Bruce, *The Manufactured Crisis*
Bloom, Allan, *The Closing of the American Mind*
Routman, Regie, *Literacy at the Crossroads*
Salzman, Mark, *Iron and Silk*

The World Wide Web

www.a1education.com—The Education Webpage
www.aspensys.com/eric/—Educational Resources Information Center (ERIC)
www.ed.gov—National Center for Education Statistics
www.edweek.org—Education Week
www.home-school.com—Homeschool World
www.petersons.com—Peterson's Education and Career Center

Movies

Dead Poets' Society
The Man without a Face
The Miracle Worker
Stand and Deliver
Up the Down Staircase

It is an axiom in political science that unless a people are educated and enlightened it is idle to expect the continuance of civil liberty or the capacity for self-government.

Texas Declaration of Independence, 2 March 1836

Climbing the Corporate Ladder

As citizens of a country influenced by its early Protestant colonists, Americans have valued hard work, self-discipline, and thrift. These qualities have become known as the American work ethic. Two hundred years ago, nearly all settlers in the United States worked at home or on their farms. Later, and throughout most of the twentieth century, the typical Americans worked from "nine to five" outside of the home for the same company throughout their whole lives. Today, however, the nature of work is changing. It is no longer uncommon to see people working different shifts, at home as well as in an office, and changing jobs every five years. Whatever the job, people's identities are so closely tied to them that in America, one of the first questions someone asks in an introduction is "What do you do?" As the British rock musician John Lennon said, "Work is life, you know, and without it, there's nothing but fear and insecurity."

> A tremendous number of people in America work very hard at something that bores them. Even a rich man thinks he has to go down to the office every day. Not because he likes it but because he can't think of anything else to do.
>
> W. H. Auden (1907–1973), Anglo-American poet

The following articles present different dimensions of the U.S. work environment today. In "The New Way We Work" from the *Los Angeles Times*, Martha Groves presents a glimpse into how technology is forcing individuals to "adjust the way they think about their careers and how to manage them." In "Happy Workers a Must," Jan Norman, a business writer for the *Orange County Register*, discusses the importance of creating a positive work environment. The third article, "Cesar E. Chavez Biography" from a collection of essays entitled *Hispanic Biographies*, gives readers background into the development of the United Farm Workers Union and the dedication of Cesar Chavez to the fight for the rights of American farm workers. Unions have been an important force in achieving America's goal to provide workers with fair wages and safe working conditions. Finally, the last reading in this chapter is a story from *Home Business News* about beating the rush hour traffic, not by leaving for work earlier but by working at home and telecommuting.

How do American workers compare to others? Discuss this question in small groups. Then talk about the picture on page 212 and answer the question: *How does this picture fit your views of Americans at work?*

On the Job

Work with a partner to decide which of these statements about the United States are true *(T)* or false *(F)*.

_____ 1. The standard American work day is from 9 to 5, Monday through Friday.

_____ 2. All Americans get at least two weeks of vacation per year.

_____ 3. The average salary of U.S. workers is $35,000 per year.

_____ 4. Most Americans enjoy their jobs.

_____ 5. People with a college education make more money than those with a high school diploma.

_____ 6. A professional athlete earns more money than a teacher.

_____ 7. Most Americans work within ten miles of home.

_____ 8. The fastest-growing occupations are in the health field.

_____ 9. About one-third of all businesses in the nation are owned by women.

_____10. About 10 percent of Americans are unemployed each year.

Test Your Word Power

Take this vocabulary quiz. Then compare your answers with a partner.

_____ 1. entrepreneur (n)

_____ 2. revenue (n)

_____ 3. incentive; bonus (n)

_____ 4. start-up company (n)

_____ 5. consultant (n)

_____ 6. network (v)

_____ 7. lay off (vp)

_____ 8. personnel (n)

_____ 9. union (n)

_____10. climb the corporate ladder (idiom)

a. person who provides advice for pay

b. to meet and exchange information with people

c. to dismiss someone from a job, especially temporarily

d. benefits that make someone work harder

e. person who starts a business and makes it grow

f. money earned

g. organized group of workers

h. new company with an innovative product

i. to move to a new and better job

j. all people working in an organization

- In the United States today, Americans no longer have the job security that they once had. As *Los Angeles Times* reporter Martha Groves points out, technology is changing the workplace. These changes are forcing professionals to adapt to new requirements and to adjust their expectations.
- As you read this article, think about the way workers are adapting to new demands. Are workers in your country facing similar kinds of changes?

The New Way We Work

MARTHA GROVES

FROM THE *LOS ANGELES TIMES*

1   When Arturo Salazar went to work as a Caltrans engineer straight out of USC in 1980, his tools were pen, ink and paper. How times have changed. Today Salazar lays out highway curves and calculates *embankments*[1] exclusively on computers in his downtown Los Angeles office. And he sits on task forces aimed at helping California Department of Transportation civil engineers, many in their 50s, make the transition to using *computer-aided design,* or CAD.

2   "Sooner or later, computers catch up with people," Salazar said.

3   Indeed, computers have caught up with most working Americans in the last two decades. . . . As a result, individuals are being forced to adjust the way they think about their careers and how to manage them. Gone are the days of the so-called corporate contract, when *bright-eyed college graduates* who worked hard and remained loyal to an employer could count on steadily climbing a prescribed corporate ladder. . . .

4   Waves of layoffs among major corporations in the last decade—a trend that appears to be intensifying after a period of decline—have spawned[2] a fast-growing class of contract workers, entrepreneurs and *self-employed consultants*. These and other workers are finding that they must *fend for themselves*[3] in directing their careers—and that technological skills are a must.

5   "In the final analysis, it's up to individuals to continue to reinvent themselves," said Sidney E. Harris, dean of the Peter F. Drucker graduate management center of the Claremont Graduate School. "That responsibility has never been greater."

6   The traditional pyramid structure of companies—thick at the bottom with *blue-collar workers*[4] and narrow at the top with *white-collar supervisors*[5]—has been replaced by what one consultant refers to as "the diamond"—thick in the middle with service providers and other self-supervising workers who produce revenue, and thin on support staff and executives. Those folks in the middle advance their careers not by *specializing,*[6] as in the old days, but by developing an *array*[7] of technological and *people-oriented skills*. . . . A software engineer at a digital telecommunications company, for example, might find himself marketing the products he *devises*[8] to clients overseas.

7   "You come in with a lead skill, but as your career develops you need to be open to other windows," said William A. Charland Jr., who wrote about the diamond *configuration*[9] in his 1993 book *Career Shifting: Starting Over in a Changing Economy.*

---

[1] *embankment* (n) mound of earth on the side of a roadway
[2] *spawn* (v) to give life to
[3] *fend for oneself* (idiom) to defend oneself
[4] *blue-collar worker* (n) laborer doing manual jobs
[5] *white-collar supervisor* (n) professional working in an office and overseeing other workers
[6] *specialize* (v) to become an expert in one area
[7] *array* (n) group
[8] *devise* (v) to create or develop
[9] *configuration* (n) shape, arrangement

8   "If you keep growing on those paths, which I think makes for a more interesting career anyway, then your career is going to be more manageable," he added.

9   The challenge is keeping a daily workload under control while juggling instruction in new technologies.

10   "It is an ongoing struggle," said Susan Morris, a Phoenix consultant. "People are working *12-hour days* to accomplish this."

11   The nation's 1,200 community colleges, Charland said, are *taking up the gauntlet*.[10] At those institutions, entering students commonly have a *four-year degree* or even a master's degree in business but turn to local schools for short courses in practical, technical skills.

12   "Sometimes," Charland said, "the first skill people need to learn is typing."

13   Steve Wade, 47, a certified public accountant in Fremont, Calif., found that out the hard way.

14   "When I started in business, the people who input the information were clerks," Wade said. "Today, we don't have input clerks. It's *CPAs*[11] and *MBAs*[12] who do their own inputting. . . . If you're not technically proficient, you're like the person who didn't graduate from high school in the old days."

15   Funny he should say that. Technology can pave the way for motivated workers to *forgo*[13] a college education yet still succeed on the job. Eight years ago, fresh from high school, Audra Pineda started as a file clerk at the Burbank company that makes Stay-Put shoulder pads, lace camisoles and other staples of women's wardrobes. By learning new technologies on the job, she has moved up to managing the company's computer system and handling most payroll and personnel duties. . . .

16   Jennifer Polanski, public relations manager at Adobe Systems Inc. in Mountain View, Calif., spends as many as five hours a week of her own time at home becoming familiar with the software company's new products. Polanski, who fell into Silicon Valley by accident after majoring in political science at Stanford University, figures that such *after-hours training* goes with the job territory these days. In an *offbeat tactic*,[14] she also took a class in teaching English

American workers constantly have to upgrade their skills to keep up with new technology.

as a second language with the intention, among other things, of becoming more sensitive to cultural diversity at a time when business is increasingly international.

17   At 29, Polanski has learned a key lesson for her generation: "A year or two [at a company] is considered long term," she said. "You don't find lifers as you used to at IBM."

18   At Claremont, Harris said, students are starting to recognize that fact. No longer is there the sense of *entitlement*[15]—quite fragile, as it turned out—that existed for previous generations.

19   "Our students are no longer thinking that the job of their lifetime will be at IBM or AT&T," Harris said. Rather, most graduates see an advantage in employment in small to medium-size companies, particularly in *start-up businesses* that have a shot at *going public*[16] one day and dramatically boosting the wealth of the pioneers.

20   It's up to individual workers, he noted, to realize that they must acquire the appropriate technical expertise to increase their attractiveness to prospective employers down the line.

21   About all that any company owes you today, Harris said, "is the opportunity to develop best-of-the-breed skills."

---

[10] **take up the gauntlet** (idiom) to accept the challenge
[11] **CPA** (n) acronym for Certified Public Accountant
[12] **MBA** (n) acronym for Master's in Business Administration
[13] **forgo** (v) to do without

[14] **offbeat tactic** (np) unusual method
[15] **entitlement** (n) right
[16] **go public** (idiom) to offer shares of stock in a company to the public

Understanding the Reading: Charting Information and Paraphrasing

A. *Fill in the following chart with information from the reading. Put a ↑ to show high expectations and a ↓ to show low expectations. Try filling in the chart first without looking at the article; then check your answers with a partner before searching the text.*

Workers' expectations to . . .	20 years ago	Today
need continued job training		
work for one company all their lives		
make a mid-life career change		
return to school after college		
advance easily in a company through hard work		
work from 9 to 5		
need to know about technology		
do their own typing		
work in a culturally diverse environment		
have more than one skill		

B. *A **paraphrase** is a restatement of the text that has the same meaning as the original. Put a check in front of the sentence that has the same meaning as the original sentence from the text. Keep in mind what the whole reading was about. To recognize a paraphrase, look for synonyms, variations in word order, and alternative word forms.*

1. Indeed, computers have caught up with most working Americans in the last two decades.

    _____ a. In the last twenty years, most Americans have had to adjust to computers at work.

    _____ b. In the last twenty years, computers have influenced the lives of all Americans.

2. "In the final analysis, it's up to individuals to continue to reinvent themselves," said Sidney E. Harris, dean of the Peter F. Drucker graduate management center of the Claremont Graduate School.

    _____ a. According to Harris, each worker is responsible for changing and growing on his own.

    _____ b. According to Harris, individual workers must make the adjustments recommended by the boss.

> The average unemployment rate during the 1980s and early 1990s was 7 percent; by 1998 it was below 5 percent.
>
> U.S. Bureau of Labor Statistics

3. Those folks in the middle advance their careers not by specializing, as in the old days, but by developing an array of technological and people-oriented skills.

_____ a. The old days were better because people could advance if they specialized more.

_____ b. The old days were different because specialization was more important to career advancement than new skills.

4. "If you're not technically proficient, you're like the person who didn't graduate from high school in the old days."

_____ a. You can't be technically proficient if you don't graduate from high school.

_____ b. Now skill in technology is as important as a high school diploma used to be.

5. . . . most graduates see an advantage in employment in small to medium-size companies, particularly in start-up businesses that have a shot at going public one day and dramatically boosting the wealth of the pioneers.

_____ a. Small start-up companies are attractive to those new to the job market because they offer good opportunities if the companies grow and succeed.

_____ b. New graduates like small to medium-size companies because they can learn more from the wealthy pioneers who started them.

> **About 12 percent of Americans in the 1990s were "underemployed"—working at jobs below their skill level.**
>
> **Economic Policy Institute**

Using the Vocabulary: Hyphenated Modifiers

A. _**Hyphenated modifiers** are adjectives made by combining words that work together to modify a noun, for example,_ hard-working _student or_ well-known _artist. See if you can match the hyphenated modifiers in the left column with the nouns used in the article "The New Way We Work." Write the correct nouns next to the modifiers. Check the italicized words in the reading to see if you matched them correctly._

1. computer-aided _____

2. bright-eyed _____

3. self-employed _____

4. blue-collar _____

5. white-collar _____

6. people-oriented _____

7. 12-hour _____

8. four-year _____

9. after-hours _____

10. start-up _____

a. businesses

b. training

c. workers

d. degree

e. days

f. design

g. college graduates

h. skills

i. supervisors

j. consultants

> The occupations that will have the highest growth rate between 1992 and 2005 will be in the area of home health aid.
>
> U.S. Census Bureau

B. *Now try to write original sentences using two of the words.*

Example

Computer-aided design has changed the way architects work.

1. _____

   _____

2. _____

   _____

Reading Graphs

*A **pie graph** is used to compare the amounts of parts to a whole. Sections of a circle, or pie, are divided and shaded. Sometimes the exact figures within each section of the pie are provided, but not always. Study these pie graphs from the Bureau of Labor Statistics on Employment Distribution by Occupational Groups in 1986 and 2006. Then answer the questions.*

1. Which occupational group makes up the smallest percentage of the work force in both 1986 and 2006?

2. Workers in which three groups will see a decline in their share of total jobs between 1986 and 2006?

3. In 1986, which occupational group had the highest number of workers?

4. In which two fields will there be the fewest jobs in 2006?

5. Which occupation is expected to grow the most between 1986 and 2006?

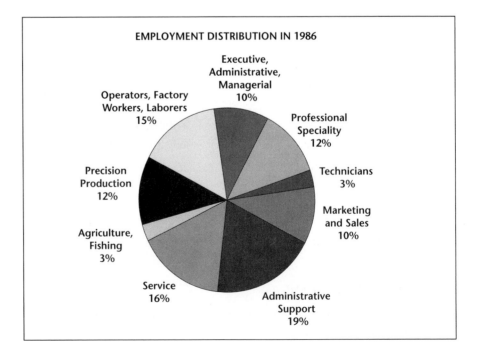

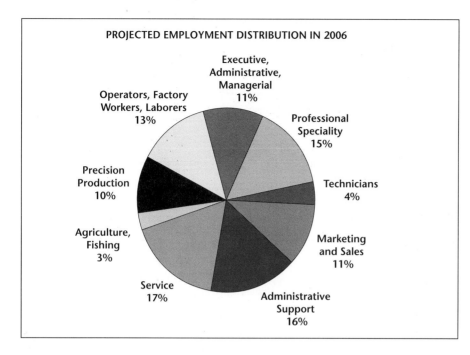

Thinking Together

The terms "white-collar" and "blue-collar" are commonly used when discussing the American work force. With your class, discuss the definitions of these terms. Then, in small groups, write down a list of jobs and professions. Make sure to include your own jobs or the ones you plan to work at in the future. Then divide a paper into two columns. Label one "white-collar" jobs and the other "blue-collar" jobs. Put the jobs into the correct column. Discuss whether the same categories apply in your native countries.

Writing about It

*Write one to two paragraphs on one of the following topics. Try to use some of the vocabulary from this reading and from **Focusing In**.*

1. Write a short summary of the things Americans have to be willing to do in order to succeed in the new job market and "climb the corporate ladder."

2. Write a short speech from Dean Harris of the Claremont Graduate School advising the students on what to expect in their future careers.

3. Write a letter from Jennifer Polanski to her college roommate describing her experiences. Imagine what she might say about what she has learned about the "real world" of work since graduating from Stanford University.

Reacting to the Reading

Do you think a company should fire someone who was hired for a particular job but is unwilling to learn new skills to keep up with the changing workplace?

> According to a *Parade* survey, in 1997 a restaurant owner in Oklahoma City, OK, earned $19,500, a social worker in Worcester, MA, earned $23,000, and a beauty salon owner in Atlanta, GA, earned $45,000.

- While workers are having to adjust to the competitive work world, American business owners are recognizing the need to create more productive work environments. Based on the title of this article by syndicated columnist Jan Norman, what ways do you think the author will suggest for keeping workers happy?
- While you read, compare how employers in your country motivate their employees and take their needs into consideration.

Happy Workers a Must

JAN NORMAN

FROM "IT'S YOUR BUSINESS,"
THE *ORANGE COUNTY REGISTER*

1 On Marcy Mighetto's third anniversary with Dalton Personnel Inc. of Santa Ana, President June Welsh gave her a little *token of gratitude*[1] for her great work.

2 Mighetto received a slice of company ownership and *net profits*.[2] Welsh also rewarded Mighetto with the responsibility for running the inside operation.

3 "The best way to run a business is to involve the people," Welsh said.

4 Mighetto's response? "I was shocked. I felt every minute I worked for her was worth it. I started as a temporary here answering the phones. I never asked for a raise. It's just that she noticed that I worked hard, rewarded it, and I worked even harder."

5 When the economy's *in the doldrums*,[3] it's especially hard for small–business owners to keep *morale*[4] up for themselves and their employees. "It's Your Business" asked local entrepreneurs how they keep spirits and motivation high in bad and good times. It can be as simple as a pat on the back or as profound as stock in the company, owners said. And the resulting enthusiasm and hard work can pay astounding benefits.

6 By following a philosophy of putting employees first, Pennsylvania-based Rosenbluth Travel has had revenue growth of 7,500 percent in the past fifteen years.

7 In his book, *The Customer Comes Second*, Hal Rosenbluth says, "Profits are a natural extension of happiness in the workplace."

8 Another company *renowned*[5] for treating its employees well, furniture manufacturer Herman Miller Inc., has had a 41 percent annual return on investment since 1975.

9 Wow! Maybe nice guys don't finish last.

10 At Dalton Personnel, Mighetto isn't the only employee whose hard work is noticed and rewarded. Every employee earns a percentage of gross profits. Many employment firms give such *incentives*[6] only to salespeople.

11 "My customers know the service people on the desk," Welsh said. "If we send a customer someone who doesn't know how to type, we'll lose that business."

12 Money isn't the only motivator at Dalton Personnel. Welsh schedules weekly staff meetings and asks for employee suggestions. She sometimes orders pizza and keeps wine in the refrigerator for the end of a particularly trying day.

13 "Motivation is like eating; you need to do it daily," said Keith Powell, head of Powell and Associates in Brea, which does marketing, motivation, and travel consulting. "One of the things that we've learned to do around our companies is to be *outrageous*.[7] Like laughter, enthusiasm is *contagious*.[8]"

14 So Powell opens staff meetings with music. He sometimes wears a costume and makes a dramatic opening to lighten the mood.

15 "To be truthful, I don't always feel as up going into those meetings," he admitted, "but

---

[1] *token of gratitude* (np) small gift of thanks
[2] *net profit* (n) earnings after deducting expenses
[3] *to be in the doldrums* (idiom) to be depressed
[4] *morale* (n) feelings, attitude

[5] *renowned* (adj) famous; well known
[6] *incentive* (n) bonus given for hard work
[7] *outrageous* (adj) unusual, shocking
[8] *contagious* (adj) catching; infectious

by the time I have *donned*[9] either a clown suit or my Indiana Jones outfit, I have improved my own attitude, which I'm sure affects everybody in the meeting."

16 Monthly sales meetings only focus on the positive, Powell added. He believes that problems and concerns are best dealt with in private. At these meetings, "we ask people to share positive ideas and give two examples of the ways they improved their mental outlook or dealt with a problem during the past week. It really works."

17 "You feel so unproductive, so you get down and do less and sink deeper," said San Clemente business consultant Sonia Powers. "Find things to do that you don't have time for when you're busy. Clean out files. Get reacquainted with old customers without expecting to get business right away."

18 Rush Short doesn't allow himself to *wallow*[10] in low morale. And it's easy in his line of work to get down. Short owns J. C. Barus, a Placentia collection-management firm.

19 When his mood sags, Short finds someone worse off than he is and offers to help.

20 "I allow myself to become totally involved in their needs or hurts and forget my business. I do this without any *compensation*[11] for my time or services," he said. "I find that when I return to my business that I have a fresh approach and outlook. This has never failed to lift my morale."

21 Pam Lontos, a Laguna Hills motivational speaker and sales trainer, stresses the value of a positive attitude, especially in the boss. "When you think positive, your *demeanor*[12] changes, your voice changes, you go out and solve problems. If the boss shows his bad

June Welsh (right) rewards Marcy Mighetto with a slice of company ownership and net profits.

mood, all the employees reflect that. People don't want to go into a business that's gloomy."

22 When it comes to morale building, Lontos recommends getting back to basics. "Treat employees the same as you would your best customer. Say hello. Smile. Give lots of praise. The most common employee complaint I hear is, 'I can go five days of working late, smiling at customers and no one says a thing. If one thing goes wrong, they jump all over me.'"

23 Make employees feel important to the company's success, Lontos continued, and let them know what's in it for them if they work hard. Maybe it's a higher sales *commission*,[13] or recognition such as employee of the month. Contests are great, and so are performance-based bonuses.

---

[9] *don* (v) to put on (clothing)
[10] *wallow* (v) to indulge in self-pity
[11] *compensation* (n) payment
[12] *demeanor* (n) behavior
[13] *commission* (n) percentage of money earned from a sale

Understanding the Reading: Paraphrasing and Making Inferences

A. *In the previous reading, you were asked to choose the best paraphrase of a statement from the text. Now try to paraphrase sentences on your own by using some of these techniques. Avoid writing a word-by-word translation of the original sentence.*

Use synonyms and change the word order:

> The unemployed suffered terribly during the Great Depression.
>
> (Paraphrase) During the Depression, people who were out of work suffered greatly.

Use alternate word forms and change active to passive:

> Corporate executives presented the new business plan.
>
> (Paraphrase) The new business plan was presented by the executives of the corporation.

Change from direct to indirect speech and vary sentence length:

> Tom's irate boss said, "Take home the report, retype it, and fax it to me by Monday."
>
> (Paraphrase) Tom's angry boss told him to take home the report and retype it. He wanted it faxed to him by Monday.

1. "The best way to run a business is to involve the people," Welsh said. (paragraph 3)

   According to Welsh, _____

   _____

2. Hal Rosenbluth says, "Profits are a natural extension of happiness in the workplace." (paragraph 7)

   _____

   _____

3. At these meetings, "we ask people to share positive ideas and give two examples of the ways they improved their mental outlook or dealt with a problem during the past week." (paragraph 16)

   _____

   _____

4. If the boss shows his bad mood, all the employees reflect that. (paragraph 21)

   _____

   _____

5. Make employees feel important to the company's success, Lontos continued, and let them know what's in it for them if they work hard. (paragraph 23)

   _____

   _____

> It's true hard work never killed anybody, but I figure, why take the chance?
>
> Ronald Reagan (1911–), U.S. president

B. *Review the instructions for drawing conclusions on page 172. Then check any inferences, or conclusions, that can be drawn from the reading "Happy Workers a Must."*

_____ 1. Treating employees well has a positive effect on the profits and performance of small businesses.

_____ 2. Business owners should only worry about workers' concerns when the economy is "in the doldrums."

_____ 3. Customers should come before employees.

_____ 4. Keith Powell doesn't mind doing ridiculous things if it helps improve morale.

_____ 5. The only way to give employees positive feedback is to give them a raise.

Using the Vocabulary: Classifying Words

A. *Classify the following words and expressions from the reading as signs of a positive work environment (**P**) or a negative work environment (**N**).*

_____ 1. gloomy	_____11. unproductive
_____ 2. incentive	_____12. trying days
_____ 3. raises	_____13. lift morale
_____ 4. in the doldrums	_____14. complaints
_____ 5. wallow in low morale	_____15. token of gratitude
_____ 6. pat on the back	_____16. profits
_____ 7. sink deeper	_____17. bad moods
_____ 8. put employees first	_____18. enthusiasm
_____ 9. keep morale up	_____19. rewards
_____10. motivation	_____20. get down

B. *Now use some of these words and expressions to complete this paragraph. Each word may be used only once. Do not change word forms.*

In spite of the competition for jobs and the abundance of overqualified workers, many American employers still want to keep their employees happy. This is especially true in small businesses, such as the ones described in "Happy Workers a Must." No one wants an office full of (1)_____ and (2)_____ workers. Bosses try to listen to their employees' (3)_____ and to increase their (4)_____ whenever possible. When a worker is (5)_____, an office manager will try to (6)_____ by giving the worker a(n) (7)_____ or some other (8)_____. At the end of the year, if a company has done well, a good business owner will share his own (9)_____ by giving his employees (10)_____.

> Much of our American progress has been the product of the individual who had an idea; pursued it; fashioned it; tenaciously clung to it against all odds; and then produced it, sold it, and profited from it.
>
> Hubert H. Humphrey (1911–1978), U.S. senator

> The Americans with Disablities Act of 1990 stated that: "Business must supply reasonable accommodations to protect the rights of individuals with disabilities in all aspects of employment."

Thinking Together

In a group, discuss your opinions on the requirements for a good work environment in your native countries. How does this compare to workplaces in the United States as described in the article? Use the diagram to compare the similarities and differences.

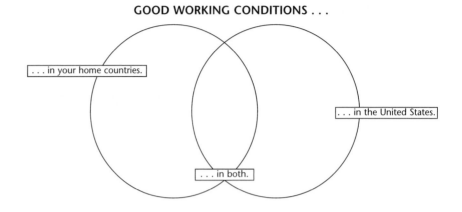

GOOD WORKING CONDITIONS . . .

. . . in your home countries.

. . . in the United States.

. . . in both.

Writing about It

*Write one to two paragraphs on one of the following topics. Try to use some of the vocabulary from this reading and from **Focusing In**.*

1. Write one to two paragraphs describing the qualities you think are most important in a good employee or a good employer. Use information from the article to help you.

2. Write a memo to a personnel manager describing the strategies that firms like Dalton Personnel and Powell and Associates use to increase their employees' morale.

3. Imagine you're a consultant for an American company. The owners want you to help them improve their workplace. Use the information you discussed in **Thinking Together** to help create a proposal.

Reacting to the Reading

Do you think it is really necessary to boost workers' morale by acting like some of the employers described in Norman's article? Why or why not?

- Industry in America relies heavily on the help of migrant workers. These temporary workers move from place to place to harvest different crops or work in different industries according to the weather and the need. Are there migrant workers in your country? What industries do they work in?
- As you read about Cesar Chavez (1927–1993), founder of the United Farm Workers Union, think about how he has changed the lives of migrant laborers. Do you know of another person who has defended workers' rights?

Cesar E. Chavez Biography

THE CALIFORNIA CURRICULUM PROJECT

from *Hispanic Biographies*

1   One night in the 1880s, a man named Cesario Chavez crossed the border from Chihuahua, Mexico, to El Paso, Texas. He was *fleeing* the hardships of his homeland to make a better life in the United States for his family. Decades later, his grandson, Cesar Chavez, would make a stand in the fields of California to fight for a better life for all farm workers.

2   Cesario and his wife, Dorotea, worked very hard. Their children married and had children. The whole family lived in the Arizona desert near the town of Yuma and worked as farmers. One of Cesario's sons, Librado, married Juana Estrada, a woman who had also come from Chihuahua. Together they had six children. Cesar was born in 1927; he was their second child and the oldest son.

3   Librado Chavez was a hardworking man, and he *prospered*. In addition to farming, he operated a general store and was elected the local postmaster. "I had more happy moments as a child than unhappy moments," Chavez later recalled. Librado was good to his children; he even made their toys, but he was too busy to spend much time with them. "My mom kept the family together," Chavez had said.

4   When Cesar was ten years old, disaster struck. Librado made a business deal with a neighbor who did not keep his part of the bargain. In the end, the Chavez family lost their farm and all their belongings. It was 1937, the period following the Stock Market crash; the country had not yet recovered from the Great Depression. There were very few jobs, and many people were homeless. To make matters worse, the Southwest was experiencing severe droughts at this time.

5   By 1938, the Chavez family had joined some 300,000 migrant workers who followed the crops in California. Migrant workers would travel all over the state, picking whatever was in season for the farm owners. The migrant workers had no permanent homes. They lived in *dingy* overcrowded quarters, without bathrooms, electricity, or running water. Sometimes, they lived in

> People don't choose their careers; they are engulfed by them.
>
> John Dos Passos
> (1896–1970), U.S. novelist

the pickup trucks in which they traveled. Like the Chavez family, most of them were of Mexican descent.

6   Going to school wasn't easy for the children of the migrant workers, since they were always on the move. Cesar and his siblings attended more than thirty schools. Many times, their teachers were neither friendly nor helpful. The teachers of migrant children often felt that since these children would soon move on to other farms in other towns, teaching them wasn't worth the effort.

7   Some of these teachers were even prejudiced against Spanish-speaking students. "When we spoke Spanish," Chavez remembers, "the teacher *swooped down on* us. I remember the ruler whistling through the air as its edge came down sharply across my knuckles. It really hurt. Even out in the playground, speaking Spanish brought punishment." He remembers hating school. "It wasn't the learning I hated, but the conflicts," he recalls. Despite all his difficulties in school, Cesar managed to graduate from the eighth grade. For migrant children in those days, graduation was an unusual occurrence.

8   Chavez had worked part-time in the fields while he was in school. After graduation he began to work full-time. He preferred working in the vineyards because grape pickers generally stayed in the same place for a longer time. He kept noticing that the labor contractors and the land owners *exploited* the workers. He tried reasoning with the farm owners about higher pay and better working conditions. But most of his fellow workers would not support him for fear of losing their jobs. As a *solitary* voice, Chavez had no power.

9   In 1944, he joined the United States Navy. At the end of his tour of duty, he returned to California to work in the fields. In 1948, he married a young woman named Helen Fabela, who shared his social concerns. They began teaching the Mexican farm workers to read and write so they could take the test to become American citizens. They hoped that, as citizens, their fellow farm workers would be less afraid to join Cesar in his efforts to improve working conditions.

10   One day, a man from the local Community Service Organization wanted to recruit Chavez. He wanted him to join the organization to help inform the migrant workers of their rights. At first, Chavez was suspicious of the man because he was "Anglo," or non-Mexican white. But the man from the Community Service Organization convinced him of his good intentions, and Chavez became a part-time organizer for the group. During the day, he picked apricots on a farm. In the evening, he organized farm workers to register to vote. He was so successful that he registered more than 2,000 workers in just two months. But he was so busy helping the farm workers that he *neglected* his own work. As a result, he lost his job in the fields.

11   He then went to work full-time for the Community Service Organization. He had to organize meetings to tell the workers of their rights. He worried because he felt he wasn't a good speaker. So at first, he did more listening than speaking. In time, he grew more confident and found that people lis-

tened to him and liked his message. But, it was still very difficult to persuade the workers to fight for their rights. They were always afraid of losing their jobs.

12   By 1962, he could no longer stand to see the workers being taken advantage of, watching as they worked long hours for low pay. At the age of thirty-five, he left his own well-paid job to devote all his time to organizing the farm workers into a union. His wife had to become a fruit picker in the fields to feed their children. Chavez traveled from camp to camp organizing the workers. In each camp, he *recruited* a few followers. By this time he had also gotten many other members of his family involved in the movement. At the end of six months, 300 members of the National Farm Workers Union, as the group was first called, met in Fresno, California. At that first meeting, they approved their flag, a red background with a black eagle in a white circle in the center. "La Causa" (The Cause) was born!

Cesar Chavez speaks out for the rights of migrant farm workers.

13   With a strong leader to represent them, the workers began to demand their rights for fair pay and better working conditions. Without these rights, no one would work in the fields. A major *confrontation* occurred in 1965. The grape growers didn't listen to the union's demands, and the farmhands wanted a *strike*. At first, Chavez wanted to avoid a strike, but he was finally convinced that there was no other way. The workers left the fields, and the unharvested grapes began to rot on the vines. The growers hired illegal workers and brought in strikebreakers and *thugs* to beat up the strikers.

14   The dispute was bitter. Union members—Chavez included—were jailed repeatedly. But public officials, religious leaders, and ordinary citizens from all across the United States flocked to California to march in support of the farm workers. Then, in 1970, some grape growers signed agreements with the union. The union lifted the grape boycott, and its members began to pick grapes again. That same year, Chavez thought that even people who could not travel to California could show their support for his cause. Thus he appealed for a nationwide *boycott* of lettuce, and people from all parts of the United States who sympathized with the cause of the farm workers refused to buy lettuce. Some even picketed in front of supermarkets.

15   By 1973, the union had changed its name to the United Farm Workers of America. Relations with the grape growers had once again deteriorated, so a grape boycott was added to the boycott of lettuce. On several occasions, Chavez fasted to protest the violence that arose. Finally, by 1978,

In 1997, the minimum wage for workers in the United States rose to $5.15 per hour.

Women and minorities will make up two-thirds of entrants in the work force between 1998 and 2000.

Odette Pollar, *Managing Diversity of Workplace 2000*

some of the workers' conditions were met, and the United Farm Workers lifted the boycotts on lettuce and grapes.

16   In 1985, after several changes in the California labor laws, the unionized farm workers began to march again for better wages and improved working conditions. Today, the Chavez children—Paul, Ana, Anthony, Fernando, Eloise, Sylvia, and Linda—all work for migrants' rights. Chavez himself continues to lead marches, often accompanied by one or more of his grandchildren. In the sixth decade of his life, he is as concerned as ever about dignity, justice, and fairness. He is still ready to make a sacrifice for what he believes is right. "Fighting for social justice, it seems to me, is one of the profoundest ways in which man can say yes to man's dignity, and that really means sacrifice," Cesar has said. "There is no way on this earth in which you can say yes to man's dignity and know that you're going to be spared some sacrifice."

Understanding the Reading: Sequencing

*To put events in **sequence** is to put them in order. That order may be natural order (the order as events happened in reality) or narrated order (the order as the writer tells them). This essay on Chavez is in natural order. However, the reading on page 4 is in narrated order. The sentences that follow are not in any order. Work with a partner to scan the article for dates to find the year when the event took place. Then number the sentences in natural order. The first one has been done for you.*

Year	Order	
1880	1	Cesario Chavez crossed from Mexico to the United States.
____	____	The Chavez family lost its farm.
____	____	Cesar Chavez was born.
____	____	The Chavez family moved to California.
____	____	Cesar Chavez joined the U.S. Navy.
____	____	Cesar became a teacher to migrant workers.
____	____	Cesar Chavez began to work organizing farm workers into a union.
____	____	The National Farm Workers Union became the United Farm Workers of America.
____	____	Cesar Chavez married Helen Fabela.
____	____	Grape pickers went on strike.
____	____	The boycott on grapes and lettuce was lifted.

Using the Vocabulary: Finding the Meaning from Context

A. *In this reading, new words are not defined in footnotes because it is possible to figure out the meanings of words from the context, without consulting a dictionary or asking for help. Review the context clues on page 44. Then read each sentence and circle the correct meaning for the italicized words. The first one has been done for you.*

1. He was *fleeing* the hardships of their homeland to make a better life in the United States for his family.

    a. running to

    b. hoping for

    (c.) running away from

2. Librado Chavez was a hardworking man, and he *prospered*.

    a. did well

    b. was unsuccessful

    c. was not lazy

3. They lived in *dingy* overcrowded quarters, without bathrooms, electricity, or running water.

    a. clean

    b. dark, dirty

    c. beautiful

4. "When we spoke Spanish," Chavez remembers, "the teacher *swooped down on* us. I remember the ruler whistling through the air. . . ."

    a. attacked

    b. followed

    c. praised

5. He kept noticing that the labor contractors and the land owners *exploited* the workers. He tried reasoning with the farm owners about higher pay and better working conditions.

    a. paid well

    b. treated fairly

    c. treated unfairly

6. As a *solitary* voice, Chavez had no power.

    a. single

    b. forceful

    c. passive

7. But he was so busy helping the farm workers that he *neglected* his own work. As a result, he lost his job in the fields.

    a. paid attention to

    b. ignored

    c. found

Something made greater by ourselves and in turn that makes us greater.

Maya Angelou (1928–), U.S. author, defining work

8. Chavez traveled from camp to camp organizing the workers. In each camp, he *recruited* a few followers.

    a. gathered

    b. got rid of

    c. lost

9. Without these rights, no one would work in the fields. A major *confrontation* occurred in 1965.

    a. study

    b. agreement

    c. battle

10. The grape growers didn't listen to the union's demands, and the farmhands wanted a *strike*.

    a. hard hit

    b. work stoppage

    c. party

11. The growers hired illegal workers and brought in strikebreakers and *thugs* to beat up the strikers.

    a. kind people

    b. supporters

    c. tough guys

12. Thus he appealed for a nationwide *boycott* of lettuce, and people from all parts of the United States who sympathized with the cause of the farm workers refused to buy lettuce.

    a. refusal to buy

    b. sale

    c. reduction

B. *Use some of the words from the list to complete the following paragraph. Change verb forms when necessary.*

boycott	flee	solitary
confrontation	neglect	strike
dingy	prosper	swoop
exploit	recruit	thrug

Labor unions use different techniques to try to change the ways the workers are treated. One activity is to call for a (1)_____ of a product. The idea is that if people do not buy a product, the company will suffer and then it will listen to the demands of the workers. A stronger form of protest is a

(2)_____. This is a real (3)_____ between owners and workers because the workers often stand outside the factory, field, or place of business and prevent anyone from entering or "crossing the line." The purpose of these activities is not for workers to (4)_____ their work but to express their concern about poor pay or working conditions. Many union organizers travel around trying to (5)_____ new members for a union because a larger union has more power.

Thinking Together

In your group, talk about the problems the farm workers had in California that led to the creation of a labor union. Find out if labor unions exist in the countries represented in your group. Make a list of as many occupations as you find that seem to have unions in all countries, including the United States. Why do you think unions are so common in those occupations around the world? Be prepared to report your findings to the class.

> Clearly the most unfortunate people are those who must do the same thing over and over again, every minute, or perhaps twenty to the minute. They deserve the shortest hours and the highest pay.
>
> John Kenneth Galbraith, U.S. economist, *Made to Last*

Writing about It

Write one to two paragraphs on one of the following topics. Try to use some of the vocabulary from this reading and from **Focusing In**.

1. Cesar Chavez died in 1993. Write an obituary for a newspaper highlighting his life and work.
2. Based on the reading, what are some of the most severe problems immigrants face in the workplace? What are the causes of most of these problems?
3. Write a letter from a follower of Chavez to the governor of California complaining about the rights and working conditions of immigrant workers.

Reacting to the Reading

Do you think workers should join or try to organize unions? Why or why not?

Keeping Track of Your Reading Rate

- Setting up a home business is one way many people like Gina Crusco are changing the face of American business while coping with the demands of working.
- When your instructor gives you the signal to begin, read this passage from *Home Business News* and mark down the time as soon as you are done. Then do the comprehension activity without looking back at the reading.

Having commuted to work for several years, Artists' Representative Gina Crusco began to feel that the daily treks to and from work were as exhaust-

Once you figure out the author's gist, or main point, you can anticipate the flow of ideas. Keep the gist in mind in order to read Crusco's article more efficiently.

> **The business of America is business.**
>
> Calvin Coolidge
> (1872–1933),
> U.S. president

ing and time-consuming as working a second job. With the confidence that she could convert commuting time into income-producing hours, she joined the ranks of thousands of other Americans and moved her business into her New York City apartment—home, sweet home. "The idea of a home-based business is an attractive idea because it allows me to juggle my many responsibilities and interests."

Crusco's business began to take shape five years ago, when she generated a mailing for a local artist that resulted in two jobs. Later that year, she signed on as festival administrator for the Arcady Music Festival in Maine. There, Crusco met another artist who eventually became a client. Her roster has since grown through recommendations and active networking. One of Crusco's clients was originally her exercise instructor.

Her business mainly consists of seeking out performance spots and dates for her clients. She charges a modest hourly fee plus postage and telephone expenses to the performing artist. Crusco receives a 15 percent commission payable upon the signing of the contract. . . .

"As circumstances in my life change, the home office setup adapts to them," she adds. "I recently got a dog who needs to be taken out three times a day. This would be impossible if I were commuting, leaving my house at 8 A.M. and returning at 6 P.M." Gina, who recently married, anticipates future advantages from her home business. "The fact that my husband is a school teacher, with an 8 to 3 schedule and summers off, will give us an opportunity to share child-rearing more equitably than the average two-career couple."

Crusco is also a realist when it comes to the down-side of working at home. "It is very important to be able to separate work and home life emotionally when there is no physical separation. Occasionally, I feel the pull of unfinished tasks when it is properly time off. I let the answering machine pick up on evenings and weekends and do not respond to business calls at these times unless the matter is urgent. From the other side, family and friends know I'm at home during the day, and I have let them know that a home office is still an office, so calls have to stay brief."

(400 words) TIME: _____

*Now mark these statements true (**T**) or false (**F**) without looking back at the reading.*

_____ 1. Crusco has never commuted to work.

_____ 2. Crusco was living in Maine when she started her home business.

_____ 3. When she first started a home business, Crusco worked out of her apartment.

_____ 4. Crusco is an artist.

_____ 5. Crusco receives a 50 percent commission from her clients.

_____ 6. Crusco and her husband have children now.

_____ 7. Crusco's husband is a teacher.

_____ 8. Crusco plans to be a working mother.

_____ 9. Crusco believes there are no disadvantages to working at home.

_____10. Crusco would probably recommend working at home for most people.

Percent correct = _____   wpm = _____

MAKING C O N N E C T I O N S

Responding to the Readings

Prepare short oral or written responses based on your personal experience and your reactions to the readings. Try to incorporate the information and the vocabulary you have learned in this chapter.

1. Do you think you are the type of person who would work best in a large American corporation, small business, or home business? Explain your reasons.

2. What experiences have you had working for someone else? What were some of the positive and negative aspects of the job?

3. Would you join a union if you were a farm worker, a teacher, or a news reporter? Why or why not?

4. Write a list of technical skills you have that will help you get and keep a job.

5. Prepare three to five questions to ask a person who works for an American company in the United States or in your native country. Then find someone to interview and summarize his or her answers.

6. Write a paragraph discussing the types of jobs most immigrants find when they first arrive in the United States. Do members of certain ethnic groups tend to work in any particular fields?

7. Discuss your reaction to one of the quotes or facts in the margins of this chapter that you find most interesting or surprising.

Editing Your Work

*A student wrote this paragraph about his decision to become a doctor but forgot to edit for verb forms. Remember to pay attention to the form of a verb (**base V, V + -ing, V + -s, V + -ed, V + -ed/-en/-t, to + V**) that follows a preposition, modal, and the verbs "be" and "have." The second verb in a two-verb phrase also has a special form, for example, learn to drive and enjoy driving. There are five errors in verb form in this paragraph.*

> By the end of the 20th century, over 10 million Americans telecommuted and more than 4 million self-employed people were working in home-based business.
>
> **Bureau of Labor Statistics**

I've did many volunteer jobs that are relate to the medical field. Last summer I volunteered at a doctor's office and had the chance to talk with the doctor about my career choice. The doctor, who is a friend of my parents, is a successful man. He works at a popular hospital in our community. He told me that becoming a doctor was not about money but about help people. He said, "If you want making a lot of money, you should became an engineer." He advised me to decide on the profession that matched my goals in life. It was good advice.

Writing an Essay

Choose one of the following topics and write an essay. As a prewriting activity, read over your shortwrites and notes for inspiration. Remember to review the brainstorming techniques on pages 262–263. In your essay, use the readings, factoids, quotes, class discussions, and personal experience to support your ideas. Try to use the vocabulary you have learned in this chapter. If you choose to write a research paper, make certain to cite your sources clearly.

1. How easy would it be for you to become a successful worker in today's American job market? Write an essay in which you summarize what you have learned about American workers, the American work ethic, and American businesses from the readings in this chapter. Be sure to include specific information about the readings to help develop your essay. For each point, discuss how you see yourself in relation to it. How do you compare to the typical American worker?

2. Compare and contrast the differences between working in your native country and working in the United States. Make sure to draw on personal experience, knowledge of other workers, and information from the articles to develop your essay.

3. Write an essay about your career choice. What influenced your decision? What do your parents and peers think about it? Why do you think you are suited for this career? What will be the rewards of this career? What will you need to do in order to have a job in this field someday, and what are you doing now to get there? Your overall goal is to show that this career choice is a good choice that fits your needs and skills.

4. If you have had a VERY interesting work experience, write a narrative essay about it with the goal of showing why it was so special. It might be your first job and how you got it, it might be a situation at your workplace and how you dealt with it, or it might be about facing discrimination when finding a job or working. What did you learn from the experience, and how did it affect you and your plans for working in the future? You could also write about the experience of someone you know well. This essay will only be successful if you

Bill Gates, founder of Microsoft, was the richest man in America throughout the 1990s.

Fortune magazine

have an interesting story to tell. You will have to develop details around the experience very skillfully.

5. Write a proposal for establishing a small company in the United States which reflects your understanding of American business and American workers. Make sure your proposal covers how you are going to address the issues that were raised in the readings. Consider including concerns such as the company organization, personnel management, available technology, location (home-based or not), and employee experience and skills.

6. Go to the library and research one of the topics in this chapter. You may want to look for information on a person famous for union organizing, such as Cesar Chavez; an entrepreneur, such as Donald Trump; or a technology wiz, such as Bill Gates. Write an essay describing this person's contributions and influence on the American business community or work force.

> **The income of the average American college graduate was over 50 percent higher than that of the average high school graduate in 1996.**
>
> U.S. Department of Commerce

Finding More Information

Magazines and Journals

Business Weekly
Forbes Magazine
Home Business News
Money Magazine
Working Woman

Books

Bolles, Richard N., *What Color Is Your Parachute?*
Fodell, Betty, *Cesar Chavez and the United Farm Workers*
Shaw, Lisa, *Telecommute! Go to Work without Leaving Home*
Steinbeck, John, *The Grapes of Wrath*
Teiger, Paul, *Do What You Are: Discover the Perfect Career for You*
Terkel, Studs, *Work*

The World Wide Web

www.careermag.com—Career Magazine
www.dol.gov—Department of Labor homepage; links to Bureau of Labor Statistics
www.homebusiness.com—American Home Business Association
www.jobssmart.com—guide to finding a job online
www.unionweb.org—UnionWeb, unionized labor

Movies and Videos

Baby Boom
Harlan County USA
Norma Rae
Wall Street
Working Girl

CHAPTER 10

Pursuing Happiness

> Entertainment is one of the biggest businesses in the United States—you have to pay for everything here . . . but there are innocent pleasures that don't cost anything. . . . Everybody just spending time together on their day off.
>
> Bastienne Schmidt, German photographer

In 1776, the Declaration of Independence stated that Americans were guaranteed the right to life, liberty, and the pursuit of happiness. Thomas Keneally, an Australian writer, describes Americans as "the first people to invoke the pursuit of happiness as a goal." Americans may have the most disposable income to spend on leisure activities, but they do not have the most vacation time to use it. Most employers only grant one week of paid vacation to full-time workers during their first few years on the job. The maximum vacation time that most Americans can ever accrue is four weeks. How they spend their free time is the theme of this chapter.

In their pursuit of happiness, Americans travel down many different pathways. The first article, "The Pursuit of Happiness: Once Upon a Time, Did More Americans Live Happily Ever After?" by Leslie Dreyfous, details how the perception of being happy has changed in the United States over the past thirty years. Americans seem to have less free time now and are under more stress both at work and at home. In the article "Pursue Your Passion," experts such as Barbara Sher advise them to find a hobby or interest that they enjoy. Surprisingly, many Americans find enjoyment in volunteering their time and energy to causes they believe in. Such a group is profiled in "ONU Habitat for Humanity." The last passage—entitled "Call Waiting: Hi, This is America. I'm on Vacation."—points out that summer is still the prime season for travel and leisure activities in the United States.

What do you know about the ways Americans spend their free time? Discuss this question in small groups. Then talk about the picture on page 236 and answer the question: *How is this family planning to spend their free time together?*

Proverbs

Each country has short, well-known popular sayings called **proverbs.** Most proverbs come from a country's folk culture and are passed on by word of mouth. Work with a partner to determine what the following proverbs and expressions tell you about Americans' attitudes toward their free or leisure time.

1. All work and no play makes Jack a dull boy.

2. An idle mind is the devil's workshop.

3. The hardest work is to do nothing.

4. The man with no business is the busiest man.

5. Time waits for no man.

Expand Your Word Power

See how fast your group can come up with the answers to these word puzzles. Then try to write one or two sentences using as many of these words as you can. Share your results with the class.

1. If a *vehicle* is a means of transportation, and *recreation* is fun, what is a *recreational vehicle* (RV)?

2. If *R and R* is a phrase meaning *leisure*, what do *R* and *R* stand for?

3. If senior citizens are required to *retire* from their jobs at age sixty-five to enjoy their *golden years*, what is *retirement*?

4. If *volunteers* are people who donate their time, do they get paid?

5. If a *hobby* can be healthy (golf), educational (reading), and creative (gardening), what is a *hobby*?

■ Most Americans feel they have the right to be happy, and they spend a lot of money to reach this goal. Do you know what a "self-help" book is? Movements to help people "be all that they can be" became popular in the 1970s. According to Leslie Dreyfous, the Esalen Institute in California is "the granddaddy of all human-potential centers," a place to get away from it all and contemplate life and nature.

■ Have you ever gone on a "retreat," a place to get away from it all? Are there support groups in your country? These resources are common in the United States. As you read this article, you will find out why.

Note: The **Understanding the Reading** activity for this article is a comprehension test. Previewing the questions at the end of a passage is one technique to focus your attention on what you will be asked. Look over the questions on page 241–242 before you read.

The Pursuit of Happiness: Once Upon a Time, Did More Americans Live Happily Ever After?

LESLIE DREYFOUS

FROM THE *SALT LAKE TRIBUNE* (ASSOCIATED PRESS)

1   BIG SUR, Calif.—Not long after dawn, the Esalen Institute's *communal hot tubs*[1] begin to fill with early risers and some *bashful*[2] others *dodging*[3] peak-hour crowds. It's quiet at first, a handful of bathers contemplating the ribbon of fog stretched along the Pacific shoreline far below. Grown-ups wearing no more than a wristwatch, sloshing about like awkward, overgrown children.

2   Bather No. 1, salt-and-pepper beard with a sizable belly and hair on his back, soon turns to Bather No. 2, a blond woman with freckled thighs, unshaved armpits and a *New Age*[4] crystal dangling from her neck. "This is definitely heaven," says the guy, who drove up from Hollywood for a weekend retreat at this, the granddaddy of all human-potential centers. "But I don't like to call it that."

3   For an instant, the woman looks puzzled. Then her eyes widen and her head begins to bob: "Ohhh," she chimes. "I know what you mean. When you come expecting heaven, things always fall short." An uneasy silence follows, broken only by the barking of sea lions at play in the surf beneath Esalen's cliffside *perch*.[5] It sounds like a *taunt*:[6] "See how easy it is?" they seem to say. "This is happiness." But evolution has played a nasty trick, drawn us into a perpetual game of *hide-and-seek*[7] with this thing the Declaration of Independence only guarantees the right to pursue. In 1992, happiness is a sophisticated business.

4   The number of books on the topic has quadrupled in recent years and the therapy industry has more than tripled in size. Frank

---

[1] *communal hot tub* (np) big wooden outdoor heated tub in which a group of people relax together
[2] *bashful* (adj) shy
[3] *dodge* (v) to avoid
[4] *New Age* (proper n) modern set of religious, health, and lifestyle beliefs that are nontraditional

[5] *perch* (n) high seat or site above the surroundings
[6] *taunt* (n) cruel remark
[7] *hide-and-seek* (n) game in which someone hides and others look for him or her

talk shows dominate afternoon TV, and entire catalogs are devoted to marketing meditational tapes and inspirational videos. People pay hundreds of dollars and travel thousands of miles to retreats like Esalen.

5   Generations born after World War II grew up hearing how happiness was theirs to grab. After all, America was No. 1, the *undisputed*[8] postwar leader in science and technology. The economy was booming, educational opportunity expanding, social barriers crumbling at every turn. Soon women were going to have equal rights, and minorities their civil rights. Drugs promised higher consciousness and the sexual revolution promised freedom from *old Victorian convention*.[9]

6   This generation of young people would have "careers" rather than jobs, spouses who were sensitive, bodies that were beautiful, goals fulfilled, selves *actualized*.[10] They would have it all, or at least have a great time trying. And so, rich and poor, many young people showed up at life's buffet assuming their plates would be filled. Maybe their Depression-era parents and grandparents were satisfied just to have food on the table, but things were different now. Something more profound than getting by was out there. It was just a matter of finding it. "We watched our parents live with misery. They basically settled," says Penny Sharbino. "For us, we were told things would be better, that we'd have all these choices. Then we became adults."

7   . . . *Baby boomers*[11] are four times likelier to say they are not satisfied with their lives than are people of their parents' generation, according to an Associated Press poll. Experts estimate the incidence of psychological depression is 10 times what it was pre–World War II. Expectations have vaulted higher and higher—perhaps so high that real life inevitably would fall short for some. At the same time, just as this thing called happiness seemed an *attainable*[12] goal, the rules were changing.

Self-help books offer solutions to problems and advice on ways to find happiness.

8   *Giddy*[13] sexual freedom ground to a halt with AIDS. Recreational drugs and drinking landed millions in rehabilitation clinics. The price of an afternoon at the movies climbed to $7 and comfort foods were *demonized*[14] for their high cholesterol. The 1980s wound down in recession and permanent layoffs for 1.4 million white- and blue-collar workers. Those with jobs sense thinner ice with each round of factory or corporate layoffs. Neither union brotherhood nor the mother company are guaranteed life preservers.

9   We know that a hole has opened in the ozone, that smoking kills, that one in four girls are sexually abused, that the known rape rate has quadrupled, that the violent crime rate has quintupled, that half the marriages end in divorce. . . . Not me, you say? Perhaps you're in denial.

10   "It seems we are all victims. And if we're not, then we're *repressing*[15] something," says the Rev. William Nolte, 69, a Roman Catholic priest in Martinsburg, W.Va. "Ever since World War II, the idea of putting on a smile

---

8 *undisputed* (adj) undeniable, certain
9 *old Victorian convention* (np) rules of behavior based on the conservative, family-oriented, middle-class values that characterized the period of Queen Victoria's reign (1837–1901) in England
10 *actualize* (v) to realize or make more complete

11 *baby boomer* (n) post–World War II child in the United States, born between 1946 and 1965
12 *attainable* (adj) reachable
13 *giddy* (adj) lightheaded or lighthearted
14 *demonize* (v) to make out to be evil
15 *repress* (v) to keep secret

and sacrificing for others has been out of style." This draws a laugh from two young colleagues who have joined Nolte in the sun-splotched rectory living room. They have heard mixed messages.

11 "People yelled at me, 'Eh, why are you leaving? You're earning good money and have an excellent future,'" says John Bocan, 28, who left the banking fast track in Pittsburgh to become a pastoral minister at St. Joseph's.

12 "Me, I had a *lucrative*[16] job in the Army. I was a helicopter pilot and homeowner. But it wasn't enough," says Herb Peddicord, 33, now director of religious education for the small-town parish. They don't make much money. They're still single and unsure of the future. But there's this banner flapping out in front of the church's 12-foot Greek Revival columns. "Come On Home," it says.

13 "Being part of a community, working with people instead of against them—that's spirituality. That's what's missing: spiritual peace," Bocan says.

14 "There's a lot of surface happiness. But deep down people—especially young people—are just very lonely," says Peddicord.

15 The majority of Americans live in urban or suburban areas, away from nature and its consoling rhythms. Communities have fragmented, children migrated to better jobs, mom and pop's Main Street store replaced by *strip malls*[17] that look pretty much the same from one town to the next.

16 We may listen to television talk at us rather than talking to one another. On warm evenings, we often are inside by the air conditioner rather than out on the porch, shooting the breeze with neighbors or passers-by.

17 Half of those polled for the AP by ICR Survey Research Group of Media, Pa., say marriage, friends and family contribute most to their happiness—four times as many as credit such individual pursuits as careers or hobbies. But the standard 1950s nuclear landscape has been reshaped by feminism and economics. More than half of mothers today work outside the home, many coexisting uneasily with a guilty sense that neither the job nor children are getting enough attention.

18 Men are supposed to pitch in, and many do. But studies indicate the vast majority still find child care and housework more or less optional activities, certainly not the sort of thing their fathers did. . . .

19 Some 92 percent of Americans say they're satisfied with their lives, according to the AP poll. But of those, one in four uses self-help books, recovery programs or counseling to increase happiness.

20 "It's a perpetual search for Mr. Goodbook, the idea that maybe the next one will be the one that solves all my problems and finally makes me happy," says Steven Starker, author of *Oracle at the Supermarket: The American Preoccupation with Self-Help Books*.

21 "It's like buying a *lottery ticket*.[18] You know you're probably not going to win," he adds. "But there's always a chance." Bill Wilson and Dr. Bob had no idea what they unleashed when they came up with 12 steps to alcoholic recovery in 1935. Today, their formula provides the blueprint for Gamblers Anonymous, Sex-oholics Anonymous, Messies Anonymous, Overeaters Anonymous, Shoplifters Anonymous, Parents Anonymous, Spenders Anonymous, Emotions Anonymous and on and on . . .

22 "Groups are developing left and right. I just got across my desk a group that's forming for people who have been struck by lightning," says Edward Madara of the American Self-Help Clearinghouse in Denville, N.J. It may sound laughable, he acknowledges, but in fact his own daughter had a boyfriend who was killed by lightning.

23 "There's a tendency to trivialize or think it's funny, but these groups are opening doors on issues and giving people some sense of community. When they walk into the room, they know they're not alone." These groups—to which an estimated 12 million to 15 million Americans belong—represent a new kind of community, a modern religion binding people together in understanding. Talking openly about incest or wife beating, alcoholism or unemployment has afforded relief to millions.

24 If even one family's destructive cycle is broken, one child protected from harm, then

---

[16] *lucrative* (adj) profitable

[17] *strip mall* (n) narrow shopping center along a busy street

[18] *lottery ticket* (n) chance purchased in a public game to win a prize

who would say the new awareness isn't all to the good? But where to draw the line? Some say we are becoming a nation of victims, paralyzed rather than empowered by what we know. Do we really need another star's confession? Another chat show featuring *born-again*[19] *cross-dressers*[20] for peace? At what point does healthy self-awareness become unhealthy self-absorption?

25   "I wonder if in the '90s we're not beginning to see a shift back toward an appreciation of close relationships and a communal mentali-ty. For all our pursuit of individual happiness, there's no evidence that we're happier today than when we had much less," says David G. Myers, a social psychologist and author of the new book *The Pursuit of Happiness: Who Is Happy—and Why.*

26   Maybe Dorothy was onto something. Forget the land of Oz, she said. Happiness is found in the gardens we tend, the people we love. Maybe, in the words of the late songwriter Harry Chapin, "It's got to be the going, not the getting there, that's good."

Understanding the Reading: Review

Most reading comprehension tests cover many of the reading skills you have been learning about in this book. Take this comprehension test on the reading "The Pursuit of Happiness." Circle the correct choice.

1. The main idea of this article is:

   a. Americans are happier now than they were thirty years ago.

   b. Even though Americans say they are satisfied with their lives, they are still searching for happiness.

   c. Americans have too many personal problems to allow them to reach a state of happiness.

2. Choose the correct meaning for the word *trivialize* from the context: "There's a tendency to *trivialize* or think it's funny, but these groups are opening doors on issues and giving people some sense of community."

   a. take seriously

   b. take lightly

   c. take angrily

3. According to a survey cited here, how many Americans say their lives are satisfying?

   a. half

   b. ten times more than in the 1950s

   c. 92 percent

> He enjoys true leisure who has time to improve his soul's estate.
>
> Henry David Thoreau (1817–1862), U.S. philosopher, author, naturalist

---

[19] *born-again* (adj) with new-found Christian beliefs
[20] *cross-dresser* (n) one who dresses in the clothes of the opposite sex

> If there's anything Americans agree about—and there hasn't been much— it's our individual and collective right to have a good time.
>
> Ian Frazier, U.S. writer

4. "It's a *perpetual* search for Mr. Goodbook, the idea that maybe the next one will be the one that solves all my problems and finally makes me happy." A *perpetual* search is one that

   a. has ended.

   b. goes on forever.

   c. will end in the near future.

5. The Declaration of Independence guarantees

   a. happiness.

   b. the right to happiness.

   c. the right to pursue happiness.

6. Groups like Gamblers Anonymous, Overeaters Anonymous, and Spenders Anonymous give people a place to

   a. get together and talk about their lives and problems.

   b. get together to gamble, eat, or spend.

   c. get together and write self-help books.

7. The author gives details to show that by the end of the 1980s, the United States was

   a. a place where the living was easy and secure.

   b. going through difficult economic and social times.

   c. a happier place than it is today.

8. Children moving away to find better jobs is given as a reason for

   a. the unhappiness of their parents.

   b. the breaking up of communities.

   c. the high divorce rate.

9. The abundance of self-help books is used to show that

   a. Americans buy and write more books than they used to.

   b. so many people are unhappy that they write about it.

   c. Americans are looking for books with suggestions for a better life.

10. The author of this article seems to believe that

    a. Americans will never find happiness.

    b. happiness will come to Americans when they get back to a simpler lifestyle and develop closer relationships with others.

    c. Americans from previous generations were clearly happier than those from the present generation.

Using the Vocabulary: Figurative Language

A. *This writer uses a great deal of imagery and idiomatic expressions in her article. In order to fully understand the meaning, you have to understand her language. Choose the correct meaning for each of these phrases from the text.*

1. A "salt-and-pepper beard" (par. 2) is one that is
   a. flecked with food.
   b. grey, white, and black.

2. The "granddaddy of all human potential centers" (par. 2) refers to one that is
   a. the oldest and most famous.
   b. the largest and most unusual.

3. If "things fall short" (par. 3), people are
   a. disappointed.
   b. not tall enough.

4. In "a perpetual game of hide-and-seek" (par. 3), the players are
   a. always searching for something they may never find.
   b. always acting like children.

5. We search for "freedom from old Victorian convention" (par. 5) if we
   a. want to preserve traditions.
   b. want to break the rules.

6. People who "show up at life's buffet" (par. 6) assume they will
   a. have many satisfying meals.
   b. taste the good life.

7. "Mom and pop's Main Street stores" (par. 15) can be found in
   a. big cities in America.
   b. small towns in America.

8. To "shoot the breeze" (par. 16) during a meeting is to
   a. sit around and chat.
   b. kill someone's idea.

9. When we "draw the line" (par. 24), we
   a. place limits on things.
   b. experiment with creative options.

> More than 40 percent of Americans reported that they were looking forward to a vacation in outer space.
>
> *National Leisure Travel MONITOR,* 1997

> I still need more
> healthy rest in order
> to work at my best.
>
> Ernest Hemingway
> (1899–1961), U.S. author

10. People who "pitch in" (par. 18)

   a. like to play baseball.

   b. join in and help.

B. *Try your hand at writing a paragraph using figurative language. Use a few of the expressions from Exercise A or others you have learned.*

Thinking Together

This article ties together many of the themes of American culture that you have read about in this book. Work with a partner to try to find as many references to the themes in other chapters as you can. Make a list with paragraph references. Did this article add anything to what you already knew about these themes?

Writing about It

*Write one to two paragraphs on one of the following topics. Try to use some of the vocabulary from this reading and from **Focusing In**.*

1. Summarize some of the problems Americans have, according to Dreyfous.

2. Given the evidence provided, do you think Americans are happier now than at other times since World War II?

3. What are some of the advantages and disadvantages of self-help books and groups like Alcoholics Anonymous?

Reacting to the Reading

Do you think the secret formula for happiness can be found in a self-help book, through a support group, or at a spiritual retreat?

- Americans are often criticized for spending too much time at work or for bringing work home from the office, which takes away from family time. In this article, Shari Caudron points out the need for interests outside of work to keep people happy and in turn to make them better workers.
- As you read, think about your own hobbies and what you do to "pursue your passion." When you are done reading, see if your hobby fits the answers to the questions on page 247.

Pursue Your Passion

Shari Caudron

from *Industry Week*

1   Are you bored, *burned out*,[1] or *plateaued*?[2] Sometimes the key to on-the-job fulfillment can be found outside your office.

2   Eric Rutberg, vice president of product development for Impo International Inc., a women's shoe manufacturer based in Santa Maria, Calif., is a connoisseur of life. He enjoys good food, fine wine, stimulating conversation, and global travel, and he zealously pursues each of them.

3   Three years ago, at the age of 42, he found a way to bring these passions together in one place. That place? Bizou, the trendy San Francisco restaurant he and a handful of partners opened in April 1993 to rave reviews by *Gourmet*[3] magazine and other publications. The restaurant, which he helped to *conceptualize*[4] and finance, has given Rutberg a unique sense of celebrity among his business colleagues. But more than that, he believes the endeavor has given him more energy and confidence and a greater willingness to take risks on the job, which is important in the highly competitive fashion industry.

"Now, more than ever, I'm likely to try anything," he says.

4   As Rutberg's experience suggests, sometimes the key to *rekindling the fires*[5] on the job may lie in off-hours avocations. If you're bored, burned out, or feel there are no challenges left, you may not need a new career or even a new job. You might simply need a new and engaging hobby.

5   It sounds simplistic. But before you discard this advice, consider the experiences of people who've been there. "We live in a culture that says if you don't have a job you can throw all your passions into, you must not be doing something right," says Rutberg. "Personally, I think there are lots of places where we can find our passion."

6   Barbara Sher, career counselor and best-selling author of personal growth books such as *Live the Life You Love* (Delacorte Press, 1996), agrees with Rutberg's assessment. "Americans think if they are not satisfied with their work, they must go out and get another job," she says. "I believe if your job isn't killing you and it provides a

---

[1] ***burn out*** (vp) to tire of doing the same thing over and over
[2] ***plateau*** (v) to reach a stage of little or no change
[3] ***gourmet*** (n) one who knows a lot about and enjoys fine food
[4] ***conceptualize*** (v) to come up with an idea
[5] ***rekindle the fires*** (idiom) to bring enthusiasm back to

good living, then you should take your talents and gifts and apply them to interests outside of the office."

7   Sher, who has helped thousands of individuals find their passion in life, says a funny thing happens when people start devoting their time to activities they love. They get sexier, more playful, and more generous. They become more energetic, open-minded, and fun to be around. Better yet, all the energy and creativity they generate in pursuit of their passion carries over into other areas of their lives, including the workplace.

8   It's probably not a stretch to say that mid- to upper-level executives are more in need of an off-hours tune-up than most. "It's a variation on the Peter Principle," explains Katy Piotrowski, director of advising for the Denver office of Bernard Haldane Associates, a career-advising firm with 62 offices nationwide. "People who do well and are ambitious typically *get promoted*[6] outside of their passion area." In fact, she says, a lack of passion is what drives many executives to seek career advice. "Over 40 percent of people we see express a lack of passion for their work."

9   Although Sher paints a much grimmer picture—"At most, only 4 percent of people are doing work they're passionate about"—she also believes successful executives don't have to give up their positions and paychecks to find passion in life. A 48-year-old banking executive she worked with, for example, came to her after a good friend and *colleague*[7] dropped dead on the tennis court just shy of his 49th birthday. Seeing how precious and short life really was, the executive thought what he needed was a new career.

10   After thinking about it for some time, the executive realized what he really loved in life

Boating and fishing are popular outlets for stress. Seventy-eight million Americans participated in boating-related sports in 1998.

was dogs. He knew he didn't want to be a vet; he'd discarded that idea in high school. Nor did he want to be a trainer. And he didn't want to give up the salary and prestige he'd acquired as a successful banker. Instead, he bought a *breeding*[8] pair of terriers, put a *kennel*[9] on his country property outside of Boston, and started selling puppies. His goal was to breed playful puppies and sell them only to people who loved animals.

11   Today, he's still a successful banker, but he's also known throughout Massachusetts for having the sweetest puppies available in that state. How does he feel about work now? "Because he's happy with life, he finds joy in everything in it," Sher says.

12   Sometimes, passion in life turns up in the most obvious places. Last year, 37-year-old Bob Price, a manufacturing manager at Eastman Kodak Co.'s Windsor, Colo., plant, thought a change in companies was what he needed to stoke the professional fires. After completing a set of personal assessments conducted by Bernard Haldane Associates, Price realized what really mattered to him in life were his two kids and living in

---

[6] ***get promoted*** (vp) to be awarded a higher job position
[7] ***colleague*** (n) co-worker

[8] ***breed*** (v) to keep animals for the purpose of reproduction
[9] ***kennel*** (n) place where dogs or cats are kept

Colorado. "By clarifying my own lifestyle needs, I'm able to bring a renewed level of commitment to work," he says. Rather than seeking a promotion that would have taken him to another state, Price accepted a *lateral transfer*[10] in April. Now he says his life is "an awesome total package."

13 John M. Clayman, president of Frelonic Corp., a Salem, Massachusetts-based manufacturer of performance textiles and "comfort" products such as camping mats, pursues his passion on the water in a sailboat. His is a 57-foot *sloop*,[11] manufactured in England before World War II and restored to museum quality. Clayman, who has been sailing and racing boats since he was a child, stopped keeping track when he'd logged more than 100,000 miles at sea. For him, sailing is not just a wonderful outlet for stress, it's a great place to refine business skills such as planning, organizing, and crisis management. "Sailing has taught me how to be cool in a crisis," he says.

"Regardless of whether I'm on the water or at work, when all hell breaks loose I've usually anticipated the emergency and know how to handle it."

14 Still, by far the most important benefit of Clayman's sailing and Price's kids and the banker's dogs and Rutberg's restaurant is the happiness and enthusiasm they bring to these executives both off and on the job. As Sher says: "Once you start doing something that makes you happy, feelings of boredom disappear."

15 So you say you don't have time to pursue anything but work? "Nonsense," says Rutberg. "I ask executives all the time how many hours their job would take if they could find a way to become more organized. Most people could do their work in a third less time."

16 And Clayman adds, "Frankly, I don't see how people don't have time to pursue their passion. No one on their deathbed wishes they had spent more time at the office."

STARTER QUESTIONS

Often, people spend so much of their lives wearing hats of responsibility—doing what they think they should be doing—that it's tough for them to know what they really want to do. These questions, prepared with the help of Barbara Sher, author of *Live the Life You Love*, are designed to help you uncover your particular passion.

- Most people who are happy in life spend time doing things they are gifted at—music, writing, leadership, speaking—things they are genetically engineered to excel at doing. What gifts do you have that you've been ignoring?
- What would you do if you knew you could not fail? Even if it is something a little far out—such as traveling the world in a kayak—the answer to this question will give you some clues as to your areas of interest.
- If you could leave the job you have had for two years without losing anything—salary, title, etc.—what would you do?
- If you were twins and one twin lived the life you do now, what would the other twin be doing?

---

[10] *lateral transfer* (n) change to a job at the same level
[11] *sloop* (n) small sailboat

Understanding the Reading: Review

Take this comprehension test on "Pursue Your Passion." Answer as many questions as you can without looking back at the article. Then work with a partner to check your answers in the reading.

1. The main idea of this article is:

   a. Hobbies help people enjoy their leisure time and perform better at work.

   b. Americans spend too much time at work and have trouble performing well.

   c. Most people do not have enough time to pursue a hobby.

2. Choose the correct meaning for the word *connoisseur* from the context: "Eric Rutberg, vice president of product development for Impo International Inc., a women's shoe manufacturer based in Santa Maria, Calif., is a *connoisseur* of life. He enjoys good food, fine wine, stimulating conversation, and global travel, and he zealously pursues each of them."

   a. a creator

   b. a rich person

   c. a knowledgeable critic

3. Choose the best paraphrase for this sentence: "No one on their deathbed wishes they had spent more time at the office."

   a. When people look back on their lives, they wish they had had a better job.

   b. When people look back on their lives, they don't think about missed opportunities to work more.

   c. When people look back on their lives, they wish their deaths could be more meaningful.

4. It can be inferred that Eric Rutberg, the vice president mentioned in paragraphs 2–4,

   a. will quit his job at Impo International Inc. to run his restaurant.

   b. will be open to taking more chances due to the fun and success of his new business.

   c. was not wealthy enough to open the Bizou restaurant on his own.

5. The question about what your imaginary twin would be doing was suggested as a means to help

   a. reveal secrets about your family life.

   b. identify your ideal spouse.

   c. discover what you might enjoy doing as a hobby.

> On an average day, one million American workers miss work due to stress-related problems.
>
> National Safety Council, 1998

6. Which of the following is not a hobby or pastime mentioned in this article?

   a. breeding dogs

   b. sailing boats

   c. gardening

7. Barbara Sher, an author mentioned in the article, writes many books about

   a. how to improve your life.

   b. hobbies.

   c. how to find a better job.

8. According to Sher, the percentage of people who are doing work they are passionate about is approximately

   a. 40 percent.

   b. 49 percent.

   c. 4 percent.

9. Which of the following summarizes the ideas in paragraph 8?

   a. Mid- to upper-level executives work harder than others so they need outside hobbies.

   b. Mid- to upper-level executives need outside hobbies because they have often been promoted to jobs beyond their original career interests.

   c. Executives need "off-hours tune-ups" because they are ambitious and competitive and lose passion for everything but work.

10. After participating in a personal self-assessment study, Bob Price decided to

   a. take a new job with a promotion in another state.

   b. take a new job at the same level so he could stay in Colorado.

   c. quit his job at Eastman Kodak and take one with Bernard Haldane Associates.

> **Eighty-four percent of households surveyed in 1996 reported that at least one of its members engaged in a craft or hobby.**
>
> **Hobby Industry Association**

Using the Vocabulary: Reviewing Analogies

A. *Review the analogies on page 179 and then choose the correct pair to complete the analogies below.*

1. *rekindle* : *renew* ::

   a. live : die

   b. fire : hire

   c. preserve : keep

2. *hobby* : *gardening* ::

   a. track : train

   b. commitment : ambition

   c. career : teaching

3. *creativity* : *art* ::
    a. innovation : technology
    b. industry : factory
    c. melody : lyrics

4. *fulfillment* : *satisfaction* ::
    a. vision : hearing
    b. pursuit : search
    c. employee : supervisor

5. *burned out* : *enthusiastic* ::
    a. playful : comical
    b. fatigued : energetic
    c. melodic : harmonious

B. *Now complete this paragraph with the correct italicized words from Exercise A.*

Today people are looking for satisfaction and (1)_____ in their lives. For those who are bored or (2)_____, finding a(n) (3)_____ can help them become more (4)_____ about their work. People who pursue their passions often (5)_____ "the fires on the job" and find more excitement in their lives.

Reading Graphs

A **line graph** is a visual representation of numerical information, such as years, percentage, and quantities. The direction of the lines shows the trends, and the points along the lines indicate specific data. When using the graph, it is important to note the title, the axis labels, and the key.

Work with a partner. Use the graph to answer these questions about the changes in Americans' leisure activities between 1994 and 1997.

1. The only leisure activity that has stayed constant from 1994 to 1997 in terms of participation is _____.

2. Two of the activities that have decreased the most are _____ and _____.

3. The activity that was enjoyed the most in 1997 was _____.

4. The activity that was enjoyed the least in 1994 was _____.

5. Approximately _____ percent of Americans found the time to go bicycling in 1997.

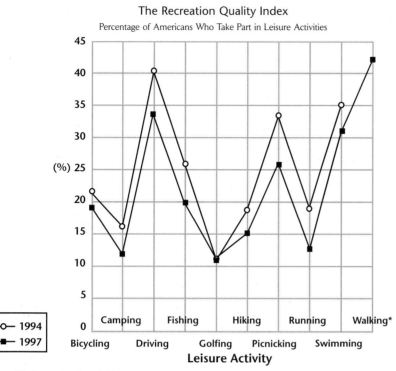

The Recreation Quality Index
Percentage of Americans Who Take Part in Leisure Activities

(%) y-axis: 45, 40, 35, 30, 25, 20, 15, 10, 5, 0

Legend:
—○— 1994
—■— 1997

X-axis activities (upper row): Camping, Fishing, Hiking, Running, Walking*

X-axis activities (lower row): Bicycling, Driving, Golfing, Picnicking, Swimming

Leisure Activity

Source: The Recreation Roundtable

* Not included in 1994 survey.

Thinking Together

Talk to the members of your class until you find one person to match each of the following hobbies. Try to find out why at least one student became interested in that pastime. Then share your findings with the class.

fishing   gourmet cooking   collecting something unusual
sewing   writing   gardening

Writing about It

*Write one to two paragraphs on one of the following topics. Try to use some of the vocabulary from this reading and from **Focusing In**.*

1. Summarize the benefits of finding a hobby at which to spend your free time.

2. In your opinion, which one of the people in this article has found the most interesting pastime? Why?

3. Write a letter to your boss explaining why you need a little time off to "pursue your passion."

Reacting to the Reading

Do you agree or disagree that in general people work too hard today and should find more time to relax?

Americans spend more than $40 billion on sporting goods each year (Sporting Good Manufacturers Association) and $2.2 billion per year on gardening supplies *(The New York Times,* 1997).

- For American college students, summer vacation is a time to work to make money for school, but spring break (usually in March or April) is a time to "party" just before the school year ends. Popular spring break vacation sites are Palm Springs, CA, and Daytona Beach, FL.
- The college students in this article by Margaret Dwiggins spend their spring break in a special way. As you read, think about whether you would really classify this as a "vacation." Would you like to spend your leisure time this way?

ONU Habitat for Humanity

MARGARET DWIGGINS

FROM THE *COURIER*

1 Like many college students, Scott Jacobson headed south for spring break with a group of friends. But rather than spending the week partying on a beach, Jacobson, a sophomore electrical engineering major at Ohio Northern University (ONU), really accomplished something. He made someone's dream come true.

2 Jacobson, a 1994 graduate of Findlay High School, was one of 47 ONU students and five ONU administrators who traveled by school bus to Jackson, Mississippi—a 17-hour trip— where they all pitched in to build a house for a family who couldn't otherwise afford one.

3 The house-building project was sponsored by *Habitat*[1] for Humanity International (HFHI), a non-profit agency which *strives*[2] to eliminate *poverty*[3] by providing volunteers who build low-cost homes, which low-income families can buy at 0 percent interest rates.

4 HFHI was founded in 1976 by Millard and Linda Fuller, a wealthy Georgia couple who wanted to use their money to help others. HFHI quickly spread from its Georgian roots—when the organization celebrated its fifth anniversary, it had 14 U.S. and seven international affiliates. In the past 20 years, HFHI volunteers have built or *renovated*[4] over 40,000 houses throughout the world, providing over 250,000 people with housing far better than what they could afford on their own.

5 Former president Jimmy Carter and his wife, Rosalynn, became active members of HFHI in 1984 and Carter regularly leads building projects throughout the world. The first college campus chapter of HFHI was started at Baylor University in 1987. The ONU chapter was founded in 1990. Current chapter president Mark Light, a senior from Leipsic, explained that this is the fifth year ONU students have taken a spring trip to assist in HFHI projects.

6 According to Light, last year members of the ONU chapter of HFHI went to Jackson, Mississippi, to assist in several building projects. The students completed in one day what the organizers expected them to do in one week. Because of that, the ONU chapter was challenged to come back to Jackson again this year to participate in a "*blitz*[5] build"—a house which is entirely constructed in one week. No other campus chapter working in Jackson received this offer.

7 For this year's project, the ONU students were divided into two groups of 25 upon their arrival in Mississippi, Jacobson said. One group was assigned to work an 8 A.M. to 12:15 P.M. shift. The two groups met each day for lunch, and the second group worked from 1 to 6 P.M.

8 Jacobson noted that the ability levels of people within the groups ranged from those who had never picked up a hammer to those who were quite experienced in construction work. The building projects were done under the

---

[1] *habitat* (n) home
[2] *strive* (v) to work hard for
[3] *poverty* (n) lack of money and material possessions
[4] *renovate* (v) to make new again
[5] *blitz* (n) rapid attack

guidance of professionals, and Jacobson said that the *foundation*[6] had already been laid for the three bedroom, one bathroom house when the ONU group started Monday morning.

9   "The first morning, all the walls went up," Jacobson said. He spent his first day working on roof *trusses*.[7] By the end of the first day of work, the outer structure had been covered with *insulation*[8] board.

10   "We basically had the whole *skeleton*[9] of the house done," Jacobson said.

11   On the second day, wood siding and roof shingles were put on, and professional *drywall*[10] contractors were inside putting up drywall. Light noted that some of the work performed on HFHI homes, particularly wiring and plumbing, is done by paid professionals because of inspection requirements.

12   Light explained that the philosophy of HFHI is to provide low-income families with quality housing, but not to provide a *handout*.[11] A family buying an HFHI-built house basically pays for the materials while the labor is provided for them. The homeowner is required to assist in the building of the house as well as other houses in the neighborhood, which gives the homeowner an added sense of appreciation for not just his home but the neighborhood in general. The homeowner pays for the home over 20 years at a 0 percent *interest rate*.[12] The money paid by the homeowner goes into a fund which is then used to finance more building projects.

13   Light estimated that the house built by the ONU students would have an approximate value of $40,000 to $50,000 with labor and material costs *factored in*,[13] but he believes the family paid between $15,000 to $20,000.

14   By the end of the week, Jacobson said he and his fellow workers were painting the house inside and out. Final touches were to be added after the students left, and the house was to be ready for the family to move into within a week.

Future homeowners of HFHI-built houses must work side-by-side with volunteers.

15   Jacobson heard about the ONU HFHI chapter through friends who were already members. The campus group meets once a week, and early in the school year members helped build a house for a family in Ada.

16   According to Light, there are three main focuses for the campus chapter. The first is to educate other students about Habitat for Humanity. Secondly, the group takes a spring break trip each year and works closely with the Hardin County Habitat for Humanity organization. Lastly, *fund-raising activities*[14] are held to finance the spring trip and to raise money for the Hardin County chapter.

17   Light explained that each student paid $50 to go on the trip to Jackson, Miss., which was donated to HFHI. Trip expenses were paid from fund-raiser income. Jacobson said the group stayed at a church youth house for the week. In their free time, the students played ping-pong and pool, went roller-blading or roamed one of the local shopping malls. One night they

---

[6] *foundation* (n) base

[7] *truss* (n) physical support

[8] *insulation* (n) material that keeps out cold, heat, or sound

[9] *skeleton* (n) basic structure

[10] *drywall* (n) wall panel that goes over wood beams

[11] *handout* (n) charity; an item given for free

[12] *interest rate* (np) percentage paid on an amount of borrowed money

[13] *factor in* (vp) to take into account

[14] *fund-raising activity* (np) event to support a cause

watched themselves on a Jackson news station.

18   Although he knew only about half the students at the beginning of the trip, by the end of the week the group had all become close friends.

19   "It was great to see how we all got along together," Jacobson said. "There were no low points, we had a great time all week." Jacobson's experiences with the Jackson trip were so good he hopes to spend next year's spring break building another Habitat for Humanity house.

20   "I wouldn't trade it for any other vacation," he said.

> There are 1,366 chapters of Habitat for Humanity in the United States.
>
> *Habitat World*

Understanding the Reading: Paraphrasing and Summarizing

A. *Fill in this chart with information about Habitat for Humanity.*

INFORMATION ON HABITAT FOR HUMANITY

Abbreviation	
Founders	
Year founded	
Number of houses built/renovated by 1996	
First college campus with a chapter	
Interest rate for loans on the house/materials	
Former U.S. president involved in the organization	

> **• H I N T •**
>
> Remember, a good way to avoid copying the original sentence is to cover it up while you are paraphrasing.

B. *When writing a summary, it is necessary to paraphrase the information provided by the author. Review the suggestions for paraphrasing on page 222. Then paraphrase the sentences that follow.*

1. In the past twenty years, HFHI volunteers have built or renovated over 40,000 houses throughout the world, providing over 250,000 people with housing far better than what they could afford on their own.
   Since 1976, _____

   _____

2. Jacobson noted that the ability levels of people within the groups ranged from those who had never picked up a hammer to those who were quite experienced in construction work.

   _____

   _____

3. The homeowner is required to assist in the building of the house as well as other houses in the neighborhood, which gives the homeowner an added sense of appreciation for not just his home but the neighborhood in general.

_____

_____

C. *Now put together the information from Exercises A and B and write a short summary of this report on the students at ONU who volunteered for Habitat for Humanity.*

Using the Vocabulary: Crossword Puzzle Review

Review the vocabulary related to leisure time and pursuing happiness by working on this crossword puzzle with a partner.

Across Clues

 1. life, liberty, and the pursuit of _____
 3. place to go to get away from it all
 6. free time
 8. time off from work
 9. tension
10. most popular leisure activity in 1997, according to graph on page 251
11. leisure activity or pastime
12. person who works for free

Down Clues

 2. National _____, preserved recreation land
 4. summer vacation month
 5. rest and _____, R and R
 7. lack of interest

> For me, vacations have always meant pulling out the cards, board games, and jigsaw puzzles and getting together with family and friends for long, relaxing days and evenings of game playing.
>
> **Hillary Rodham Clinton,** (**1947**–), **U.S. first lady**

> Habitat for Humanity
> is an excellent
> example of
> Americans working
> together for the good
> of our nation.
>
> William Clinton (1946–),
> U.S. president

Thinking Together

Work in a small group. Plan a volunteer activity in which the students from your school could make a contribution to the community. Assess the needs of a small group in your community and think of ways to meet those needs. Try to plan something that you would really be able to do if you wanted to. What would you need to carry out your plan?

Writing about It

*Write one to two paragraphs on one of the following topics. Try to use some of the vocabulary from this reading and from **Focusing In**.*

1. Owning a house is a big part of the American Dream. Describe Habitat for Humanity, its founders and workers, and how it helps poor Americans achieve this dream.

2. Explain the contributions that the prospective homeowners have to make to their new homes.

3. Write a short report for the school newspaper about how a group of students at Ohio Northern University spent their vacation.

Reacting to the Reading

Do you think that giving college credit for activities such as the one Dwiggins describes would encourage more students to volunteer?

(Keeping Track of Your Reading Rate

tip

Looking over the comprehension questions before reading a passage will help you find the answers more quickly. Use this strategy here. Although this will not be a true test of your reading speed, this is a good technique to use on a standardized reading test.

- The following article by David Barton—"Call Waiting: Hi, This is America. I'm on Vacation"—appeared in the *Sacramento Bee*.
- When your instructor gives the signal, read the passage as quickly as possible and record your speed when you are done. Then answer the comprehension questions that follow.

Sallie Floyd is not at work. Instead, she is visiting Sacramento with her husband, Ed, and 10-year-old son, Jason. On a sunny Monday morning that's getting warmer by the minute, they're seeing the sights of Old Sacramento before heading up to the Gold Country and then on to visit family friends in Reno.

"It's heaven!" she responds when asked about her family's vacation. "We've only been gone since yesterday, and it feels like a week. It's so great to get away." When she's at work, Floyd, 39, is a bookkeeper for a small insurance firm in Wausau, Wisconsin. But they're just having to do without her for a couple of weeks. "Oh, they'll miss me, I guess," she says. "But it's a slow time for us now anyway." She tilts her head back and lets the hot Sacramento sun warm her face. When she speaks, it's a declaration: "I feel no guilt whatsoever."

Those who call for Floyd will just have to call back. Or leave a message. No one can be expected to work *all* year. . . . It's vacation season, the peak of which is late July and early August. Anyone phoning around, for whatever reason, is almost as likely to get an answering machine as the person they were calling. It's not as pronounced a lull as it is in August in France, where the entire country goes on vacation. . . .

It's also the most practical time for many people. Although an increasing number of schools are adopting year-round schedules, early August is still the best time for many families with school-age children to get away. And they do. Andrew Wachlis, a Sacramento-based free-lance telemarketer who hires his services to different businesses, says that he gets more answering machines around this time of year than at any other. . . .

Chuck Ross is spending his money at home this August. He works for a Tennessee-based company, Smith Travel Research, which keeps statistics on hotel occupancy rates. He says that the July-August peak is reflected in those occupancy rates. . . . So summer is still the time most people choose to escape. "There's a trend for people to take shorter but more frequent vacations, which is characteristic of the two-income family," says Ross on the phone from Nashville. "So people take more extended weekends or short week vacations. But families still travel in the summertime; the vacations just aren't as long as they used to be."

(400 words)   TIME _____

*Now mark the following statements true (**T**) or false (**F**) without looking back at the reading.*

_____ 1. Sallie Floyd is on a vacation traveling with her family.

_____ 2. Sallie Floyd feels guilty about being on vacation.

_____ 3. Most Americans with schoolchildren take vacations in early July.

_____ 4. Some American children go to school in July and August.

_____ 5. Hotel occupancy rates decrease during the summer.

_____ 6. The percentage of French on vacation in August is higher than that of the Americans.

_____ 7. Americans take longer vacations now than they did in the past.

_____ 8. Some factors that influence vacation plans are working parents and school schedules.

_____ 9. A long weekend is considered a vacation for some Americans.

_____10. It's likely that a machine will answer the phone in a business office during the summer.

Percent correct = _____   wpm = _____

> **More than 250 million tourists visited America's national parks in 1997.**
>
> **National Park Service**

MAKING CONNECTIONS

Responding to the Readings

Prepare short oral or written responses based on your personal experience and your reactions to the readings. Try to incorporate the information and the vocabulary you have learned in this chapter.

1. Describe some of the volunteer groups in your country and what they do.

2. Would people around the world say they are happier today than they were thirty years ago?

3. When do most people go on vacation in your country? Why?

4. Answer one of the Starter Questions from "Pursue Your Passion" on page 247.

5. What kind of charitable organization would you like to volunteer for? Why?

6. What are some of the most popular places to spend vacations in your country?

7. Some self-help books listed at an online bookstore (www.amazon.com) include *100 Ways to Motivate Yourself; 101 Ways to Happiness*; and *The 10-Minute Stress Manager*. What type of self-help book might you buy to improve your life? Why?

8. Discuss your reaction to one of the quotes or facts in the margins of the chapter that you find most interesting or surprising.

Editing Your Work

This passage was written by a student who forgot to edit for verb tense shifts. Remember to pay attention to time words when writing a description or narration that covers a span of time. Correct the five errors in verb tense in this student's paragraph about his hobby.

> The hot months used to be about growing crops and getting closer to God. Suddenly, America had an idea. And summer, in the beach-and-potato-chip sense, was born.
>
> Ian Frazier, U.S. writer

I have many friends who have different pastimes, but most of their hobbies are in sports, video games, computers, and so on. Photography is my all time favorite hobby. When I am depressed, desperate, or bored with my daily routine, I pick up my photographic equipment and began my adventure.

My grandfather, who is a photographer back in the early 1900s, also has a huge photography studio, but I never saw it because it was torn down during the invasion of China. When I was small, I love to play with cameras. Perhaps my skill was inherited from my grandfather because now whenever I see something interesting and beautiful then I naturally imagine a picture in my brain. I get my equipment together and I tried to get a better perspective of it.

Writing an Essay

Choose one of the following topics and write an essay. As a prewriting activity, read over your shortwrites and notes for inspiration. Remember to review the brainstorming techniques on pages 262–263. In your essay, use the readings, factoids, quotes, class discussions, and personal experience to support your ideas. If you choose to write a research paper, make certain to cite your sources clearly.

1. Shari Caudron says that if you are tired or stressed out, "You might simply need a new and engaging hobby." Write an essay about a hobby or leisure activity that you enjoy. When did you start pursuing this interest? Why? How much time and energy do you spend on it? Make sure you show the readers the benefits of "pursuing your passion."

2. Tell the story of a memorable (good or bad) vacation. Give background information regarding your plans and your expectations. Who were your traveling companions? Where did you go? What kinds of experiences did you have? Did the vacation meet your expectations, or were you disappointed? Convince your readers that this vacation spot is worth visiting.

3. If you have ever spent time volunteering, write an essay about this experience. Describe how you got involved, what you did, and what rewards you found. Do you think you made a difference in someone's life? Was this a valuable way to spend your free time? Would you recommend this as a way to give something back to society?

4. Compare and contrast the things people do in the United States and in your country to unwind and have a good time. Refer to the readings for details on activities that Americans enjoy. How much leisure time do people have in your country? How do they typically choose to spend it? Are people in your country as overworked as Americans are?

5. Research a travel plan for a vacation you would like to take somewhere in the United States. Find out about major cities and attractions, weather, and special foods. Look into the costs of hotels, restaurants, airfare, and local transportation. Write a detailed itinerary in essay form describing your plans.

Finding More Information

Magazines and Journals

American Collector
Outside Magazine
Sierra
Sunset
Travel and Leisure

> **You could go to a different Hawaiian beach every day for a year and have sixty-six left over on New Year's Eve.**
>
> *Hemispheres*, Fascinating Facts

> Success is getting
> what you want.
> Happiness is liking
> what you get.
>
> H. Jackson Brown Jr.,
> U.S. author

Books

Kraus, R., *Leisure in a Changing America*
Kuralt, C., *On the Road*
Lowery, L., *How to Enjoy Your Leisure Time*
Schwartz, A., *Hobbies*
Shor, J., *Overworked America: The Unexpected Decline of Leisure*
Steinbeck, J., *Travels with Charley*

The World Wide Web

www.cyso.com/leisure.htm—leisure activities in sports, entertainment, and hobbies
www.eas.ualberta.ca/elj/als/als1.html—Academy of Leisure Sciences
www.fodors.com—Fodor's Travel Online
www.nps.gov—U.S. National Park Service

Movies and Videos

Mr. Hobbs Takes a Vacation
Summer Rental
Touring America's National Parks
Wind
Ferris Bueller's Day Off

Suggestions for Reading and Writing

Reading More Efficiently

Good readers are not passive. They focus in on the topic before they begin and constantly assess their understanding while they read. Try to use some of these strategies to improve your comprehension.

1. Preview the reading. Carefully read all titles and subtitles. Look at pictures, graphs, and artwork and read the captions to start thinking about the topic.

2. Before you read, ask yourself questions about the text to see how much you already know about the subject. Ask yourself: *What do I know about this topic? How does my knowledge of the subject relate to this article? Have I read anything else by this author?*

3. Read any introduction. It may give you some background information on the author and help orient you to the topic. Prereading activities often ask you to reexamine your preconceptions or to think about a question as you read.

4. At times, look over comprehension questions at the end of a passage before you actually start reading it. This strategy may help you to anticipate some of the important points the writer is trying to convey.

5. Quickly read or skim the reading once. Do not stop to look up unfamiliar words. Most likely, you won't understand every word in every paragraph. Try to get the gist or overall meaning of the passage. Then reread it more slowly to gain a better understanding.

6. As you read, ask yourself questions to see how much you really understand. Some of these questions might be: *What is the author trying to say? What do I think will come next? Is this what I expected the author to say? Do I agree?*

7. Make predictions about the text and then see if you are right.

8. Refer to a dictionary or glossed vocabulary only when necessary. Always try to figure out the meaning of new words by the context.

9. Read in chunks or word groups, not word by word. Reading too slowly causes you to lose the writer's train of thought.

10. Pay attention to signal words and phrases, such as *on the one hand . . . on the other hand, as a result,* and *although/even though.* These expressions signal changes in the direction of a writer's thoughts and can help you follow the meaning.

11. Use study skills such as annotating (writing notes/comments in the margins), highlighting, outlining, and note taking to help you retain information. Underline main ideas and important details. Mark any difficult words, sentences, or passages to refer to later or to discuss in class.

Writing More Effectively

Good writers always have a purpose for writing. As they write, they keep their audience engaged by making sure their work is clear, informative, and focused. Try to keep some of these tips in mind as you develop your writing skills.

1. Keep a journal of your activities, thoughts, and reactions to readings and class discussions.

2. Practice your writing skills on short pieces. In *American Perspectives,* many writing topics can be found in **Reacting to the Reading, Writing about It,** and **Keeping a Journal.** Use these activities to help build up to longer essay topics.

3. Vary the types of responses you write. Try a narrative, a summary, a letter, or a news report.

4. Review short responses you have written. They will help you develop ideas for your essays.

5. Use brainstorming techniques such as clustering, mapping, outlining, and Venn diagrams to help get your thoughts down on paper before you write. They will also help you to organize your material.

Here are some examples of outlining, diagramming, and mapping for part of an essay on holidays in different cultures.

Outline

An Important Holiday

I. Introduction—Holidays in Vietnam and the United States
   A. Common Holidays—Celebrating the New Year
   B. Different Holidays
      1. Halloween
      2. Moon Festival
   C. Thesis: Although the Vietnamese and Americans both celebrate the New Year, there are more differences than similarities in the way this holiday is celebrated.

II. Differences
   A. Dates
      1. Lunar New Year
      2. Calendar New Year

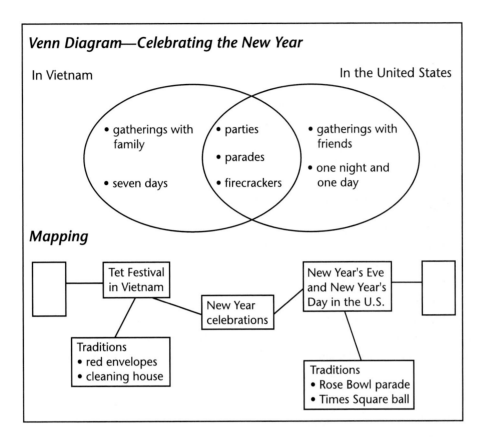

Venn Diagram—Celebrating the New Year

In Vietnam

In the United States

- gatherings with family
- seven days

- parties
- parades
- firecrackers

- gatherings with friends
- one night and one day

Mapping

Tet Festival in Vietnam

New Year celebrations

New Year's Eve and New Year's Day in the U.S.

Traditions
- red envelopes
- cleaning house

Traditions
- Rose Bowl parade
- Times Square ball

6. Carefully consider the *purpose* of your essays. What are you trying to show through your writing? Choose examples and supporting details that fit the assignment and illustrate your points.

7. Think about your audience. What will your reader know about your topic? Remember to explain the context of situations and circumstances you are writing about. Define any new or unfamiliar words or expressions. Clarify any references to materials you have used. What language and style of writing are appropriate? Words like *kid, lots of, kind of, stuff,* and *guys* are usually considered too casual and vague for academic writing.

8. Don't expect perfection in one draft. Leave yourself time to write several drafts of your essay. As you revise, you can pay attention to different areas such as content, organization, details, and form.

9. Remember that careful editing should always be part of the writing process.

10. Don't be put off by your instructor's red ink or peer readers' negative comments. Suggestions and constructive criticism go with the writing territory.

11. Read, read, read! Notice how writers weave sentences together, present their ideas, and create powerful descriptions. Write down interesting expressions, idioms, and vocabulary choices. Review your notes regularly and try to include them in your own writing.

Tips on Revising and Improving Your Essay

- Make sure your reader can recognize the purpose of your essay and can understand your main idea. This may be apparent in a clearly written thesis statement or it may be implied. Ask someone to read the first page of your essay. See if he or she can restate your central thought.
- Check the first and last sentences of each paragraph. Do the ideas flow smoothly? See if adding a transition or repeating a key word or phrase will help make your essay more cohesive.
- Reread your introduction. Does it clearly present your topic? Make sure it is not too long. Remember to leave supporting details for later paragraphs.
- Check to see that each paragraph relates to your overall theme and develops only one clearly expressed point.
- Read each paragraph to see if irrelevant details or repetitious phrases can be deleted.
- See if there are places where you can support your ideas by adding information from the readings or, for example, from the facts and quotations in the margins of this book.
- Review passages where you have referred to outside sources to see that you have given credit to the writer for his or her ideas. If you have not used a direct quote, make sure you have not inadvertently plagiarized. Check the tips on paraphrasing on page 222.
- Reread your conclusion. Did you stay on topic? Does your conclusion tie together your ideas without going beyond what you have shown in your essay?

Tips for Editing Your Essay

- Meet with your instructor for comments and suggestions.
- Read your essay out loud several times.
- As you edit, focus on one writing problem at a time.
- Put your paper aside for a while before editing it so you can be more objective.
- Be aware of your editing weaknesses and edit for those problems.
- Check verb tense consistency by marking time expressions and their appropriate verb tenses.
- Use a learner's dictionary (such as the *Longman Dictionary of Contemporary English*) to check for correct verb forms, word forms, and count/noncount nouns.
- If subject-verb agreement is a problem for you, mark the subjects and verbs and check for agreement.
- Avoid repetition by using pronouns and synonyms.
- Check to make sure your pronouns have correct and clear antecedents.
- Run the spellchecker on your computer and proofread your essay before you submit it.
- Make sure you understand the correction symbols used by your instructor.
- Pay attention to your instructor's feedback; ask him or her to clarify any comments you don't understand. Be sure to make any necessary revisions.

Idioms and Expressions

The following is a list of useful expressions and idioms related to the topics in *American Perspectives*. Try to use them when you discuss issues in each chapter.

Chapter 1

to go back to your roots—to connect to your ancestors and heritage

to trace your family tree—to find out who your ancestors were

to be fresh off the boat—to be a recent arrival in a new country

to set foot on—to first arrive in a new country

Chapter 2

to cut the apron strings—to free oneself from parents' influence

to be a mama's boy—to be a child spoiled by his mother

to come of age—to reach maturity, usually 18 years old

to stand on your own two feet—to be independent

to take after someone—to look or act like a relative

Chapter 3

three strikes and you're out / strike out—to fail after three chances

to get to first base—to start successfully

out of one's league—beyond someone's level

to bat 1000—to be very successful

to go for the gold—to try your hardest to succeed and be the best

Chapter 4

to be a couch potato—to sit around and watch TV

to be buff—to be in great shape, to be muscular

to pump iron—to lift weights to strengthen muscles

to be under the weather—to feel ill

Chapter 5

to dance the night away—dance all night long

break a leg!—a wish for good luck in a performance

to be music to someone's ears—to sound sweet, like good news

to keep the beat—to maintain the rhythm

Chapter 6

to surf the net/travel on the information highway—to visit websites on the computer

to voice an opinion—to speak out about an issue

to make a point—to say something important, relevant

to hit it off—to get along well together

Chapter 7

to put on a pedestal—to admire someone greatly and never see his/her faults

to receive a hero's welcome—to be greeted with special recognition

to go where angels fear to tread—to put oneself in dangerous or risky situations

to go from rags to riches—to go from poverty to wealth

to pull yourself up by your bootstraps—to rise out of poverty and become successful on your own

Chapter 8

to pull an all-nighter—to stay up late studying

to be a teacher's pet—to be the teacher's favorite student

to hit the books—to study hard

to play hooky/cut school/ditch school—to be absent from school without permission

Chapter 9

to get to the bottom line—to make the main point, to summarize the issue

to work one's fingers to the bone—to work very hard

to roll up one's sleeves—to get ready to get to work

to fall down on the job—to fail to work well

Chapter 10

to have a blast—to have a great time

to have the time of one's life—to enjoy oneself a lot

to loosen up—to relax

to live off the fat of the land—to live well without having to work

to get a life—to stop worrying and do something meaningful

APPENDIX C
Keeping Track of Your Reading Rate

Use this chart to record your time and comprehension score. First, go down the left column of the chart to find your time. Then check the number opposite your time in the right hand column. This number represents your words per minute (WPM). Write your comprehension score (0–100%) in the box that corresponds to the correct time for each chapter.

Time	Ch. 1	Ch. 2	Ch. 3	Ch. 4	Ch. 5	Ch. 6	Ch. 7	Ch. 8	Ch. 9	Ch. 10	WPM
1:00											400
1:10											345
1:20											300
1:30											265
1:40											240
1:50											220
2:00											200
2:10											185
2:20											170
2:30											160
2:40											150
2:50											140
3:00											135
3:10											125
3:20											120
3:30											115
3:40											110
3:50											105
4:00											100

APPENDIX D

Map of the United States

Some Facts about the United States

Population: 272,478,217 (1999)	**Largest Cities (1999)**
Area: 3,536,278 square miles	**New York**: 7.3 million
Number of states: 50, plus the District of Columbia	**Los Angeles**: 3.4 million
Capital: Washington, D.C.	**Chicago**: 2.7 million
Government: Federal Republic with a democratic	**Houston**: 1.7 million
tradition	**Philadelphia**: 1.5 million

State Mottoes and Postal Abbreviations

State	Postal Abbreviation	Motto
Alabama	AL	We dare defend our rights.
Alaska	AK	North to the future
Arizona	AZ	God enriches.
Arkansas	AR	The people rule.
California	CA	Eureka (I have found it.)
Colorado	CO	Nothing without Providence
Connecticut	CT	He who transplanted still sustains.
Delaware	DE	Liberty and independence
Florida	FL	In God we trust.
Georgia	GA	Wisdom, fortune, and moderation
Hawaii	HI	The life of the land is perpetual in righteousness.
Idaho	ID	It is perpetual.
Illinois	IL	State sovereignty—national union
Indiana	IN	Crossroads of America
Iowa	IA	Our liberties we prize and our rights we will maintain.
Kansas	KS	To the stars through difficulties
Kentucky	KY	United we stand, divided we fall.
Louisiana	LA	Union, justice, and confidence
Maine	ME	I direct.
Maryland	MD	Manly deeds, womanly words
Massachusetts	MA	By the sword we seek peace, but peace only under liberty.

State	Postal Abbreviation	Motto
Michigan	MI	If you seek a pleasant peninsula, look about you.
Minnesota	MN	The star of the north
Mississippi	MS	By valor and arms
Missouri	MO	The welfare of the people shall be the supreme law.
Montana	MT	Gold and silver
Nebraska	NE	Equality before the law
Nevada	NV	All for our country
New Hampshire	NH	Live free or die.
New Jersey	NJ	Liberty and prosperity
New Mexico	NM	It grows as it grows.
New York	NY	Ever upward
North Carolina	NC	To be rather than to seem
North Dakota	ND	Liberty and union, now and forever, one and inseparable
Ohio	OH	With God, all things are possible.
Oklahoma	OK	Labor conquers all things.
Oregon	OR	She flies with her own wings.
Pennsylvania	PA	Virtue, liberty, and independence
Rhode Island	RI	Hope
South Carolina	SC	While I breathe
South Dakota	SD	Under God, the people rule.
Tennessee	TN	Agriculture and commerce
Texas	TX	Friendship
Utah	UT	Industry
Vermont	VT	Freedom and unity
Virginia	VA	Thus always to tyrants
Washington	WA	By and by
West Virginia	WV	Mountaineers are always free.
Wisconsin	WI	Forward
Wyoming	WY	Equal Rights

ANSWERS TO FOCUSING IN QUESTIONS

CHAPTER 1

Can You Pass This "Citizenship" Test?

1. **F**—Many immigrants remain permanent residents. **2. T 3. F**—Christopher Columbus, an Italian, discovered America; his trip was funded by Spain. **4. T 5. F**—There have often been quotas set to stem the tide of immigration; in 1921 and 1924 the quota was based on country of origin and in 1917 it was based on language skill. **6. T 7. T 8. F**—Most immigrants come from Asia and Latin America; Asians and Latinos/Hispanics topped the list of 1.1 million people who took the U.S. citizenship oath in 1996. **9. F**—Spanish is the second most common language. **10. T**—for example, the state of Colorado (Spanish), the city of Milwaukee (Native American), and the street name Avenida del Mar (Spanish)

Test Your Word Power

1. a **2.** g **3.** j **4.** c **5.** d **6.** i **7.** h **8.** f **9.** e **10.** b

CHAPTER 2

What Do You Think?

Background Information for Responses:

1. Our definitions of togetherness are related to our cultural perspectives. It is true that Americans do not usually live in extended families. They move an average of 11.7 times in their lifetimes, but mostly within the same state. However, over 7 million Americans attend 200,000 family reunions a year.

2. While it is true that most of the elderly do not live with their children, according to the Census Bureau, in 1993, 30.9 million elderly Americans lived in the community, not in institutions; fewer than 5 percent of senior citizens over the age of 65 lived in nursing homes.

3. Most American children look forward to moving out on their own or going away to college when they are 18 because they want to be independent. Although children may choose to move out, and parents may expect them to leave home, they are not forced to. In fact, in 1998, 59 percent of boys and 48 percent of girls between the ages of 18 and 24 lived at home.

4. In 1998, 43 percent of new marriages were expected to end in divorce. However, more than 40 percent of people who divorce later get remarried. In fact, in 1998, only 10 percent of all Americans over 18 were still unmarried following a divorce.

5. Our definitions of respect are related to our cultural perspectives. It is true that American children are encouraged to be independent and to voice their own opinions, which may make them seem disrespectful. Most American children call their parents *mom* and *dad,* although divorce and remarriage cause some children to call their step-parents by their first names. This is not seen as disrespectful by most Americans but may be perceived differently by other cultures.

Expand Your Word Power

1. jealousy between brothers and sisters **2.** all of one's relatives, including parents, children, grandparents, aunts, uncles, cousins **3.** when they are related through only a mother or a father due to divorce and remarriage **4.** No; legally the child now has living parents and is no longer an orphan.

CHAPTER 3

Are You a Sports Fan-atic?

1. baseball **2.** beach volleyball and surfing **3.** football **4.** basketball **5.** private donations and fund raisers **6.** American high school students in general take one hour of physical education (P.E.) per day for at least two years; only Illinois requires one hour of P.E. per day in elementary school. **7.** American Youth Soccer Organization **8.** 30,000 runners **9.** golf **10.** eleven

Test Your Word Power

1. c **2.** a **3.** f **4.** h **5.** d **6.** b **7.** e **8.** i **9.** j **10.** g

CHAPTER 4

What Do You Think?

Background Information for Responses:

1. False—Obesity is a problem in the U.S. However, thirty-five percent (not most) of Americans over 18 were overweight in 1997.

2. True—The fitness revolution has created a $3-billion dollar industry in the U.S. There were over 16,000 U.S. health clubs registered in the Global Health and Fitness Health Club Directory in 1998; however, 60 percent of American adults do not achieve the recommended amount of exercise. Americans spent over 5 billion dollars on vitamins in 1997.

3. False—Americans eat out often, but they do not always eat fast food (hamburgers, tacos, hot dogs). *Longman Dictionary of American English* defines fast food as "inexpensive food that is prepared and served quickly in a restaurant." According to Simmons Market Research Bureau, in a nationally representative survey of U.S.

households, 46.9 percent of Americans eat fast food at least once per month, but not every day.

4. Somewhat true—Americans live by the proverb, "Cleanliness is next to godliness." According to the Bureau of Economic Analysis, Americans spent $49.9 billion on hygiene products in 1996. American foods must pass rigorous government inspections by the Food and Drug Administration (FDA). Whether this is an obsession could be open to debate.

5. True—Because theirs is a youth-oriented culture, this is true for many Americans who risk their lives for elective surgery. For example, in 1998 more than 2 million North Americans tried to improve their appearance through plastic surgery and each year an estimated 126,000 women undergo cosmetic breast enlargement in spite of the suspected dangers.

Test Your Word Power
1. b 2. d 3. c 4. j 5. e 6. h 7. f 8. a 9. i 10. g

CHAPTER 5

Can You Hear the Beat?
1. Music Television 2. Elvis Presley 3. Pete Seeger, Joan Baez, Woody Guthrie, Judy Collins, Burl Ives, Bob Dylan 4. Jazz 5. Grammy Awards, Election to the Rock and Roll Hall of Fame, MTV Music Awards, Kennedy Honors, Country Music Awards 6. ballet 7. an outdoor rock concert that attracted 500,000 fans 8. folk music 9. violins, recorders, flutes, trumpet 10. "The Star Spangled Banner" written by Frances Scott Key during the War of 1812 between Britain and the U.S.

Test Your Word Power
1. g 2. d 3. f 4. c 5. i 6. h 7. a 8. b 9. j 10. e

CHAPTER 6

Are You Part of the Information Generation?
1. a 2. b 3. b 4. b 5. a 6. a 7. b 8. b

Expand Your Word Power
1. break the ice 2. surf the net 3. gets the message 4. shoot the breeze 5. go on the air

CHAPTER 7

How Heroic Are You?
1. e 2. c 3. h 4. f 5. d 6. i 7. g 8. b 9. a 10. j

Test Your Word Power
1. e 2. d 3. c 4. g 5. h 6. a 7. f 8. b

CHAPTER 8

What Do You Think?

Background Information for Responses:

1. Although many say this is true, statistics do not support this statement. The 1995 Gallup Poll indicated that although only 20 percent of parents gave high marks to public schools in general, 65 percent gave high ratings to the public schools their own children attended. Even though there is a movement in the U.S. to approve school vouchers to use public money to attend private schools, according to the National Assessment of Educational Progress, there is only a small gap between public and private school achievement.

2. This statement is false if parental involvement is viewed as participation of parents in school activities. In a 1996 National Center for Education Statistics (NCES) study, 80 percent of parents reported meeting with teachers at least once. Forty percent reported volunteering on at least one school committee in elementary schools, and it is common to see parents volunteering as aides in the classroom. Every U.S. school has a chapter of the Parent-Teacher Association (PTA) which raises funds for the school, supports extracurricular activities, and offers suggestions on how the school can run more smoothly.

3. True. The U.S. has ranked behind many countries in both math and science in studies of 8th graders by the International Association for the Evaluation of Educational Achievement (IEA) Mathematics and Science; however, the U.S. educational system tests all students, including recently arrived immigrants and vocational students, not just those on an academic track. When the most advanced students in the U.S. were compared to similar students in other countries, the U.S. students came closer to the international averages in math and science.

4. Our definitions of "enough time" are related to our cultural perspectives. Compared to students in many other developed countries, American children spend less time in school. The average American school year is 180 six-hour days. Some states now have year round schools with nine weeks of instruction followed by three weeks off.

5. From an outsider's point of view, this may seem true but most parents in the United States would not agree. The goal of American education is to produce well-rounded individuals; therefore, schools offer a wide variety of extracurricular clubs, volunteer and leadership groups, and sports activities to enrich the standard curriculum. In 1994-95, 83 percent of high school students reported spending time in after school activities, the most popular being sports.

Test Your Word Power

1. h 2. i 3. g 4. b 5. a 6. f 7. e 8. c 9. d 10. j

CHAPTER 9

On the Job

1. T—The average work week is 40 hours, with time given for breaks and lunch. **2. F**—Average paid vacation after one year is 8.1 days (11.9 after 5 years) but on average there are also 7.6 paid holidays per year. **3. F**—The average salary in 1998 was $26,500. **4. T**—A 1996 Inc. survey indicated over 70 percent of Americans were satisfied with their jobs. **5. T**—50 percent more **6. T**—Public school teacher salaries start at about $20,000; the average salary for college professors in 1995 was $49,000; the average salary for a major league baseball player in 1998 was over a million dollars. **7. T**—Average travel time for all commuters is about 21 minutes for a typical journey of about 10 miles. **8. T**—Six out of ten of the fastest growing occupations according to the U.S. Census Bureau are in health-related fields. **9. T**—according to U.S. Census Bureau figures **10. F**—The rate was below 5 percent in 1997-98.

Test Your Word Power

1. e **2.** f **3.** d **4.** h **5.** a **6.** b **7.** c **8.** j **9.** g **10.** i

CHAPTER 10

Proverbs

1. Being a workaholic is not healthy or productive. People need to have hobbies and outside interests in order to be happy.

2. This is an old American proverb stemming from the belief that if people have too much free time, they might get into trouble.

3. Even though Americans believe that "All work and no play makes Jack a dull boy," they find it hard to break away from the work ethic. For example, 75 percent of executives in a Hyatt survey reported calling into work while on vacation.

4. There are several interpretations to this saying. One is: A man who works for someone else is busier than his boss. Another is: A woman who is unemployed works hardest to find something to do. Yet another is: People feel uneasy if they have too much free time, so they try hard to fill it.

5. This saying indicates that Americans feel they must be busy and get as much done as possible because time passes too quickly. A common American saying is: "Time is money."

Expand Your Word Power

1. Recreational vehicles (RVs) are large motor homes that allow people to be mobile. Since they have electrical and water hookups and are equipped with bedrooms, kitchens, and bathrooms, travelers have the freedom to go long distances and stay anywhere. RV parks are popular throughout the U.S.

2. *R* and *R* stand for *Rest* and *Relaxation.*

3. Retirement is the period of time when people are expected to stop working because of their age. Americans born before 1959 can retire at the age of 65 and receive Social Security benefits from the government, which include a nominal monthly income and health benefits.

4. The word *volunteer* means someone who does not get paid for the work he or she does.

5. A *hobby* is defined as "an activity that you enjoy doing in your free time." (*Longman Dictionary of American English*).

Answers to Physical Activity IQ Quiz, Chapter 4, page 98

1. T 2. F 3. T 4. T 5. F 6. F 7. F 8. T 9. F 10. T